Also by the Author

Dr. Spock on Parenting

▷ Sensible Advice
from America's
Most Trusted
Child-care Expert

Benjamin Spock, M.D.

SIMON AND SCHUSTER
New York   London   Toronto   Sydney   Tokyo

Simon and Schuster

Simon & Schuster Building
Rockefeller Center
1230 Avenue of the Americas
New York, New York 10020

Published by the Simon & Schuster Trade Division
SIMON AND SCHUSTER and colophon are registered trademarks of
Simon & Schuster Inc.

Designed by: Helen L. Granger/Levavi & Levavi
Manufactured in the United States of America
10   9   8   7   6   5   4   3   2   1

Library of Congress Cataloging in Publication Data
Spock, Benjamin, date
    Dr. Spock on parenting: sensible advice from America's most trusted
child care expert/Benjamin Spock.
        p.   cm.
    Includes index.
    1. Parenting—United States.   2. Parent and child—United
States.   I. Title.
Q755.8.S69   1988   88-15792
649'.1—dc19   CIP
ISBN 0-671-63958-7

Much of the material in this book first appeared, in different form, in
Redbook.

Acknowledgments

I want to thank the editors of Redbook for letting me use articles that have appeared in that magazine over the past ten years as the basis for most of the chapters in this book, though the material has been rewritten and reshaped to bring it up to date and up to my current thinking, and to make it into a book.

I am most grateful to my super secretary Lynda Long who has never mislaid any piece of the manuscript in any of its stages and who has always known where to find the pieces I have mislaid. She is invariably skillful, speedy, and sympathetic.

Carole Lalli, senior editor at Simon and Schuster has been the ideal editor, selecting with her fresh perspective the material to be considered for inclusion, detecting repetitions, passing expert judgements, but never fussing over picayune details.

DEAR GINGER,

For many years I yearned for a daughter, but without success. Then I was rewarded by acquiring you, as a rich bonus of my marriage to Mary, a daughter who has remarkable grace, generosity and beauty, and from whom I have learned much.

Contents

CHAPTER ELEVEN
Health and Nutrition   273

INDEX   303

Introduction

Parenting is a strange mixture of stress and joys. I realized when my sons were young that I was always under slight tension when I was with them, watching, worrying and correcting, much more than was necessary. But when I was away from them, on a speaking trip, for instance, I would be overcome by feelings of pride and love. I would feel ashamed that I couldn't show my approval and enjoyment of them while I was with them—for my sake and for theirs. Grandparents helped me to understand. They often asked me, "Why couldn't I enjoy my own children the way I'm enjoying my grandchildren?" I gradually realized that it is not the exception but the rule when good parents worry and correct. For parental love is not just hugging and beaming and bragging. It includes wanting your children to be approved of by your relatives and friends for their helpfulness and politeness and to be appreciated by their teachers for their good work habits. It means wanting them to grow up to be responsible workers, respected neighbors, devoted spouses and parents. At the simplest level it's keeping them healthy, and safe from accidents. All these concerns condemn you to be a fusser. You have to wait for your rewards: the occasional compliment or achievement. So be patient.

Of course some fortunate parents are able to enjoy their children most of the time—even in adolescence. I remember how startled I was, at a high school ball game at which my step-daughter was leading the cheers, when a mother said to me, with spontaneous enthusiasm and sparkling eyes, "Aren't teenagers wonderful! I just love to be with them." I'd always thought of them as being more difficult than younger children because their need to rebel and, as part of that, their need to look down on their parents' ideas and standards had made me feel that they were the enemy, lined up to pooh pooh me behind my back, and that I was relatively helpless to control them. Actually, my sons and step-daughter were never out of control; it was just my own lack of self-confidence that put me on the defensive. Another factor, no doubt, since we all get our most basic feeling about children's attitudes and how to cope with them from the way our parents dealt with us, was my mother's vigilance that expressed her fear that children would kick over the traces unless they were kept constantly under stern control.

By contrast I always felt self-assurance and pleasure in getting along with other people's three-, four-, and five-year-olds. They not only aren't looking for opportunities to rebel, they think that adults are marvelous—full of interesting wisdom on all subjects, always good for a story, magicians in making things work, and rich enough to buy anything that children want. They pay adults the great compliment of wanting to be like them, practicing being like them most of the day.

Six-to-eleven-year-olds are no longer grateful, flattering, and charming like younger children. They do not pattern themselves on their parents but ape their peers in being messy in appearance, unattractive in table manners, rough in language, argumentative. They quote teachers to prove the parents wrong. They resist the niceties that their parents are trying to teach. But they are not skeptical or scornful of their parents' beliefs. They are not defiant. They don't go in for tobacco, alcohol, drugs and sex, in order to be sophisticated.

Some parents are scared of one- and particularly two-year-olds. They express it by calling the latter the terrible twos. That attitude is unfairly prejudiced. To be sure, it takes tact and a little ingenuity to manage them because they are feeling their first oats of independence, but they are easily distracted and full of curiosity about everything. You have to be slightly pigheaded yourself not to be able to find ways to manage them.

Quite apart from the difficulties caused by the clashing personalities of parents and children at different ages are the general problems that our society throws in the way of families today.

People on low and lower-middle incomes have been getting

poorer while the rich have gotten richer. This misfortune has several causes. During the early years of the Reagan administration taxes were greatly reduced for the wealthy and for industry. Appropriations for weapons were raised extravagantly, without any serious effort to negotiate disarmament. To try to compensate for these shifts, repeated cuts were made in services that particularly benefited the poor, the old, the sick, children and women. (Two nations defeated in World War II, Japan and Germany, were denied nuclear arms and their resources went into the civilian economy instead. They are outstandingly prosperous.)

As real income has declined (as well as for other reasons), more and more mothers have joined fathers in outside jobs in order to support their families. Half the mothers of pre-school children now work, exposing the fact that there is not nearly enough high-quality day care for those families that need it. Good day care is too expensive for people on modest incomes; it should be subsidized by government or by industry, as it is in many European countries. Children are being grossly short changed in our country.

Half of all marriages now end in divorce which suggests that we've somehow lost our way. Whatever the causes, divorce produces symptoms of distress in all the children and makes both parents miserable for at least two years. Remarriage introduces the strains of the stepfamily, which I learned about personally with a lot of pain.

Teenage pregnancy, drug abuse, and suicide have all increased alarmingly, which means to me that there is a serious dearth of spiritual beliefs to sustain adolescents during this often scary transition, and that their parents too must be lacking in beliefs to inspire them with.

Our society has many, many times as many murders (most of which occur among family members) as any other nation, and we have disturbingly higher figures for rape, wife abuse, and child abuse.

The fear of nuclear annihilation frightens and depresses humans of all ages.

Some parents, seeing the statistics about the steady decrease in the number of old-fashioned families with two parents and a couple of children, believe that the family is disappearing for good and all. For me this is not the central, the major problem. To be sure, the family is under increasing strain. But children who have had any semblance of a family will idealize it and, when they are grown, will try to recreate its positive values for children of their own.

The larger threat, I feel, comes from the tense, unloving conditions under which the family sometimes exists: excessive competitiveness and materialism, lack of spiritual convictions, jobs that give no gratification or joy, the disappearance of the extended family and the small, tight-knit community.

My main answers to these deficits and strains, as I try to explain in this book, are first to bring up our children with a strong drive not so much to get ahead but to serve their fellow humans with cooperation, kindness, and love. They will find this not a sacrifice but an inspiration.

The other answer is for people to reclaim their government from special interests such as the arms makers and the other giant corporations that deny any other aim than maximal profit. Of course there has to be profit in our system but it can be humanized. People must become much more politically active so that our government will serve *their* needs.

Dr. Spock
on
Parenting

CHAPTER ONE

Anxieties in Our Lives

▷ CAN WE EASE OUR TENSIONS?

▷ TO WORK OUTSIDE OR NOT

▷ LATE PARENTING

▷ CAN YOU RAISE SUPERKIDS?

▷ ABDUCTORS AND MOLESTERS

▷ CAN WE EASE OUR TENSIONS?

I believe ours is the most stressful country in the world, though this doesn't need to be. We aren't more conscious of our distress because a majority of us are still financially more comfortable than the people of other countries, and this material wealth anesthetizes us.

Why are we so tense? To begin with, we've lost sources of security and comfort that our ancestors relied on up to a few generations ago. We aren't even aware of what we've lost.

Back when so much in the universe was considered mysterious and known only to God, a far greater number of us had a strong sense of having been created in his image and of being guided every hour of the day by his concern. Today, the sciences have appeared to take over much of the authority that was formerly God's, yet they are too impersonal to serve as guides; worse, they have fragmented and demoted us into feeling that we are merely biological and psychological mechanisms, only a little more complex than other animals, adapting to various sociological backgrounds. So we have lost much of our sense of dignity as individuals. We don't have souls anymore.

People used to live with or close to their relatives, in the extended family. Young couples could get prompt help with child care, marital difficulties, financial crises, illnesses; sitters were always at hand. This added up to a great emotional security but we don't know enough to miss it. In fact we pity the couple who takes in a grandparent: "The poor Jenkinses, they have to have *her* mother living with them."

Most Americans once lived in small, tight-knit communities where they were well known and could count on caring neighbors. They felt a corresponding obligation to help others and to participate in local affairs. Nowadays young couples hurry to large cities for better jobs, where they can depend only on themselves and feel isolated. They are apt to move often. It's a rootless existence; we take this for granted, but it surely takes its toll.

Mothers as well as fathers take outside jobs in 50 percent of families with preschool children. Whatever the reason—financial or emotional—they have every right to jobs and careers. Unfortunately, however, in this country we haven't solved the problem of providing high-quality day care. Good day care must be subsidized by government or industry for families with modest incomes, but our government says it can't afford to help. So children are being neglected in large numbers and will show the effects in their characters for life.

The tensions of our society must contribute to our high divorce rate, which has doubled in the last fifteen years. Then divorce itself creates new symptoms of distress—in all the children and in both parents—for at least two years. Then come the distresses of the stepfamily, which may last for many years and can't be imagined until experienced, as I found out myself. It is predicted that by the middle of the 1990s there will be more stepfamilies than nonstepfamilies in the United States. For the first time, original nuclear families will be the minority.

Factors contributing to divorce are briefness of acquaintance before marriage and marriage at an early age. I suspect another factor is that very many American youths have been favored with all the possessions and privileges their parents could possibly afford, including, in some families I've known, a car for the sixteenth birthday. This is far beyond what youths expect in other industrial nations. Money has been relatively easy to earn. Most high schools and universities have not been academically difficult compared to those in other countries. In other words, many youths have been able to get most of what they wanted without great effort. So they expect marriage to provide all imaginable pleasures and satisfactions. They haven't realized—and their parents haven't told them —that marriage is like a garden, which must be constantly cultivated to survive, let alone improve.

Our species by nature gets great satisfaction, in nonindustrial societies, from creating well-made and beautiful objects, whether for our own everyday use—pots, containers, implements, clothing, ornaments—or for sale. But the assembly line approach—in factories and offices—is more efficient and profitable, so it has robbed millions of any satisfaction in their job, except for the money earned. Industrial workers in Europe as well as in the United States have complained increasingly of the boredom and tension of doing meaningless work.

Our society is ferociously competitive in spirit. Children are compared with each other, in the family and in school, to spur them to greater effort. Some parents sign them up for different after-school lessons every afternoon of the week—music, dance, athletics—or send them to specialty camps to learn computing or tennis or soccer. In sports there is diminishing emphasis on fun, from Little League to university, and more on perfection and winning.

A ludicrous example of excessive competitiveness is the effort to make "superkids" by teaching children to recognize Beethoven's picture on flash cards at one year, or to read at the age of two, though no one has shown that such precocious skills have any beneficial effects whatsoever. (At least we haven't yet reached the degree of pressure on children that exists in Japan, where a shocking and increasing number of *elementary* school children commit suicide because they fear their grades will not satisfy their parents.)

In the adult years, too, the most successful executives have high rates of stomach ulcers and often neglect their children and spouses in their race to get to the top and stay there.

Part of the problem in America is that our society is so exclusively materialistic. All societies have to be practical, but in most parts of the world the materialism is balanced by compelling spiritual beliefs such as the duty to serve God (as in Iran), or to serve the family even at the sacrifice of personal desires (as in certain European countries), or to serve the nation (as in Israel).

The rate of suicide in teenagers in America has quadrupled in the past twenty years. The main reason, I believe, is that youths don't have strong enough beliefs to sustain them through those stressful, bewildering years. Another reason, well authenticated, is their depression about the likelihood of nuclear annihilation before they can start their careers or marriages.

Our country is the most violent in the world in murders within the family, rape, wife abuse, and child abuse. Domestic violence is both an expression and a cause of the seething tensions in many of our families. Ours has always been a rough society, slipping easily into brutality, as in our treatment of Native Americans, slaves, and each new wave of immigrants. Now brutality on television and in movies is multiplying the violence. For it has been proved scientifically that each time a child or adult watches violence it desensitizes and brutalizes to at least a slight degree. Yet it's estimated that the average American child has watched eighteen thousand murders before the age of eighteen. So we are creating insensitive, violent people by the hundreds of thousands. It's not that a child brought up by kind parents will be turned into a thug. But everyone is being edged in that direction to a greater or lesser degree.

Then there's the fear of nuclear annihilation, which half of all Americans expect in the not-too-distant future, but which few think of taking political steps to prevent. Their fears are justified. Each president gives lip service to disarmament but then finds excuses to pile up more and deadlier nuclear weapons. Sixty to seventy percent of our people in opinion polls favor a negotiated, verifiable disarmament, seeing that the arms race has brought not more security but less. It seems clear to me that disarmament is our only hope of being able to turn the world over intact to our children and grandchildren. It also seems clear to me by now that governments—presidents and Congresses—can't disarm because of several pressures: the financial and political power of the arms makers, the Pentagon's endless hunger for more and its alarmist cries that the Soviet Union is about to pull ahead, and the fear most elected officials have of being accused by their political opponents of neglecting national security or of being dupes of the Soviet Union. So I believe that only people can get disarmament—by voting and by endless political pressure. But so far only a small percentage of those who believe in disarmament are activated to apply such grass-roots means.

We have other serious sources of anxiety that should be self-evident. Unlike Canada and most European countries, we lack universal health care of high quality, paid out of social security or other taxes. Much of our housing is decrepit, and only the well-to-do can afford to pay for new, good housing today. There is a gross lack of recreational facilities for those in modest circumstances. Only a bare beginning has been made in overcoming the social cancer of discrimination against minorities and women.

I didn't assemble this list of stress and horrors to depress or paralyze you. I believe that we can solve our problems provided we first recognize them. My solutions come under two main headings: child rearing and political activity.

A Different Child Rearing

I think we should bring up our children with *much* less pressure to compete and get ahead: no comparing one child with another, at home or in school; no grades. Let athletics be primarily for fun and let them be organized by children and youths themselves.

Instead of raising our children with the chief aim of getting ahead, I think we should inspire them with the ideals of helpfulness, cooperation, kindliness, and love. These don't need to be preached with solemnity. The parents' example is the most effective means. Besides, human beings who've been raised with plenty of love love to be helpful to others, and it makes children feel good and grown up.

By two years children want to set the table. They should be allowed to set out the silver, which can't be harmed, complimented for their helpfulness, and spurred on occasionally by promises that they will be able to set the plates someday. However, when they forget to be helpful, we should squelch the impulse to scold. They can be reminded politely of how much you need their help, as you would remind a good friend who's staying with you. (In day-care centers the staff count on the children to put things away and to help serve and clean up, month after month.) Teenagers can be encouraged or expected to do volunteer work in hospitals or to tutor younger children.

There should be no grades in school. (I taught in a medical school that had very successfully abolished grades.) Grades pit each student against the others. They mislead students and teachers into thinking that learning comes from memorizing the teacher's words. But usable learning, the purpose of which should be to prepare the individual to contribute maximally as worker, citizen, and family member, comes from doing, thinking, feeling, experimenting, taking responsibility and initiative, solving problems, creating. The teacher provides the environment and the materials and calls attention to what is happening. The students do the rest.

I hope American parents can outgrow the conviction, which a majority have, that physical punishment is necessary to bring up well-behaved children. Certainly almost all parents have had an impulse to strike when, for instance, a child deliberately handles and breaks the parent's precious possession. But there are parts of the world where it has never occurred to any adult to strike a child. I have known personally or professionally dozens of families in which the parents never lifted a hand—or otherwise punished or humiliated their children—and yet the children were ideally cooperative and polite. Children are eager to be ever more grown up and responsible.

When an effective foreman or supervisor wants to correct a worker, he doesn't haul off and swat him on the behind or slap his face. He calls him into his office and explains how he wants the job done; in most cases the worker tries to do it better. It's just the same with children when they are treated with respect.

There are several things mistaken, I think, with physical punishment. It teaches that might makes right. It helps turn some children into bullies. And, to the degree that it makes a child behave, he behaves because he's afraid of being hurt. Much better for him to behave because he loves his parents and wants to please them and grow up to be like them.

I feel strongly that children should not be permitted to watch violence on television or in movies, whether in cartoons or with live actors. Just say, with conviction, "There is too much killing and hurting in the world!"

With similar words I'd decline to give a child guns or other military equipment, though I wouldn't run after him if he used a stick for a gun, to keep up with his pals.

Politically Active Parents

How are we to get federal subsidies for the adequate day care that so many millions of young parents and their children are now doing without? How will we get better elementary and high schools, with smaller classes and better-trained teachers, especially for the children in deprived areas? (They need inspiring schools most, in order to catch up with the children from advantaged backgrounds.) How will we get universal, high-quality health care for everyone? How will we get decent housing and recreation facilities for all our families? Not by wringing our hands. The solution can come only by greater political activity of our people. At present only half of us bother to vote. And many of those who do vote seem to do so not on the basis of the issues, but on personality preferences. (Sixty to seventy percent want disarmament but they elected and reelected Nixon and Reagan, openly dedicated to the arms race.)

Americans have shown that they will barrage with letters and telegrams their officials in Washington in opposition to a proposed tax or to a cut in social security for retired people. Yet few will be stirred to political activity in favor of disarmament. Is it that taxes and social security seem like citizens' issues but that armament is the government's business, too overwhelming or too technical for ordinary people? Political activity—even letter writing and demonstrating—seems inappropriate to millions of Americans. I've heard them dismiss all politics as dirty business though they speak proudly of our democracy. I've heard fathers say to their sons, "Never mind politics. Your job is to get ahead." People have criticized me for seeming to step out of my professional role to become undignifiedly political. I'd say it was belated realization that day care, good schools, health insurance, and nuclear disarmament are even more important aspects of pediatrics than measles vaccine or vitamin D.

Conservatives say that we can't afford to meet our social needs. But European nations, not nearly as well-off as ours, are doing more for their people and especially for their children. The main problem of course is that our government is spending trillions of dollars for additional fiendish arms in the vain hope that we can so far outdistance the Soviet Union that they will be intimidated and surrender without a fight. We must take control of the country away from the arms makers.

We must vote and vote discriminately. When incumbents seem hopeless, we can work in the nominating campaigns of candidates who share our views. After our officials are installed, we must keep track of their votes and keep after them. Letter writing and tele-graphing are not namby-pamby; they are effective in impressing the president and the Congress with how people are feeling. Officials calculate that for every letter received there are thousands of non-writers with the same urgent opinion. Don't worry about the word-ing. You only need to be clear about which side you're on.

You don't have to go to Washington to lobby your senators and representatives. Find out from their in-state offices when they will next visit and make an appointment for your committee. Give it an impressive name and include at least twenty earnest members. Don't go alone; they can dismiss you as just a nut.

You can attend big demonstrations in Washington, New York, Chicago, Los Angeles. Or you can organize a small local demonstra-tion, with signs, in front of your federal building, post office, or official's office. If you've tried all the proper approaches and feel desperate because you are getting nowhere, you may want to think of nonviolent civil disobedience. It attracts much more media atten-tion. It's wise to enlist at least one courageous clergyman, to reas-sure yourselves that your cause is just and to impress the police. It is necessary to recruit a public-spirited lawyer or two, to find out what the law says about the action planned, to notify the authori-ties, to organize bail and fines, and to represent the demonstrators in court.

So there is a wide range of political activities to choose from in working for a cause or crusade. Choose what feels comfortable to you. The most important thing, though, is to keep working at it, month after month, year after year. It's the quantity and duration that count.

▷ TO WORK OUTSIDE OR NOT

Whether a mother of a baby or preschool child should go back to an *outside* job (caring for a baby can be a full-time inside job) is a complicated matter, as every one who has tried can tell you. There are many factors to be considered. How important to the mother is the job, financially, emotionally, or psychologically? Could mother and father dovetail their working hours so that between them they can cover most of the child's waking hours? Is there a grandmother, aunt, or other relative whom both parents like who could care for their child?

Has the mother worked before, in her chosen field, long enough and successfully enough that she has confidence that she could always find work at her former job or at another, if she decided to quit her job for now? What's the local situation as to quality and availability of day care? Would the mother prefer to stay home for one or several years, perhaps until the youngest child is in first grade or three years old at the least and able to attend a good day-care center or nursery school? (There should be government subsidies for such parents who can't afford to stay home.)

A few professionals in the child development field believe that only a mother or father can give a baby or small child ideal care, because of the intimacy of that relationship and its permanence. But a majority feel, as I do, that a well-trained teacher in a high-quality day-care center, or a woman providing excellent day care in her home, or a compatible grandparent, aunt, or uncle, or a full-time sitter can do a satisfactory job during the parents' workday. It is essential, however, that his/her personality and attitude are good.

The substitute care giver should be able to give a *parental* kind of care, by which I mean loving each child with real warmth, appreciating each child's individual makeup, showing pleasure in the child's tiny achievements (which will encourage the child to keep on developing), and being able to manage the child with a kind touch (without severity and without oppressiveness).

In the three-to-five-year-old day-care situation, there should not be more than seven children in the care of one adult. And there shouldn't be more than three children per adult when the children are under three. The latter situation is called family day care when it is provided in the care giver's home.

If you are considering day care or family day care, you should visit the places under consideration for several hours on two or more occasions to be sure that the *spirit* of the care as well as the physical situation fits with your ideas. A good question to keep in mind is whether the teachers are spending most of their time giving general directions to the group or whether they are keeping their eyes open for children who are having difficulties. Is a child getting frustrated with a plaything and in need of tactful help; is he getting into tugs-of-war or fights and in need of help to learn the fun of cooperative play; is he getting hurt and in need of comforting?

Of course there should be enough constructive playthings. For the three-to-five-year-olds there should be blocks, dolls, doll's equipment, housekeeping equipment, easel and finger paints, modeling clay, toy cars, tricycles, wagons, a jungle gym, a sandbox. For children under three the playthings and activities will be simpler, but they must be available.

In past decades women who expected to have outside jobs tended to have their babies relatively soon after marriage and then they went to work when their children were one to six. But in recent years increasing numbers of women have gotten well started on their working careers first and then had their babies in their late twenties or thirties. In this way they have first settled any inner doubts about whether they are capable of holding good jobs. And when the babies have come, the mothers have been in a better position to decide whether to get back soon to the outside job on a full- or part-time basis, or whether to take off a year or more for full-time care, until the child was ready for day care at three, kindergarten at five, or school at six. By then the father might be earning more, thus making it more financially possible for the mother to quit temporarily.

Studies have shown that the old adage "Have your children when you are young, strong, and flexible" is not necessarily sound. On the average, older parents are more flexible, tolerant, understanding, and happy in child care.

Babies and children up to three years are highly sensitive to separation from the person who has been their principal care giver. Babies as young as six months will go into a depression if abruptly separated from their mother and left with an unfamiliar person. At two or two and a half they will become subdued if the mother abruptly leaves them with an unfamiliar care giver. The depth of the child's despair only shows when the mother returns. Then the child, let's say it's a girl, will rush to the mother and cling to her. She will cry in alarm when her mother goes into the next room. She will bat away the sitter, whom she accepted while the mother was gone. When her mother tries to leave her in her crib at bedtime, she will cling with a vicelike grip. If her mother can pry herself loose and head for the door, a two-year-old who has never climbed out of her crib before will unhesitatingly vault over the side and race after her. It will take months to reassure a child who has been frightened in this way.

The answer is to prepare thoughtfully for the separation over a period of at least two weeks by introducing the sitter or substitute gradually. She can come to the home for increasing periods of time for a week without trying to do anything directly for the child, just making friends at a distance. When she is accepted, she can try helping the child to dress or bringing her some food. When this step goes smoothly, the mother can leave the home for not more than half an hour, the next day for an hour, and so on, gradually. At any sign of panic, the sitter should back off and proceed more slowly.

If the young child is going out to family day care, the same principles should apply: several brief visits *with* the mother until the child feels at home; then the mother can leave the child for half an hour and gradually increase the length of her absences. This may all seem expensive—in time and money. But it is well worthwhile to prevent a separation panic that could affect the child for months and perhaps make the mother's outside job impossible.

After they reach the age of three years, children are much less likely to develop a severe separation anxiety. But I'd still recommend a *gradual* introduction to a day-care center, at least for the first few days, to see how fast the child takes to it. Then proceed, slowly or fast.

Full-Time or Part-Time Work?

For many women the best compromise, when it is possible, is to start with part-time work. This gives the mother much of the closeness to the child that she wants during the most formative years, yet keeps her hand in the work she wants to pursue. Furthermore it gives her the sense of escape from the confinement of home that many women feel they need, especially with the first child, the one who ends the mother's freedom.

In fairness, a father should be willing to cut down to a part-time job so that the mother won't have to sacrifice so much of her outside work time. But some fathers are still not ready to think of themselves as care givers, and even in families where the father is willing to assume such a role, this may not be practical. The fact is that, unfairly, men earn much more than women for equal work, so when a father goes on part-time it usually means a greater financial sacrifice for the family than when the mother does all the cutting down. And when companies do provide long leaves for infant care, it's almost always maternity leave, not paternity leave.

Good day care and family day care are expensive, more expensive than families on modest incomes can afford. Most European countries have gone a lot further than the United States in subsidizing day care through contributions of government or industry or both. Our country is the richest the world has ever known and there is no good reason why it should be shortchanging our children— except, of course, for our obscene defense budget.

In past generations and centuries most women felt that the family was the most important aspect of existence. (I myself have felt that is.) But in their crusade for equality and justice, particularly in the women's liberation movement beginning in the 1970s, many feminists have thought of equality primarily in terms of equal pay and equal access to the prestigious jobs, which they are certainly entitled to. But pay and prestige have been two of men's highest aims, in our excessively competitive, materialistic society. So, in a sense and to a degree, many women are now accepting men's values. Or, to put it in harsher terms, many women are joining the rat race. Incidentally, they are getting more stomach ulcers and heart attacks, once considered the particular disease of tense, ambitious men.

This issue—what values we should emphasize in America in the future—is one that is very close to my heart on several scores. All through my career as a medical school teacher, one of my main jobs has been to try to help students (predominantly male in most schools) to be sensitive to the feelings of their patients, because these feelings have close connections with their diseases. In other words, I was trying to counteract the tendency in the upbringing of so many boys in America to suppress their feelings and to depersonalize their relations with other people, in their family life and in their work. This tendency is particularly handicapping in the work of physicians, who will misdiagnose many conditions if they fail to recognize emotional factors.

In my pediatric practice and in writing *Baby and Child Care* I've been trying to persuade fathers to get involved in the care of their children—for the sake of the children and for the sake of the fathers themselves.

And as a peace activist I am dismayed by the encouragement of aggressiveness and violence by television, movies, and war toys as influences that will continue to push us ever further in the arms race and into military interference in the affairs of other countries. At the same time excessive aggressiveness and violence are corroding our daily existence in our own country.

It would have been so much better if, instead of women's taking on men's excessively competitive values, men had had the sense to see that they have been pursuing harmful ideals and to recognize that family life; participation in neighborhood affairs; and warm, cooperative relationships—at home, in the community, and at work—are the vital aspects of existence and that both sexes should demote the outside job to third priority.

What does all this have to do with women's outside work? I'm trying to encourage women, whether they work by choice or necessity, to avoid falling into the male fallacy of thinking of outside work as more important, more challenging than family.

▷ LATE PARENTING

In the past it was usually believed that a couple should have their children while they are young. Parents are thus more resilient, nearer to their children in spirit (somewhat as if this were an athletic contest that went to the side with more endurance). Parenting takes endurance all right. But a study a generation ago showed that, even more, it takes understanding and tolerance, and that these qualities are in greater supply *on the average* in parents in their thirties than those in their twenties. And the parent–child relationship and the child's adjustment are on the average judged to be better when the parents are in their thirties.

In trying to explain this outcome to myself, I conclude that younger parents are still so close to childhood themselves but so proud of having outgrown it that they don't want to admit any connection. I'll give two examples of this intolerance. When I was interviewing a fourteen-year-old girl and asked her what her ten-year-old brother was like, she was so irritated by his crudeness, his lack of sophistication, that she was able only to give a loud, disgusted grunt. If she were a few years older she might have been able to cast her eyes to heaven and smile indulgently at his uncouthness. Another example of intolerance: A sixteen-year-old mother, asked how her new baby was doing, scowled and declared,

"He's *bad!*" Questioning brought out that what she was disapproving of so indignantly was just the usual amount of fretfulness in a young baby.

In other words, you may enjoy your babies more and they may enjoy you more if you have them in your thirties.

In reading about and listening to young women who are going to work for the first time, I've learned that in our discriminating society, where they've often heard such remarks as "Women are not good as engineers" or not good as physicists, or not good as executives, many of them have self-doubts about whether they will be able to succeed in their chosen fields, especially if their ambitions are high. From this point of view, it may work out better for such women to start their careers early, advance through several levels, establish a reputation, and convince themselves that they have what it takes. Then they can more comfortably take off a period for full-time or part-time child care, with the idea of going back to the full-time career later. I'm not saying that starting a career first and postponing children till later will prove best for all women. But I've known a number for whom it turned out to be quite satisfying. It fits, too, with the recent tendency to postpone marriage until the later twenties.

Parents in their thirties are more secure in their adulthood. They aren't so self-centered. They can see and feel what a baby is and what he needs.

I don't want to emphasize the difference between parents in their twenties and thirties so much that I discourage couples who want their babies in their twenties. I only want to overcome the belief that the twenties are always better.

▷ CAN YOU RAISE SUPERKIDS?

Can you raise superkids? At least a few psychologists and parents think so.

When anxious parents hear that in a certain program two-year-olds are being taught to read or that one-year-olds are taught to recognize Beethoven's picture on flash cards, they may jump to the conclusion that they themselves should be seeking similar training for their own child, even though there is absolutely no evidence that this has long-term benefits.

I remember one New York City mother years ago who complained that her eleven-year-old daughter was becoming increasingly tense and cried easily. Questioning brought out that the mother had enrolled her in riding lessons on Mondays, ice-skating lessons Tuesdays, social dancing class Wednesdays, music lessons Thursdays, ballet on Fridays—and on Saturdays, opera appreciation. Besides, her school had high academic standards and the teachers ordered lots of homework. When I suggested that fatigue could be a part of the problem, her mother exclaimed, "But all those classes are so important!"

I've known parents who worried that if their son didn't give up his bottle by the age of one or stop sucking his thumb by the age of three, he'd never get into the college, the law school, and the law firm of his father's choice. This kind of anxiety is particularly common in highly successful families; you might say it's how the upper crust stays upper.

The drive is passed down from generation to generation. If during their own childhoods parents were expected to do superior work and made to feel anxious if they didn't, they are likely to apply the same pressure when they have children of their own. Other parents may explain that it's their duty in these tough times to give their kids every educational and cultural advantage.

We do live in a society that depends increasingly on intelligence and education. And we do know that drastically neglecting an infant's or child's emotional and intellectual needs may sharply limit her ability to learn. But such cases don't prove that stimulation beyond a natural amount is beneficial. In fact, I believe that too much of the wrong kind of stimulation can be harmful.

What is the harm? One basic defect in all such schemes is that the impetus to excel comes not from the children but from parents who are driven by their own preoccupation with high achievement. So the children may balk, to preserve their integrity.

When parents do sometimes succeed in pushing their children to excel in some field, such as ballet or music, the children may end up somewhat lopsided in development, perhaps self-centered or humorless or unsociable. They may also grow up feeling that their parents value them only for their unusual talent.

Conversely, if they don't succeed to an unusual degree, some children may feel keenly that they've let their parents down and end up with a long-lasting sense of failure.

Pressing children too hard may turn them into adults so obsessed with being first that they get no joy out of life except in the narrow field of competition. They neither give nor get pleasure in their relationships with spouses, children, friends, and fellow workers. Or they may simply develop ulcers or early heart disease.

Overscheduling and overcontrolling rob children of part of their inborn drive to learn for themselves and to strive for healthy independence. They also rob children of opportunities to develop their own interests and hobbies, which are valuable if they are to develop into well-rounded, successful adults. In fact, a study of the childhoods of unusually creative individuals has revealed one common denominator: as children these people all became deeply interested in some hobby or project (not necessarily related to their later occupation) and stuck with it.

How are babies and children normally stimulated to develop emotionally, socially, intellectually? Love plays a vital part in this process. Children work hard at learning to behave like people they love; unloved children do not imitate.

When a baby is loved, her inborn patterns keep unfolding; when she is ready for the next step, she reaches out to activities and to things. Fond parents who have been watching and waiting for her first smiles respond delightedly with smiles of their own. If this encouraging delight is repeated for months, and she is regularly fed, hugged, and comforted, she will learn that she is loved and that her parents can be trusted. These feelings—love and trust—form the foundation of all the child's future development and future relationships. Even her interest in the outside world, and later her ability to deal with ideas, will spring from this foundation. Children who've been deprived of these feelings in infancy suffer serious limitations.

Parents also naturally encourage their babies' development by noticing the kinds of things they respond to at different stages and by supplying appealing objects—bright pictures or mobiles to watch, later dolls and cuddly toys to examine and manipulate endlessly.

One-year-olds are never still. They get into everything, taste specks of dust, climb stairs before they can walk. Their instinct prompts them to do everything possible by themselves; they'll insist on taking hold of the spoon when being fed. Even more noticeable is their resistance to suggestions that are not made tactfully; they may say, "No!" at first to a favorite activity. They don't want to be dominated.

By the second year, children mature by striving to copy their parents' actions, from brushing teeth to dressing and undressing. Parents instinctively encourage development by showing their pleasure in each tiny accomplishment. Vocabulary and sentences come with a rush toward the end of the second year; parents do their part by listening.

In the years from three to six, children watch with particular intensity the parent of the same sex, and they strive to be like that parent—in manner, interests, and feelings, as well as in actions. This is a crucial step in maturity, and one that can be seen most clearly in societies in which all the men have the same occupations and all the women, others. Through an emotional identification with their parents, all young children acquire a lifelong drive to do their parents' jobs well. First they play at their parents' occupations. When they are considered old enough, their parents take them on as apprentices and helpers. (In our complex industrial society it is unfortunately much harder for children to visualize what their parents work at outside the home, and there is a bewildering variety of jobs.)

At this age children love being read to. It stimulates their imagination and increases their desire to read to themselves eventually.

All these strivings to grow up can be nurtured or suppressed, depending on the attitude of the adults. The drive for autonomy can be strengthened by giving children the opportunity to practice new skills until they are mastered. At the same time, as children grow older, their urge to learn and mature can be impaired if their parents and teachers are constantly directing and dominating them unnecessarily, filling every waking minute with dictated activities.

There are a number of very human and enjoyable activities that school-aged children themselves get involved in, without any planning—spending time with friends, playing with dolls, organizing games, reading books, and engaging in working at self-selected hobbies and projects of all kinds. These are not just pleasant pastimes. These activities keep children's feelings alive and warm in a society that is pushing us further and further into cool technology. They teach sociability, cooperation, leadership, followership, creativity, responsibility, independent thinking, and self-discipline. In these ways they help prepare children for satisfying careers and good relationships with people.

Compared to these benefits, the value of special, imposed lessons seems to me to be secondary. It's not that special instruction is bad or unimportant. But lessons or prescribed activities should not be allowed to take the place of spontaneous ones.

When both parents work outside the home, after-school scheduling can be a way of providing supervision for the child. Ideally the child should be in an after-school group program, preferably at her regular school, that offers activities she can pursue for her own interests and enjoyment. The value will depend on whether the child made the choice and how much enthusiasm she continues to feel; it also depends on whether the leadership, responsibility, initiative, and creativity are mainly left to the group. Instructors should be selected for their popularity with children. There should be no grading. The possible offerings are endless: athletics (with coaches who will emphasize teamwork and enjoyment instead of perfection or winning at all costs), computer operation, carpentry, electronics, painting, music, story writing, newspaper editing, stamp collecting and trading. Parents should demand such programs in their children's schools, whether or not both parents work.

I started with the example of a child who was sent to six activities outside school each week. She didn't have much time for friendship, reading, hobbies, or fun. It seemed clear that, while her parents may have been hoping to make her more accomplished, the child was instead becoming tense under the pressure.

I can picture other children who are just as busy every day after school but with their own spontaneous interests. In these activities they are being themselves, cultivating their curiosity and developing their character. So it's a question not of how many hours a child should spend or how many interests she should have, but of the spirit in which activities are entered into and carried out.

Why have I bothered listing the well-known activities of children? Simply to remind us that there is a beautiful system by which children who are well loved reach out to their parents and to the world for what they need. Through the centuries, this has been enough to produce plenty of bright people who have succeeded in life as well as in school.

So you don't have to seek out special, newfangled, advanced courses. I do feel that the preschool and the regular school should foster creativity, initiative, responsibility, and problem solving; they should be joyful places, rather than prisons that teach memorization and conformity. To be sure, the courses in high school and universities have to keep pace with computers and other technological advances. But children who have grown up secure and curious will have no serious difficulty adapting to these. It's those who have grown up with stunted curiosity and insufficient love who won't catch on.

▷ ABDUCTORS AND MOLESTERS

Two child safety proposals have been much discussed lately and put into practice in some localities: the fingerprinting of children and the inviting of police officers to give talks in schools warning children against abductors and molesters. There is an obvious appeal to these suggestions. I myself would be in favor of any proposal that offered real protection. But I believe that on balance these particular precautions are likely to do more harm than good, because they will make millions of children fearful without a redeeming benefit.

There is no doubt that children have morbid imaginations and are easily frightened. Studies have shown, for example, that children entering a hospital for as ordinary an operation as a tonsillectomy have developed all manner of dreads—that the operation is necessary because they have not obeyed their parents, that their necks would be sliced open from ear to ear, or that their parents would never be able to find them again to take them home.

You can guess, then, what a child's imagination will make of a policeman's lecture on kidnapping, rape, and murder. For one thing, to many children, police do not represent protection but punishment. And I can easily imagine a young girl who has passed a raggedy-looking man on the way to school exclaiming to her friend, "I saw a kidnapper this morning and he was looking at me!"

In fact, the overwhelming majority of molesters are people the child knows well—a relative or a friend of the family whom the child is accustomed to respect. How can a police officer explain sexual molestation or warn children not to trust close relatives? I feel that these are jobs better done by parents, who know their child's sensitivities.

An overwhelming majority of the children who "disappear" fall into two categories. The first are those picked up by a divorced, noncustodial parent who feels resentful about unsatisfactory visitation rights. Obviously, having children fingerprinted will not prevent such abductions. The second large group are young teenage runaways, mostly girls, who have felt misunderstood or insufficiently loved by parents. Their fingerprints will not help anyone to discover them. When they *are* eventually picked up by the police it will be because of their evasive behavior. They soon identify themselves anyway.

Actually the only real use of fingerprints that I can see would be to hasten the identification of recently murdered children, who usually get identified anyway because police and parents are on the alert. (I say "recently murdered" because decomposition of the body soon destroys fingerprints.)

How can parents themselves go about protecting their children against molesters, to the extent that this can be done at all?

To me it seems easier and less traumatic to talk first about sexual proposals from other children, of your child's age or older. The subject might come up through some sex question your child asks or her report of such an incident, or because you've discovered sex play. Children get interested in the origin of babies and also get involved in sex play at three and four years. You can say to a girl that if a boy asks to see or touch her vulva (or whatever the family word is), she doesn't have to let him. She can just say, "No! I don't want you to do that!" Then the parent, say it's the mother, can repeat the same advice as applying to an older boy. Finally she can repeat it as applying to a man. The repetition is valuable to help any child take in a new idea and to prepare the child to make the same speech herself. In fact the parent can invite the child to practice the recitation with her, right then: "Let's say it together: 'No! I don't want you to do that.' " This should to some degree help the child to call her body her own if and when a suggestion comes from an adult relative or family friend.

To give a young child some protection against abductors, I'd say, matter-of-factly, "Don't get into a car with anybody but us. And don't go with anybody to his house. If somebody asks you to, you tell them, 'No! I don't want to!' and run the other way." You are telling the child that she doesn't have to obey a stranger (abductor or molester), and that there are a couple of things she *can* do, so she has some power. If she wants to know what a stranger might do, I'd say, "There are a few mean people in the world and they might be mean to a child."

If a child, having heard some report of molestation from a friend or television, asked why a person would do such a thing, I'd try to be low-key. "There are a few men," I might say, "who are mixed up in their heads; instead of falling in love with grown-up women, they fall in love with boys and girls and want to take them home to live with them." I would be trying to put the mildest interpretation on such behavior because that would be sufficient warning, and I feel it is important to raise children with as much trust as possible in their fellow beings.

If the child were reacting to a specific television report of a murdered boy or girl, I would say more: "A few people were treated so badly when they were children that now they want to hurt others —not only children but grown-ups too."

Whether children have been molested in a brief, incomplete way or more aggressively, it's essential for parents to realize that the children always feel guilty and that you should do your best to minimize this guilt. "It's not your fault at all," you might say. "You didn't want him to do that. He was mixed up. He was mean." You shouldn't pretend nothing has happened: that tells the child that it's too awful to talk about. At the same time, don't carry on as if a terrible tragedy has occurred, one that can never be overcome.

It is wise to secure help for the child and for yourselves from a family guidance clinic, an agency that specializes in sexual trauma, or a family social agency.

The long-range solution for all kinds of violence toward children, including sexual abuse, is to raise future generations in such an atmosphere that they will grow up to be kindlier adults—parents, teachers, and people generally—than many who are alive today. In other parts of the world the figures for violence of all kinds— toward adults as well as children—are much lower than here, which should give us hope that we too can make a better society if we will recognize the problems and work on them.

All schools should be friendly, creative places like the best I've seen. We should wean ourselves away from physical punishment. We should demand challenging television and movie programs in place of the present violence. We should have more and better social services to rescue the children who are presently being ne- glected and abused so that the pattern will not be passed down.

CHAPTER TWO

Being a Father Today

▷ WHAT A CHILD NEEDS FROM A FATHER

In this chapter I want to take up various aspects of the father's role as model, as companion, as disciplinarian, and as a teacher of sexual equality.

At the start, I should review the matter of the boy's identification with his father, because that is by far the most potent mechanism by which a boy's character is shaped. I need also to review the girl's romantic attachment to her father, because it is on this that her relationship to the entire male sex is first oriented. In both these respects children are molded to a much greater extent by the personality of the father and by how he acts than by what he preaches.

In earlier centuries it was assumed that girls and boys grew emotionally to be women and men by their very nature—by inborn instinct. We know now that though the glands, instinct, and inborn temperament play a part, the main influence is the relationship between the child and the parents. A boy from around three years of age begins to sense that he is destined to be a man. He watches his father, identifies with him, and tries to act just like him. This is how he acquires his sense of being masculine. To a much lesser degree a boy also identifies with his mother, and that is how he comes to sense most of what he'll ever know about females.

In the usual course of events a girl identifies predominantly with her mother, but also to a lesser extent with her father.

A few children make their major identification with the parent of the opposite sex. The boy, for example, who grows up to be what our society calls effeminate has made his main identification with his mother instead of his father. There are a variety of factors that may cause this reverse identification in a boy, such as a poor relationship with the father and particularly close ties to an unusually possessive mother. Similarly, the girl who grows up to be distinctly mannish in outlook and manners probably has made her major identification with her father instead of with her mother. (I'm not referring here to the many girls who go through a tomboy phase.)

Of course, what is called feminine or masculine in activities, interests, dress, and manners is not a fixed matter but depends on the patterns of the society and of the individual family. In one part of the world, being masculine means being macho, tough, aggressive. In another country or on another social level, it means to be philosophical, interested in ideas. In recent times most young

American women have grown up without the appearance of passivity, helplessness, and fragility that were considered the essence of womanliness a century ago.

A small boy assumes that his father is the strongest, wisest, richest man in the world. He attempts to imitate his father's mannerisms, his tone of voice, his phrases and even his curses. He copies in play his father's way of driving the car and his remarks when doing it. He acts out going to work at the factory or the office. In playing house he takes on the exact roles that his father plays in the family. He cares for his play children—live or dolls—as his father does, showing affection, approval and disapproval, and perhaps dealing out punishments.

He converses with his play wife, expressses his affection or irritation, discusses the day's plans with her, and shows or fails to show helpfulness and respect, sticking as closely as he can to an imitation of what he sees as his father's attitudes.

At three and four years old, in his play with other boys and in dealing with men, a boy already has taken on some of his father's manner of heartiness or reserve, of scrappiness or agreeableness.

He is not simply playing here. He is learning to be a man, a husband, a father. When he is fully grown, his way of carrying out these roles will still show strong traces of the way he learned them before the age of six.

A father doesn't have to take much of the initiative in shaping his son's character. The son eagerly does nine tenths of the work. By this I don't mean that the father doesn't have to shoulder his full share of the daily requirements of guidance and discipline; he does, because children are inexperienced and impulsive. But parental guidance mostly involves the details of duties, politeness, safety, and health, rather than basic attitudes toward others and self.

For a father to have a favorable influence on his children, the children need to feel that the father is genuinely interested in them, loves them, and fundamentally approves of them, no matter how much he has to correct them. This is also true of the mother. It's the feeling of being loved by the parents that makes children want to please the parents and grow up to be like them.

Of course, the father has to be with his children, at least from time to time, for them to understand his character and to feel his attitude toward them. This is why, in the case of the divorced father who lives far away, visits as frequent as possible are extremely valuable and why letters and birthday presents help to fill in the gaps. If the father lives far away, has disappeared, or has died, the mother can keep his favorable influence alive by emphasizing his good qualities more than his bad ones—even if she herself now believes he was mostly a scoundrel—and by recounting stories that show he loved and enjoyed his children.

Children have such a need of a father figure that when a father is permanently gone, they create and preserve one in their imagination, made up partly from what they've heard and partly from the characteristics they appreciate in the other men they see in their daily lives: grandfathers, uncles, stepfathers, teachers, and friendly tradesmen. The same applies to the absence of a mother.

As everyone knows from experience, if a father has several sons, they will not all turn out to be replicas of him. Inborn temperament —whether a person is quiet or vigorous, for instance—will have an influence. Place in the family—whether oldest, middle, or youngest —also helps to shape personality. The oldest, for example, is more apt to turn out to be serious, responsible, and self-conscious, but not as easy in his social relationships as subsequent children in the family. Another molding influence is the parents' attitude toward each of their children. For obvious or unconscious reasons they may be more critical with one child and more tolerant with another.

When it is said that the average boy identifies predominantly with his father but to a lesser degree with his mother (and that with a girl it's the other way around), this could mean, for instance, that a man might have taken mainly from his father his pattern of personal appearance, his manner of dealing with men and women, his ambitiousness; but from his mother he might have acquired an absorbing interest in children that led him, for example, into a career of schoolteaching or psychology. But any such formulation is oversimplified. An individual's manner or drive will have several roots in addition to the influence of the parent.

A girl learns how to be a woman and how to get along with women primarily from her mother. But she learns from her father in early childhood how to get along with the other half of the human race. Some of what she learns are the obvious and simple things, such as getting used to the low voice (which makes some girl babies who are not used to it cry in the beginning); she learns to enjoy the rougher, more daring kinds of play that fathers are apt to go in for, such as being tossed in the air or being galloped around piggyback; she learns how to take kidding, how to flirt.

These may not sound like important steps in development, such as learning the three Rs, but that's because we take them for granted. They are basic. The girl who has never had these experiences or has never had a father-person to know in early childhood has a harder job finding out later how to get along with males.

A girl develops an intense romantic attachment to her father in the three-to-six-year period. She thinks he's the handsomest, most fascinating, and most appealing man in the world. What he looks like, what his job and interests are, what his personality is, what his relationship is to his wife and to his daughter, all will have an influence on the image his daughter eventually forms of what she will want in a husband someday. All these things, along with her mother's activities and interests, will help to form her activities and interests.

I'd say, then, that what a daughter particularly needs is a father whose devotion to his family can be counted on, who is warmhearted and who can appreciate girls as much as he can boys. It will help if he is affectionate. But he shouldn't be so emotionally seductive to his daughter as to arouse exaggerated rivalry between her and her mother or make it hard for her in adolescence to turn to boys her own age.

It's a boon to all parents that during those years when children are most intently watching, imitating, or developing romantic attachments to their parents—particularly the ages of three to six—they tend to idealize their mothers and fathers, to be enthusiastic about their admirable qualities, and to overlook their less appealing ones. In fact, the need to be critical of the parents doesn't become strong until adolescence.

So a parent doesn't have to be a paragon of all the virtues—only to be a decent, kind person who is reasonably approachable. If a father happens to be shy, for example, this may have at least a slight influence on his son. But if it does, in most cases it won't be unfortunate. The world can only bear a certain number of hearty extroverts. Many productive scientists, writers, musicians, and inventors have been on the shy side. For another example, timidity in childhood may be transmuted, by compensatory drives, into extraordinary indomitability.

All I mean is that parents can never know in advance which of the attitudes they endow their children with will prove most valuable in the long run.

▷ LEARNING TO BE A FATHER

I once led a discussion with half a dozen fathers. The purpose was to bring out directly what young fathers are concerned about these days.

Nathan, aged twenty-three, got us off to a dramatic start by confessing, "I'm a father of a week! I have no idea what being a parent is like. In the latter part of my teens I was scornful about what gave people the right to be parents; it was really one of my pet peeves. Now all of a sudden *I'm* a parent. I'm faced with all these responsibilities. In a way it scares me—although I'm not usually one to let things like that bother me. I'm really looking for all kinds of information and trying to find the best way to raise my son."

I asked the other fathers, whose ages varied up to twenty-nine years and whose children's ages ranged up to seven years, to tell Nathan the most valuable thing they'd learned from their earliest experiences as parents. Mike spoke of the need for self-confidence about one's ability to raise a child with the right attitudes and morals. Leon confessed how strange his baby seemed to him at first; only gradually did he come to realize that her crying and smiling and babbling were *her* ways of communicating and that he had to respond to these, not wait until she could speak in sentences. Nathan also spoke of his feelings of helplessness and frustration when his baby cried.

The gist of my contribution to the discussion was as follows:

Self-confidence in raising your children is a tremendous boon. It's what makes parenting most comfortable and enjoyable. It's hard to come by in the twentieth century, though—especially with the first child.

Back in earlier centuries there was no "psychology," and nobody ever had suggested that parents were constantly molding their children, for better or worse. It was just assumed that you'd do the "natural" thing—in most cases a repetition of what your parents did.

If a child turned out bad, they used to think it was because the devil had got into him. The nearest they came to blaming anybody was when, for instance, a child grew up to be an alcoholic: then a parent would say that this trait was inherited from his uncle Charles.

I'm sure that this innocence about psychology made being a

parent much easier, for I've known some parents—there are some even today—who never blamed or questioned themselves. But most of us start out burdened with doubts about whether we will be wise enough to raise sound children.

The doubts come partly from all our schooling, which teaches us that we start by being ignorant and learn by attending classes. If we don't study, we'll flunk. Most of us haven't taken courses in child development. If we have, we've learned about phases, not about feeding and diapering and crying and vomiting.

The doubts come more specifically from having picked up enough psychology—from taking courses and reading books and articles—to gain the impression that only the professionals, the experts, know the answers. Furthermore, we've learned from them to blame our parents for what they did to us that we didn't like; the backlash comes when we become parents ourselves and realize that we are apt to stir up resentments in our children too.

The man who's never had contact with children before expects any relationship to start with some kind of greeting and then with finding a common topic of conversation. But it takes most babies a couple of months to learn even to smile, and a year to say one word.

Most women are encouraged from childhood to feel empathy with tiny creatures of all kinds, including dolls, and to talk baby talk to them. Nevertheless, many of them find the first baby hard to relate to at first. If you can get into a confidential conversation with them, in the hospital or soon after they've gone home, they'll confess that they were distressed to find that they had no maternal feelings when the baby was brought to them the first time. They'll say they didn't even feel the child was theirs.

Incidentally, there is much less of this sense of strangeness if the mother has seen her baby born by natural childbirth and has been allowed to keep the baby with her in the hospital. The same applies to the father if he has participated in the childbirth.

I believe that fathers and mothers learn to be parents mainly by taking care of their first child. That's one of the big advantages, it seems to me, of breast feeding: it convinces a mother more than bottle feeding that she's a good mother, because the baby seems so pleased with her milk and thrives on it.

If beginning parents have had a great deal of experience in being sitters with neighbors' babies, that will help some. But there's no such thing as being born with a mother's or father's instinct.

The nearest thing to instinct is what parents learned early in their childhood from the way their parents managed them. You can see three-, four-, and five-year-olds caring for their dolls, scolding or praising them in just the way their parents praise or scold them; twenty years later they'll be doing it the same way with their own children.

So you learn some of your basic attitudes toward your future children in your earliest years. The rest you learn by practicing parenthood. If a father lets his wife do it all for the first year or two, she becomes the expert and he tends to be out in left field, just watching.

This doesn't necessarily mean that a father must give exactly the same number of bottles and baths and change exactly the same number of diapers as his wife does. (He can give a breast-fed baby two or more bottles a week.) He should do enough so that he's one of his baby's regular care givers and also do his share in trying to comfort the baby when she is miserable. All this not only helps him to feel comfortable about caring for the baby and to feel she's truly his child, but also helps him develop a sound, deep relationship with her right from the beginning.

The majority of mothers who stay at home to care for the first baby while their husbands go out to work are apt to experience much more strain than their husbands. They have to shift from being free souls without heavy responsibilities to staying home all day, having to be concerned about the baby and about whether they are doing the job right.

Today, in the United States, in most families children are brought up with very little responsibility. Maybe they have a chore or two, but no serious responsibilities. There's also extraordinary freedom during the high school and university years, and even in a nine-to-five job. Then all of a sudden a couple is responsible for the life of another person, a completely helpless one. This is an awfully sudden imposition of one of life's heaviest obligations.

In many simpler societies a boy from the age of ten or twelve is already assisting his father, working at fishing or farming or hunting or whatever else the society lives by, and a girl actually is taking care of her mother's latest baby. From the time she is four or five she is carrying the baby around on her hip all day. So children take on serious adult responsibilities from the time they are very young. But in our society children are excused from most of this because they go to school.

The result is that many Americans are quite unprepared for the demands of parenthood. I remember that when I started pediatric practice in the 1930s, young people felt less secure than they do now and some mothers cried as they left the hospital because they felt so unprepared and frightened. Most young people have a more natural self-confidence now, so that you don't see many mothers crying anymore. However, there is still some anxiety in a majority of cases.

The situation is much worse if the first baby frets and cries a lot. (Of course, the crying of a first baby will seem *much* greater than the crying of a second baby, even if the amount of time is actually the same.) The parents will be obsessed with the feeling that there must be something seriously wrong, no matter what the doctor says. In any case, it's impossible for them to relax. They are convinced that they somehow are lacking as parents if they can't satisfy or comfort their child.

A baby who continues to cry hard despite the parents' efforts can give them the feeling that she is angry with them, and a baby with colic seems to be purposefully kicking the parent who is holding her.

Underneath, a parent can't help beginning to resent a baby who seems so unappreciative and so hostile. But the mother who, because she is at home all day, takes the brunt of this isn't allowed to say, "I'm sick of my baby!" Such an idea is unacceptable, out of the question, in our society. So the mother has to keep denying and burying the feeling of resentment at being confined with this small, difficult creature.

This is a situation in which the husband can be supportive and loving. If he returns from work and finds dishes in the sink and supper not yet started, he can pitch in, suppressing the impulse to be critical. He can give the baby her bottle, if this is how she's fed, and can bathe her, if this is a good time for it. He can listen sympathetically to his wife's recital of the day's difficulties.

A great tonic is for the father to insist that the couple go out for an evening—to a restaurant, to a movie, or to visit friends. If they can't find or pay for a sitter, then he should at least make his wife go out while he holds the fort.

Most important, perhaps, is for the father to encourage his wife to be aware of and express her irritation and resentment toward the baby. He might begin by openly admitting these feelings in himself, thus helping his wife to admit her feelings too. I've known cases in which a joint confession relieved the tension dramatically and brought the parents closer together than they ever had been before.

▷ A FATHER'S COMPANIONSHIP

Some American fathers worry about the amount of companionship they give—or fail to give—to their children. It's an American preoccupation. As far as I'm aware, it doesn't concern parents nearly as much in other countries. Americans don't love their children more or make greater sacrifices for them than parents in other countries. But they worry more about whether they are doing the right thing for them and about whether their children love them.

In simpler societies parents take it for granted that they are managing their children correctly. They assume that their children love them—at least in the sense of respecting them. They would consider it an upside-down situation for parents to be worrying about whether they are approved of by their children: let the children worry about whether they have won the approval of their parents.

I think that these preoccupations in the United States come at least partly from the feeling of the first pioneers and subsequent immigrants that they would willingly endure any hardships in order to provide their children and grandchildren with a better life. In the old country the children had a great obligation to the parents. Here it was the other way around—a child-centered society.

Because of the absence of old traditions and often because of the lack of grandparents nearby, Americans have been particularly receptive to psychoanalysis and child psychology, which have focused a lot of attention on the mixture of loving and hating feelings that coexist in the relationships of most families. Bringing negative feelings into the open has made conscientious parents guilty about them, has made them anxious to hold antagonism to a minimum and to try to be, first of all, friends with their children.

The fathers who worry are especially those who have become so involved in their businesses or in community service or both that they have little time left for their families. But in actual practice they find it difficult to reverse their priorities.

Then there are the fathers who don't feel really comfortable with their children. Most often this applies to their sons, because at unconscious levels fathers and sons tend to feel rivalrous and critical—as mothers and daughters also do. Some of these fathers had unusually tense relationships with their own fathers. Some are uncomfortably shy with adults too. Most people with problems like these don't like to dwell on them or even admit them. It's mothers who often worry openly when their husbands have little contact with the children, and it's mothers who sometimes turn to professional people for advice on how much harm is being done, especially to a son, and whether anything can be done.

Mothers who don't have an outside job are rarely concerned about their closeness to their children. They're closed in with them from 7 A.M. until well into the evening, except for school hours. In most such cases, though, there's not much time for play together. It's the working mothers of young children who sometimes feel anxious and guilty. But that's another story.

It is all to the good when a father naturally feels companionable with his children and wants to do things with them. The more exciting things are, for example, visiting museums and zoos, attending concerts and athletic events, going on fishing trips, picnics, and visits to historic sights. Before he makes big investments of money and time in special excursions like these, however, a father should test the child or children once or twice, unless they are unusually mature. He may find, as I did with my own children, that a child at a ball game may be more interested in the refreshments and souvenirs than in the play; that's okay, but only if it doesn't bother the father. A child on a fishing trip may want to spend all the time building a dam in a stream. On a picnic he might like to throw all the food to the birds or squirrels. Anyway, excursions should be fun for everyone or they are a mistake. Sometimes it works better if the father and the child each take a friend, so that both can enjoy the trip together but in their own ways.

It isn't necessary or wise for a father to provide special events for his children all the time. This applies to divorced fathers as well. There are simpler activities in or near the home that usually give more opportunity for knowing each other, such as an occasional pickup ball game, a practice session roller-skating or throwing a baseball or football. A father can work side by side with his child at a carpentry bench, a puzzle, or in a cooking session. His voice and attitude give a new flavor to story-reading hours. He might occasionally be drawn into playing a game of checkers, chess, or Monopoly.

In carpentry, playing with trains or in any other activity, a father should be careful not to impose his elaborate ideas on his child, which are apt to make the child feel inadequate. On the other hand, a father shouldn't pretend to lose at every game of skill. A child senses a fake victory and gets no satisfaction from it.

Instead of thinking of how the father can play with a child to be companionable, it's often more sensible to think of how the child can be encouraged to participate companionably in the parent's activities. In an industrial society it's not possible for a father to take his son to help him at the plant or office. But at home there are lots of jobs parents must do that children should help with, such as food buying, preparation, and serving; washing and drying dishes; house cleaning; yard care; car washing; and caring for younger children and babies.

Too often, I believe, parents do these jobs themselves until they think their children are able to do them; then they turn them over to the children—at least at times. I think it is better for the parents to ask for the children's help at an earlier age, and then, even when the children can do such jobs by themselves, to keep on doing them together. Companionship on a job seems to me more comfortable than companionship all by itself. If parent and child temporarily run out of things to say, they may work silently for a while and then open up the conversation again when the spirit moves them.

Besides, when a father works with his children it keeps them from forgetting their chores or putting them off indefinitely, which are common problems.

But suppose a father feels he's too busy to be able to do lawn work or housework with the rest of the family and frankly has no interest in carpentry, athletics, or excursions. Will his children suffer? I'd first want to ask him whether he's really too busy or whether he really doesn't enjoy keeping company with children. If he's too busy, he shouldn't be.

I've talked with a number of fathers who, when they were getting started in their careers at the time their children were young, felt that their jobs (or community service) always came first. Then when their children reached adolescence they realized that they'd never become friends and regretted it deeply, especially if the children had gotten into some kind of trouble. Such fathers saw too late that the slavish subservience to the job that meant neglect of the family had not been essential to their advancement in the firm or in the community. It was simply an obsession, an expression of anxiety.

In a country like America, where getting ahead has been widely preached as the greatest virtue, it takes courage and forsightedness for a young father to see that a good family life and the raising of fine children is not only a greater contribution to society but also brings greater satisfaction in the long run. The decision has to be made in the beginning, when the children are very young.

As for the fathers who don't quite know how to enjoy themselves with children, the time to practice and get over the hump is when the first one is a new baby. At that stage some men say, "I think I'll feel more natural with her when she's a little older and is more of a human being."

I believe it works the other way around. It is caring for a child that teaches the adult what she's like, what she needs, what she wants, what fun she is to be with, how to communicate, how to show love to her, how to win love from her. These lessons can't be learned through words, only by living them.

To be able as an adult to get along well with other adults doesn't necessarily carry over into getting along with babies and small children; you can charm adults by appealing to their intellect or their vanity, but you can't get far with small children by these means.

The way for a father to become companionable with his children is to participate fully in the care of his first baby from the day she comes home and to keep on participating. When she is two or three years old he can expect her to begin to be helpful to him as he goes about his home chores, whether in the market, yard, or house. His participation in her care and her assistance in his work are the best bases for sound companionship. Then games at home and excursions outside are just extras, the frosting on the cake.

One last point. Quite a few fathers love to go wild with their children. They toss their babies up to the ceiling. They pretend to be lions with their small children. They get into pillow fights with older children. Child psychiatrists have discovered that in some cases, at least, this is too exciting. It stirs up turbulent emotions that don't settle down again completely and lead to nervous symptoms. When you tell this to fathers, many of them are impatient. They point out how much the children love these games and beg for more. That's true, but it doesn't negate the advice. A little excitement goes a long way.

▷ THE PLEASURES OF BEING A PARENT

We think of parenthood mostly in terms of the obligations and the problems. When my sons were small I always forgot to think of the pleasures until I was away on a trip and realized how much I missed them, or until the children were grown and lived at a distance. This made me sorry and a little bit ashamed each time, but it didn't seem to change my behavior the next time I was with them.

The main reason is that most of us feel we always have to be keeping after our children—about their eating, their clothing, rubbers, their chores, their manners. Or about the dangers of fire, of being run over, of poisoning, of falling out of a tree or an upstairs window.

Grandparents have often asked me why they couldn't have enjoyed their own children they way they are now enjoying their grandchildren. I thought this over for years and finally decided that there is no magic way for parents to get around their constant preoccupation with their children's behavior and safety. That's what parents were made for, although, to be sure, the amount of fussing varies greatly from family to family.

Grandparents, on the other hand, feel close enough by blood to their grandchildren to take pride in their accomplishments and delight in their charms; but most grandparents—though not all—manage to escape that anxious sense of responsibility they themselves had as parents.

So I don't believe I can point out ways for parents to take a *lot* more pleasure in their children, but I'll try to help just a little.

First, it's important to remember that all the worrying and fussing do no good and may even set you back some. The main factor that makes children's characters turn out sound is their deep desire to grow up to be like the parents they admire and love. Most of that work is done by the children themselves. But the more they are nagged, the less is their eagerness to copy and to please. Of course, I'm not recommending that you let children misbehave or get into trouble—only that you try to avoid the automatic and often unnecessary watching, warning, directing, forbidding, and chiding.

I learned in pediatric practice that the effects of parental preoccupation and worry can frequently be seen in the contrast between first and second babies in the first year or two of life. Many mothers have told me that they had yearned to have a cuddly baby. But their first child usually foiled them by twisting away impatiently when hugged. Their second child was *much* more embraceable. "Why the difference?" they would ask.

Of course, this contrast doesn't hold in all families, by any means. But I think that many first babies feel crowded by all the attention they get—especially by the worrisome attention, but also by the eager, proud attention. Why is he hiccuping? Does his stuffy nose mean that he has a cold? Why isn't he sitting up yet like our nephew? Is this thumb sucking a sign of insecurity? Why doesn't he go to sleep? And then: "Don't put that in your mouth!" "Make patty-cake for Aunt Mabel." "Say *Daddy.*"

With a second child parents make allowances for individual differences. They take it for granted that there are many quirks in every baby, quirks that can't be adequately explained but that have no particular significance. They've learned that a baby is tough and durable despite his smallness. Most important, they've learned from their first baby that they themselves are adequate as parents and usually manage to do the right thing. So they can trust themselves and act in a more relaxed manner with the second.

I believe that a baby or young child knows instinctively that he must have some freedom to make his tiny decisions—to choose his own activity, to play with a toy in just the way he wants to, to turn down a food today that he liked yesterday and will again tomorrow. He senses that he must not allow his parents to control him too much, physically or psychologically. If they direct him too exactly in how to use a crayon or put on a sock, if they try to snuggle him too long, if they want to clean his ear or peer in his mouth for more than two seconds, he feels a strong impulse to fight his way free.

The second or third child, usually given more freedom to go his own way, is less ready to suspect that people are trying to dominate him. So when he feels he'd like some loving or when his mother feels she'd like cuddling him, he can enjoy a hug for five or ten seconds or sit in his mother's lap for a whole minute before sliding off to go about his business.

Now for some positive suggestions. A great pleasure for parents comes from reliving the delights of their own childhood by identifying with their children through every new experience. When you pat a dog for your eighteen-month-old, you can see him shrinking back with caution, reaching out to touch with fascination, smiling in response to the dog's friendliness, and feeling proud of his own courage—all at the same time. The first time a three-year-old sees a steam shovel working, you realize that it takes him a long time to absorb all the impressions: the noise, the jolting of its motions, the enormousness of the bite of earth and the huge hunks of rock that it takes, the sudden vomiting of the shovelful into the waiting truck that shakes as it is loaded, the fact that an ordinary-looking man can control such vast power with levers. A child will talk about his first sight of a working steam shovel for hours afterward, his eyes sparkling, and a parent can share in the wonderment.

Excursions to zoos, museums, circuses, woods, streams, and beaches are intensely stimulating. However, it isn't necessary to go on elaborate excursions to delight a child and enjoy his reactions. Watching a worm or a bug in the backyard or the park can give both of you pleasure for half an hour.

And don't forget about the simple pleasure for both of you in reading aloud. Children of all ages and all sorts are fascinated by stories. The libraries are bulging with children's books. All you have to do is get in the habit of reading aloud. One reason this is an ideal way to have fun with a child is that you drop other obligations for the time being and give him full attention. Let the child set the pace in the reading. Let him ask questions, hear one page over again if he wishes or hear the whole book a second time. This is the way for him to get what he wants from the story and for you to get in harmony with him.

To work at hobbies with children—carpentry, sewing, bead stringing, model building, gardening, fishing, picture painting, cooking—can be friendship-building and soul-satisfying. But I know from my own experience as a father that it often can be frustrating instead—for both generations—if the parent sets the standards too high or is too controlling or too critical.

I ruined the fun of model trains for both my sons by buying equipment that was way beyond their stage of development, making track plans that were much too complicated, and always directing the work. You have to be able to let the child take the lead in a cooperative project. Even if you and he have separate projects in the same hobby, you have to be tactful about not making yours so elaborate that it puts his to shame.

Working together at home chores of even the most humdrum kind can be mutually enjoyable for parent and child. But adults have to remember that children can pay attention to business only for limited periods of time, are not very efficient, and tend to go off on imaginative side projects of their own after a while. So a parent has to be ready to suggest that the child has done enough when he sees enthusiasm running out. Of course, you can and should expect more as a child grows older.

Last but not least is conversation itself, one of the fundamental ways in which human beings enjoy each other. Conversation can be just as delightful between parent and child as between two people of the same age. Of course, the reason it is not fun oftener is that the parent so frequently uses the verbal channel for directing or correcting and the child uses it for begging or complaining. So both acquire the habit of turning a deaf ear.

The way to have an agreeable, meaty conversation—even with another adult—is to put yourself in tune with the other by listening to him attentively and sympathetically, with your eyes meeting his and your facial expression mirroring his mood, whether that mood is humorous, indignant, or awed. Then when it's your turn to speak you take off from his remarks, showing that you respond to them in thought and feeling. So a conversation is woven by two sympathetic souls working with the same threads.

There has to be a feeling of wanting to share something on the part of the first speaker and a real response on the part of the other. A conversation between a parent and a child can't start with a prying or probing question from the parent such as, "What did you do in school today?" This never brings the smallest nugget of significant information.

If it is the child who speaks first, the parent has to resist any tendency to seem critical or bored. For if the child says, "Charlie hit me in school today," and the parent answers, "Are you sure you didn't do something to him first?" that will be the end of the conversation. So will it be if the parent's tone of voice suggests that he (the parent) really isn't paying any attention at all.

One of the most delightful aspects of children, I think, is the originality of the things they say, especially during the preschool years. Their remarks, their ways of interpreting things, are usually fresher, more vivid even than those of great philosophers and writers. Yet lots of parents never think of paying attention to these gems of perceptiveness and even correct their children for using unconventional language. Most children will begin to be more conventional around six to eight years of age and will soon enough be speaking in the platitudes and clichés of adulthood like the rest of us.

I recently read an article by two parents who described one of their ways of communicating with their children, a way that never would have occurred to me and probably wouldn't to most parents. They watched some of their children's television programs with them, especially on Saturday mornings.

The parents said they found several values in this unusual occupation. They could keep track of what their children watched and veto the brutal programs. They found it easy to fall into natural, uncritical conversation about programs and related topics. The children took the occasion to ask many questions about matters that confused them, and the parents enjoyed being able to enlighten them.

They found their children's comments surprisingly sophisticated and amusing—especially their cynicism about commercials. The parents were amazed to find that they even enjoyed some of the programs. But best of all to the parents was the discovery that this was a pleasant, easy way for the whole family to be friends.

▷ TEACHING SEXUAL EQUALITY

My discussion group of six fathers tackled the general theme of what they were concerned about in raising their children. Scott, a twenty-nine-year-old father with a son of eight months, asked: "When can you tell from a child's reaction if one parent is more dominant than the other? I'm talking about parents' molding a child —I'm worried about that. My wife is very close to the baby. She's with him all day every day. I'm glad for her to be that close. But I'm away from home four nights of the week and I need to know what I can do to have an influence on the child too. I don't want him growing up weak-wristed, unmasculine. If I have to take extra time to be with him, what age should he be when I start doing it?"

Jim broadened the question: "How do you keep your boys masculine and your girls feminine? And how much time should a father spend with his sons?"

Leon said, "I'd like to ask it in still another way: should a boy be treated differently from a girl?"

My responses to these questions were along the following lines:

This is a broad and controversial issue today. We can't really start with the question, "How should we raise boys and girls?" We first have to answer the question, "What roles do women and men want for themselves in our society today?" This debate can be acrimonious, as you know from the fight over the Equal Rights Amendment, and people are still shifting sides.

When women and men have made up their minds about the roles that they want to play, then they can more easily tackle the secondary issue: how do you prepare girls and boys for those adult roles?

The question posed—how to foster "masculinity" in boys and "femininity" in girls—is also difficult to answer rationally, because definitions of masculine and feminine vary widely in different societies and have varied in different centuries. Those definitions continue to change in our own society today.

In eighteenth-century England, gentlemen wore lace ruffles on their collars and cuffs and walked somewhat mincingly, carrying silver-headed canes. In prehistoric Crete, bare-breasted women fought bulls in an arena. In Victorian society, women fainted when they heard men use crude or obscene language; today many women use these words themselves. In various parts of the world the mannerisms of the men and women who work in the fields—their walk, their speech, their gestures—have always been very much the same for the two sexes. So what's called masculine or feminine behavior is taught—and taught differently—by each society.

Most people in past generations assumed that you should keep boys on the straight "masculine" track by giving them "masculine" toys, "masculine" chores, and "masculine" clothes. They encouraged boys to hide and deny their feelings of pain and fear and sorrow, and shamed them if they didn't do so. Boys were urged to fight when challenged, to participate in competitive sports, and to prepare themselves for "masculine" adult occupations. Competition and success in their future careers were glorified, and they were taught to feel at least mild scorn for those who chose "unmasculine" occupations or showed "effeminate" behavior.

In earlier times people assumed that girls should look forward to marriage and motherhood as the most admirable female roles, and they were encouraged to develop the feeling and nurturing sides of their natures rather than their ambitious or competitive inclinations.

Several powerful forces have been changing people's perceptions and attitudes during the twentieth century. Two world wars propelled women into industry, in which they performed well, and this gave them a taste for financial and emotional independence. The ever-increasing number of technical jobs that do not depend on physical strength also brought women out of the home and into the work force. Men had to get used to their wives' working and not feel shamed by it. The advertising of new products such as automobiles, kitchen appliances of a dozen kinds, television sets, and air conditioners made couples feel they must have more income than husbands alone could earn and that it was all right for wives and mothers to earn money.

Participants in the women's liberation movement since the 1970s have cried out against the cruelly unjust prejudice and discrimination against their sex that is still rampant. They point out that its persistence is to some extent due to the fact that from the beginning of childhood, boys are arbitrarily treated one way, girls another, without any scientific justification. If we face this injustice honestly, it compels us to at least reexamine earlier assumptions about masculinity and femininity and about the preparation of boys and girls for their adult roles.

Meanwhile psychologists and psychiatrists, their attention focused on these social changes, have had to reconsider their previous arbitrary definitions of "masculine" and "feminine" behavior and have come around to a much more flexible attitude. Most of them now realize that every individual is partly male in his or her identification and partly female. The majority of boys identify predominantly with their fathers, but to a lesser extent they also identify with their mothers and copy them in certain interests and attitudes. The majority of girls identify predominantly with their mothers but also with their fathers.

To take a couple of examples: I realize now that the main reason I went into pediatrics was through a partial identification with my mother. I was the oldest of six children and did a lot of caring for babies. Like my mother, I loved babies, wanted to feed them right, comfort them, get them well when they were sick, and bring them up to be responsible and happy. I didn't see my father participating in baby care—that was not a man's role in those days—though he loved us dearly. Many of the young women of the past who first fought their way into medicine, law, engineering, and aviation probably benefited from a stronger-than-average identification with their fathers, which helped them to object to the very limited roles assigned to their sex and to break through the many obstacles erected against women.

So it's simply not true that a boy is 100 percent masculine in identification or that a girl is 100 percent feminine. There is no such thing. In fact, the macho male who acts exaggeratedly tough and who sneers at men who have gentler interests usually turns out, on analysis, to be an individual who has an excessive fear that underneath he may be weak or effeminate. And some of the women who cultivate an intensely seductive "femininity" in dress and manner reveal themselves, on better acquaintance, to have hostile attitudes toward men.

This mixture of identifications in boys and in girls is different in every individual. What the particular mixture will be in each case depends on the subtle relationship of each child to father and to mother and on the attitudes of the parents toward each child. There are all kinds of attitudes and emotions, interactions and influences at work—admiration, anxiety, rivalry, envy, ambition, longing. And each individual will be most productive in adult life if he or she feels comfortable with whatever his or her combination of identifications are.

Let's take ballet dancing as an example. In the United States in the past, ballet dancing for boys was disapproved of in some families as unmasculine. (I was interested to see, years ago when the Russian ballet first came here, that there was nothing "effeminate" about male Russian ballet dancers. Some of them were husky, like football guards, and none of their mannerisms were the least "unmasculine.") I would say that if a boy has a persistent drive to be a ballet dancer, it would be sensible for him to become a ballet dancer. Certainly you won't accomplish anything significant by trying to shame him out of that desire. That wouldn't change his personality or his interests or make him more "masculine." It would only make him feel uncomfortable, insecure, and inadequate, and he would be less effective, whether he ended up a ballet dancer or anything else.

I start now from the assumption that women are still being grossly discriminated against for no valid reason. The discrimination is built up step by step from early childhood.

In the stories that are read to them, boys have adventures, girls watch or stay at home. Girls are told by well-meaning parents that they are physically frail and shouldn't try to climb up trees or onto garage roofs. They are taunted by rivalrous, insecure boys who say girls can't run fast or throw a ball, regardless of the facts. Menstruation, if not handled tactfully by teachers and parents, seems another proof of infirmity. People say that girls should play with dolls, boys should play with trucks; girls should wear pretty dresses, boys should wear sturdy, boyish clothes; boys should rake the leaves and clean the garage, girls should help with the housework. There is nothing particularly vicious about any one of these views. But the cumulative effect of hundreds of discriminatory statements like these is to give boys and girls, by the time they're grown up, the conviction that the two sexes are as different as two separate species and that females are inferior. We still hear people saying, "Women are no good at mathematics or physics," "Women are poor drivers." These are wild generalizations that have no scientific basis and that rob women of their self-confidence.

The superiority claimed by so many boys and men may seem like an advantage to these males. But it is not really an advantage. Men who have not been inspired to raise their own consciousness level are not merely childishly boasting to support insecure egos. By insisting on some notion of male superiority, they also are doing psychological damage to themselves.

Their lifelong posturing, their arguments with women, the time they spend worrying about whether they are being accorded their due rank and respect—all mean a constant drain of emotional energy away from more constructive, creative, and enjoyable interests. Such men fail to make the most of their relationships with women because they are unable to relate to them on a basis of mutual respect and democratic equality.

Furthermore, in the past at least, men and boys have felt a constant pressure to perform in standard "male" patterns, whether or not these were congenial. They tried never to show fear or to weep, to wear only the accepted styles, to avoid occupations, hobbies, and interests considered feminine. As adults, most of them have felt the compulsion to strive endlessly and competitively for higher position and salary and to house, clothe, and transport their families at the finest level they could afford.

In other words, men too are victims of sexual stereotyping—of a quite different, self-imposed pattern.

Male and female stereotypes are merely two sides of the same coin. As the woman has been considered limited in her capacities and expected to play a mainly passive role, the man has felt obligated to be successfully aggressive and able to ignore his feelings. Both sexes need liberating from such obligations.

Psychiatrists long ago came to understand the importance of good masculine or feminine identity from having worked with unhappy individuals who, although they knew rationally which sex they belonged to, were mixed up in their feelings about being male or female, or wished to be the opposite sex, or really felt and behaved as if they were members of the opposite sex.

I used to assume that a father as a matter of course would help his son develop a strong masculine identity by buying him toy cars and pistols, by assigning him jobs in the yard and garage, by chatting with him about such topics as the standing of the ball teams, and that he would buy dolls for his daughter and discuss quite different topics with her. I recall ruefully the scornful reproach of feminists because I said in the early editions of *Baby and Child Care* that a father, to show his appreciation of his young daughter, might compliment her on her new dress or on the cookies she had baked!

Now I'm convinced that though sexual identity is psychologically important, in the sense that a person should be comfortable about her or his sex, emphasizing differences in such matters as clothes, toys, and chores is not necessary. In fact, sometimes it can be detrimental. Girls and boys gain their sense of being female or male primarily from a satisfactory identification with the parents of the same sex, as well as from their glands and the shape of their bodies.

When a father makes a big issue about different playthings or chores or clothes for his son and for his daughter, this is apt to express principally his own insecurity—whether conscious or unconscious—about the adequacy of his maleness. I still remember, when in 1936 our son, at the age of three, asked for a doll and his mother suggested buying it, with what anxious indignation I said, "No!" All men have some degree of insecurity about the adequacy of their maleness, but European sociologists have noted that the fear of being thought effeminate or homosexual has been particularly strong in America.

When a father makes anxious distinctions between what is boyish and what is girlish, his son senses his uneasiness. The boy absorbs some of this anxiety, and it may hinder his acquisition of a comfortable, assured identity.

The fact that each child identifies to a lesser degree with the parent of the opposite sex is part of what fosters understanding of the opposite sex throughout life. It also adds diversity, flexibility, and depth to the personality of both sexes. Since all people do have a mixture of male and female identities, it's important that they be able to accept these aspects of their nature, rather than be forever ashamed, confused, or anxious about them.

So I now believe that for the benefit of their sons as well as their daughters, parents should try to overcome their conscious and unconscious sex prejudice and avoid discrimination. This will take great good will, effort, and many, many years. If we could manage to bring up a generation of children free of such prejudice, the battle would be more than half won. Fathers, as members of the sex that the prejudice presumably favors, will have more leverage than mothers, if they choose to use it. The process must be begun in early childhood.

Here are my suggestions; perceptive parents will be able to think of many more. I think that when daughters and sons want to wear the same style of T-shirts and jeans, always and forever, including through the college years, parents shouldn't hint that it's more important for girls to dress "attractively."

Of course, any woman will be different from her husband in a hundred ways, and her young daughter will copy her eagerly in many of these respects. A girl may want to wear dresses because her mother or her friends wear them. But for a girl to choose to do so voluntarily is quite different from being told, "You ought to wear dresses because this is what girls do."

So I wrote in the 1976 revision of *Baby and Child Care* that parents shouldn't discriminate in playthings or in clothes but should let their children decide what they want to play with and wear, without the parents' fear of the effect on identification. And the same chores should be assigned to girls and boys.

When assigning raking, mowing, or car-washing jobs, I think a father should assume that his daughter is just as eligible as his son and might like to work beside her brother and father, whether or not her mother does yard work too. But if the daughter prefers house chores alongside a mother who does too, that's all right. The point is that she shouldn't feel she's being pushed into certain roles or being denied others.

If a father is thinking of taking his son to an athletic event or on a fishing or camping trip, he also should invite his daughter and his wife, unless they have expressed a permanent disinterest. Or, if a son and daughter are irritatingly rivalrous and quarrelsome with each other, it may work better for the father to invite first his daughter and then, on another occasion, his son.

A son, and therefore his father, should share in all the various domestic activities, I feel. I'm thinking of the whole list: food shopping, preparation, and serving; dishwashing; laundry; and general housekeeping—vacuuming, bed making, tidying up. Child care is another aspect of family work that should involve both sexes and all ages, I'd say: the feeding of babies, the changing of diapers, the bathing and dressing of small children, reading to them, and, for older siblings who can take the responsibility, staying home with them when the rest of the family goes out. It's particularly important for young children, who are acutely sensitive to all aspects of the loving care they receive, to see that the giving of it is shared by everyone. This will make a deep impression that will be passed on automatically from generation to generation.

When a mother does all or almost all these home jobs by herself, she's the universal servant. When only mother and daughter do housework, this appears to mean that it is women's work and, by implication, less important than what men do; worse, it suggests that the role of women is to serve and support men. But if all participate, according to their age and according to the proportion of the day they spend at home, then the work has dignity as well as utility and neither sex is diminished by it. Besides, the work goes more enjoyably when done in company and in the spirit of equality.

In my view, if the mother has a full-time job, the father should shoulder an equal part of the work at home. But if the mother doesn't have and doesn't want an outside job, the father can share equally in the home jobs that must be done before he leaves in the morning and after he comes home in the afternoon on weekdays, and he can share these jobs all day on weekends.

Each child's share of family work will depend on age and capability, of course, and on the school assignments to be done at home. But nobody should be exempt—for the family's good and for the individual's good. A three-year-old can assist in setting the table and can fetch the baby's clean diaper. Even the hardest-pressed high school student will be able to help at suppertime during the week and more on weekends.

Sharing equally between husband and wife, between boy and girl, doesn't necessarily mean washing the same number of dishes and forks at every meal, of course. Jobs may be rotated day by day or week by week. A child under eighteen, unless a great chef, will be only an assistant cook. If one member of the family dislikes washing dishes and another dislikes drying, there's no harm, when they are the cleanup team, in their trading jobs to suit themselves. But it goes against the spirit of sharing and equality if the females gradually agree to take over all the chores within the house, trading all the outside ones back to the males.

I realize now that almost all boys at the ages of three and four want to play with dolls and want to have a doll of their own. This isn't because they'd prefer to be girls; it's because they want to be parents. This is why boys, like girls, play what they call "house" so much of the time at three, four, and five years of age. I'd say that it is good for boys not only to play house but also to have dolls, if they ask for them. This will help them to be good fathers when the time comes.

The only exception I would make to this tolerant position is when a boy is very predominantly feminine in his identification, wants to play only with girls, wants to act out in play only what he knows as women's roles, and is unhappy about being a boy. Then I'd try to get him into psychoanalysis, on the basis that deeply unconscious fears have scared him away from identification with his father and that these fears should be brought to the surface and dissolved. This is on the assumption that he will be happier the rest of his life if his primary identification corresponds to his sex. And if a girl is *always* playing boys' roles and is *consistently* unhappy about being a girl, I'd advise at least a consultation. However, I would not say the same thing about the many tomboy girls who *sometimes* want to play ball with boys and occasionally grumble about being a girl.

It was amply demonstrated during World War II that a boy's identification with his father does not depend primarily on the amount of time they can be together. The father might be away in the armed services for two years, during the child's most important formative years. Yet the son would make a good predominantly masculine identification through a combination of things: The mother would talk lovingly, admiringly, about her husband. The father's picture would be on the mantelpiece. The mother would tell the boy, when he had been particularly helpful and grown up, that his father would be proud of him when he heard. His father would write him letters occasionally. The boy would be seeing other friendly males, such as grandfathers, uncles, tradesmen. So you can't say that a good identification depends solely on a father's presence for a certain number of hours of the week.

I think the identification can take place more easily if the father is around a lot. But I don't think the father who can't be around should be pessimistic. It depends on the *kind* of relationship there is between them. The important thing is for the father and son to feel reasonably comfortable about each other, to enjoy each other *most* of the time. That's what makes a boy want to be like his father.

But what I mean by *reasonably comfortable* will take some more explaining.

▷ FATHER AND SON COMFORT

A boy obviously won't have much drive to pattern himself after his father if his father is always picking on him, belittling him, laughing at him scornfully, or just looking at him with an expression that says he is trying to find something to criticize. It also is unfortunate if a father ignores his son all the time, as if the boy simply doesn't exist.

But now I have to turn around and explain that the relationship doesn't have to be a perfect, idyllic one either. Father and son don't have to be "buddy-buddy" all the time or completely relaxed with each other. There's lots of psychoanalytic evidence that boys are unconsciously more scared of—or at least in awe of—their fathers, on the average, than they are of their mothers, and that fathers are stricter with their sons on the average than they are with their daughters.

It tends more to be the father's responsibility to keep his sons in line as they grow older and more the mother's responsibility with the daughters. If you ask a father why he is stricter with his son, he'll say it's because his father was strict with him. But being a Freudian I'd also say that it's because there's more rivalry between fathers and sons than there is between fathers and daughters, as there is more rivalry between mothers and daughters than there is between fathers and daughters.

Some conscientious fathers try so hard to be pals that they keep doing things with their children that they don't enjoy. Eventually, however, they are apt to come to resent these activities. In advising mothers who've wanted me to put pressure on their husbands to play with their sons more, I've said, "Don't try to *make* your husband put in a certain number of hours with the boy if he dislikes it, because he'll be increasingly gritty and the play will do more harm than good." Of course, a father should try to find something that they *do* enjoy doing together. It may be going to ball games, fishing, reading stories, looking at the comics, or watching a favorite television program. Or it may be no more than making agreeable remarks to each other at meals.

Back in the nineteenth century and earlier, few fathers played with their sons. Middle- and upper-class fathers carried themselves with dignity in those days. They wore dignified clothes, they went out and earned a living, and they came back and presided over the family table. But that didn't necessarily mean there wasn't a good relationship or that the sons weren't making a good identification with their father.

My father never roughhoused with me or played ball. He didn't take me to sporting events or on fishing or camping trips, because he didn't do any of those things himself. He did take me, two different years, on a steamboat to Maine to look at summer cottages that were for rent, which certainly made me feel grown up. He loved opera and once took me on the train from New Haven to New York to hear *Madame Butterfly*. The singing and the acting were of no interest to me, but I was fascinated that the technicians were able to change the lighting on the stage gradually from daylight to a rosy sunset and then to night. This seemed to be incredible magic to me. (You never know what will impress your children and what will leave them cold. I remember watching on television the epoch-making splashdown of the first American astronaut with my grandsons when they were about five and seven, and they lost interest in a couple of minutes.)

What probably made me identify most strongly with my father was that he taught me when I was about twelve to tend the coal-burning furnace when he went out of town and to grease the family car. You got underneath a car on your back in those days and repacked a dozen grease cups, while the dirt you dislodged fell in your eyes. What impressed me was that he trusted me with these responsibilities, though on two shameful occasions I forgot the furnace and let it go out; it took hours to build a new bed of coals, starting with kindling wood. My father had me paint the family car too—and paid me five dollars, I remember. (That was about 1915, when unskilled laborers earned a dollar a day, the ten-cent-store carried nothing more expensive than that, and a new car could be bought for three hundred dollars.) He solemnly introduced me to adolescence by teaching me how to press my first long trousers and the sleeves of the jacket.

What I've been emphasizing is that there are many ways, apart from playing, in which parent and child can form a relationship that leads to identification.

Another element in a good relationship between father and son, mother and daughter, is physical affection, beginning in infancy and continuing. There has been a tradition in many families, especially those of Anglo-Saxon background, for fathers to be reserved physically with their sons. That was certainly true of my father's relationship with me, and I automatically carried it over to my sons. After they were adults they reproached me for this, explaining that it made them feel such affection was wrong, even though they yearned for it. My sons became aware of how I differed from other fathers when they attended schools where there were children from different backgrounds, in some of which open displays of affection between father and son were taken for granted. The children I knew as a child came from much more homogeneous backgrounds, which was too bad in many ways.

Physical affection between fathers and daughters, mothers and sons, also is good, as long as it is not too ardent, too drawn out.

It's easier in most families for a father to get along more agreeably with his daughter than with his son—because of the natural attraction between the sexes, because of the lack of rivalry, and because traditionally it is the mother who does more of the leading and controlling of her daughter.

But unfortunately it is also easier for some fathers, including those who get along agreeably with their daughters, to make them feel less important than their sons. A father may be much more eager to talk with his sons—about sports, about cars, about some repair project in the house—because all his life he has assumed that these topics belong exclusively to males. It may never occur to such fathers to take a daughter to a ball game or a science museum. This kind of bias may convince a girl not only that males and females are entirely different, but also that females are inferior and that a father loves his daughter less than his son. This may produce a femininity in his daughter that is of the old-fashioned, self-handicapping kind, or a femininity that is somewhat soured by resentfulness toward males, or a rebelliousness that makes her try to play an ostentatiously male role in all possible ways.

The ideal kind of femininity, I believe, is simply for a girl to grow up *happy to be a woman,* more or less in the pattern that is set by her mother and that is respected by her father, provided the parents show support for her particular combination of identification and aspirations. For a boy too the ideal is to be *glad to be a male* as he senses his father's and mother's approval of the particular combination of identification and aspirations he has derived from each of them.

▷ A FATHER'S ROLE IN DISCIPLINE

I'll never forget a conference of a dozen young mothers who met to discuss with me some of their concerns about child care. There was no advance planning about what aspects of child care we would discuss. But when we began chatting, the mothers soon got around to the subject of how reluctant some fathers are to participate in the disciplining of their children.

(The trouble with the word *discipline* is that some people think of it as meaning only punishment. By derivation it means simply teaching. I think of it as including the leading, managing, training, correcting, and, in some cases [I myself don't advocate punishment. See Chapter Six], the punishment of children.)

I had always known that there are a few fathers who evade participating in the disciplining of their children. But I was startled that a majority of the women in our group joined in the accusation and that they felt so indignant.

The women complained, for example, about how, after coming home from work, their husbands would continue to leave all the managing and correcting of the children to their wives while they read the evening paper or puttered around the house or even played with the children. When it was bedtime for the children, the mother would have to ask or beg her husband to exert his authority to get them to move. An hour later, when the children knew they should be quiet, there still would be sounds of excitement or quarreling from their rooms. A mother would say to her husband, "Every night they break the rules this way! I wish you'd give them a scolding they won't forget!" But the father would only call gently, "Please be quiet and go to sleep."

What are the explanations that fathers give? Some say that after being away from their children all day they want to enjoy them, not scold and punish them. Others explain that they think their wives are too critical or irritable with the children—at least by the end of the day—and then insist that the fathers go at the children in the same cross spirit. And a few mothers do keep track of their complaints about the children all day and then repeat them to their husbands, who are expected to reinforce the scolding and punishing; such fathers protest that they don't want to be cast in the role of punishers at the end of every day.

Certainly it's not fair to ask fathers to become Scrooges the minute they return home. Generally speaking, I think the parent who's with the children during the day should take care of the correcting, scolding, or punishing that's called for at the time. Only unusual misbehavior needs to be reported later.

Sometimes a woman's irritability with her children and with her husband is due to her smoldering resentment at what she considers the boring parts of child and home care and the general lack of respect for it, compared to what seems the challenge of an outside career. Such a major underlying issue has to be got out in the open and resolved before arguments over child management can be settled.

Of course in many families it is the mother who is obliged to be the family disciplinarian most of the day. Her authority has worn thin by suppertime and she yearns for help from her husband. A father's authority is usually fresh; with a quiet word he may be able to get conformity that would take a lot of arguing for the mother to achieve. I think that if the shoe were on the other foot and fathers were more often the stay-at-home parents, mothers might be the more efficient disciplinarians in the evening.

Though some mothers are unfair in wanting their husbands to be sterner than is necessary, I think more are correct in saying their husbands are dodging their share of the leadership.

Visitors from abroad have often noted how many mothers here seem to wield the major share of the home authority, in contrast to the commoner pattern in European countries, where the father is considered the senior family official. There are several reasons, I think.

In those families in which the father tends to evade his share of discipline it is sometimes apparent that in behavior he is as much one of the children as he is a husband and parent. He may expect his wife to buy his clothes; he may turn over his paycheck to her and leave to her all the decisions about how it is to be spent; he may call her "the boss."

I've known a few families in which it was obvious that the father was mischievously in league with the children to undermine the mother's discipline, or at least to keep teasing her. This pattern forces the mother to become increasingly aggressive in the home in order to stand up to the alliance against her. This in turn further encourages the group to thwart her.

A young father who appears reluctant about participating in the disciplining may explain that he doesn't want his children—especially his sons—to resent him the way he remembers resenting his father during his own childhood. He wants his children to think of him more as a pal. This is an understandable wish but it usually doesn't add up to a practical program. It represents a carryover into adulthood of a critical attitude toward parents that is more or less universal in adolescence and youth but usually is outgrown later.

When young people are going through the final struggle to break free of their childhood dependence, they find their parents old-fashioned, restrictive, and harsh. They may vow that they'll never be that way themselves. (I remember saying that a hundred times.) But a majority, by the time they have a job and a family of their own, come around to a closer emotional identification with their parents. They may say, "Now I see what my parents were up to, and I think they did a pretty good job." They may take over more of their parents' attitudes and methods in child rearing than they would have anticipated.

But there is a minority of parents who remember more of the negative feelings they harbored in childhood and rightly want to raise their own children quite differently. I think it's more often fathers who dread stirring up in their sons the kind of resentment they felt in childhood against *their* fathers. This is because on the average there is more rivalry and subconscious hostility between fathers and sons than there is between fathers and daughters or between mothers and their sons. The conflict between mothers and daughters can be severe too.

To the father who is particularly concerned that his children not fear him, I'd point out what seems a contradictory finding in child guidance clinic work. Generally speaking, boys are found to be more afraid of fathers who try hard not to scold or who particularly try not to show anger. Such boys know from the behavior of adults in general that they do become disapproving and even angry at times with children who misbehave. So when such a boy sees his father holding back, he assumes that he really is angry and fears this hidden anger. He has a greater fear of it than the average boy because he rarely, if ever, has seen his father let go; childlike, he imagines a rage worse than the reality.

Child guidance clinic experience shows that the boy also assumes his father is holding back because he fears the destructive power of his own rage. This may sound too farfetched to be plausible. You may be able to understand it more easily if I put it the other way around: The *average* boy experiences his father's disapproval fairly

often and his anger once in a while. These experiences are unpleasant while they last but they are soon over. And the boy realizes
each time—with a certain sense of triumph—that he has survived
the storm. Each episode augments the boy's self-assurance, just as
he gains more self-confidence each time he dares to go upstairs in
the dark or deliberately chooses the direct route to school that takes
him past a barking dog.

I'm not recommending that a father fly into fits of anger to
toughen his son. But I'm sure that whenever a father is disapproving or irritated with his son, it is much better not to try to conceal
it but to take up the issue openly and promptly.

Correcting doesn't have to be angry or disparaging; in fact, if a
parent takes up each little crisis of management as it arises, parental
resentment doesn't need to accumulate to the point of anger. Child
management can consist mainly of very positive directions or of
corrections that can be matter-of-fact and quickly over, without
leaving bad feeling. Leaders, whether they're generals, captains of
industry, or parents, can remain basically friendly and respectful of
those under their authority if they know what they themselves
want, make their wishes clear, and don't tolerate impositions.

Another factor that can contribute to a father's reluctance to
share in discipline may be his having been reared by an overly bossy
mother whom he didn't dare to defy openly but whom he often
resisted subtly, in a teasing, pesky way. A male raised in this kind
of relationship unconsciously may seek a wife who's on the bossy
side too. Even if that quality was not important in his original
choice of spouse, after marriage he still may try unconsciously to
provoke his wife into being a nagger by failing to live up to his full
responsibility as husband or father or by being in league with the
children in everyday disobedience. Unconsciously he compels his
wife to become a scolding mother to him just as his real mother
was. Freud called this an example of the "repetition compulsion."

If a reluctant father is to change sufficiently to take on his fair
share of the management of the children, he must be mature
enough to realize what he has been doing—or failing to do.

And his wife must make it possible for him to assume his role by
giving him the opportunities. I've known cases in which a mother
complained bitterly of her husband's failure to discipline, but when
he tried to make some of the decisions for the children and to
correct them, she tended to contradict him or to countermand his
directions.

I myself feel that when a father comes home he should take on —without having to be prodded by his wife—a major portion of the managing of the children during the evening, including the especially tough job of getting them off to bath and bed.

All this is not to say that a father has to be grim or that he can't be a pal to his children. It's a great advantage to children to have a friendly father. But if he is to have an ideal influence on his children as well as a good relationship with his wife, he must be first of all a father, which means being a leader of and a model for the children. A boy gains his main inspiration about how to grow up to be a person and a man from his father. He watches intently how his father behaves toward his children—leading them, respecting them, asking for respect from them, assigning them responsibilities, being able to say no and to show clear-cut disapproval; a boy sees how a father treats his wife and other women; how he gets along with other men, companionably and competitively; how he meets, with resourcefulness, dignity, and courage the demands and minor crises that come up every day.

If a father shows himself to be only a good-natured, overgrown child, he deprives his son of a strong model to pattern himself after. He also deprives his daughter of a good male pattern on which to build her future relations with the whole male sex and particularly with her future husband.

Children will have many friends as they grow. They'll probably have only one father. It is fine for the father to be a companion, but it is vitally important for him to be a father first.

The father's part in guidance and discipline can't wait until his sons and daughters are a certain age, and he can't suddenly pop into view when an issue looms and disappear when it's resolved. Discipline is only one thread in the whole fabric of the father-child relationship, which continues to be woven at least until the child finally leaves home. The time when the father's relationship with each child should be firmly established begins at birth. The father and mother should become experts together. The father's participation in guidance and discipline grows naturally out of other earlier acitivities—feeding, diapering, bathing, dressing, comforting, explaining, reading and telling stories.

As the children emerge into adolescence it usually and naturally works out that the mother does more of the guiding of a girl in the family and the father of a boy. By this age a boy has an exaggerated sense that his mother is so different from him because of her sex as almost to belong to a different species; it's hard for him to think of her as understanding his feelings and needs. He wants and is entitled to have his father as chief guide and controller—though he should still listen to and show respect for his mother.

A girl, as she gets into adolescence, correspondingly feels that her father cannot possibly understand her feelings and problems, so a father will tactfully leave most of the guidance to her mother. But it's still vital that a father be a companion and support to his daughter, showing interest in her ideas and activities, sharing his with her, including her in trips and treats, standing ready to explain the peculiarities of the male sex to her when she is perplexed or hurt.

▷ I DIDN'T KNOW HOW TO BE A STEPFATHER

I wrote an article once about the problems of stepparents that I thought contained a lot of wisdom. But eleven years ago, when I myself became stepfather to an eleven-year-old girl, I found I didn't know beans about actually being one. Frustrated and unhappy, I visited a counselor who specializes in such matters. She gave me hope. I had been living in a fool's paradise, she told me, naively thinking that *any* child would accept a stepparent in just a year or two. Feeling better, I settled down to work on the problem, with the help of a family therapist and the insights provided in the many books and articles that I read on this subject.

I'll start by boldly declaring that the steprelationship is just naturally accursed, just naturally poisonous. It's no accident that the villains in so many fairy tales are wicked stepmothers or cruel stepfathers. Stepparents *seem* evil to the children involved. After all, the children didn't fall in love with this outsider or give this interloper permission to take up half of the true parent's attention. And the stepparent often barges into the family at a time when the children and parent have become unusually close because of divorce or the death of the other parent. So the stepparent stirs up intense jealousy and resentment. To justify these feelings, the children exaggerate the stepparent's defects and ignore his or her good qualities.

I'm focusing on the negatives, of course. Children are sometimes quite cordial to the stepparent. But beneath the surface, the readiness to turn bitter is usually lurking and may show up as uncooperativeness or rudeness. Sooner or later this gets under the skin of the stepparent, even if he or she is understanding and patient. The stepparent eventually gets cross, perhaps openly angry, and starts to seem disapproving of the children, who, seeing this as proof of hostility, start behaving even worse.

The stepparent then reproaches the parent for having brought up such badly behaved children and asks that they be corrected. The children, therefore, think that the stepparent is trying to turn their parent against them. The unhappy parent feels torn. To make a move in either direction is certain to hurt and alienate someone.

What I've described is a typical situation; it certainly was mine. Ginger, my stepdaughter, had her mother pretty much to herself— in the sense of having no serious competitor—from the age of seven, when her parents were divorced, until I stepped in four years later.

Mary and I fell in love when we first met at a conference in California, so we were partly committed before Ginger even had a chance to meet me. From the start she was robbed of any participation in her mother's choice of a partner. Then Mary and I, in our enthusiasm for each other, gave too little weight to Ginger's feelings.

Ever since my retirement as a medical school professor, I have lived a great deal of the year on a sailboat—winters in the Virgin Islands, summers off the coast of Maine. Throughout my life, sailing had been a passion; once I retired, it became an essential element in my life, and it was important for Mary and me to know if she could share it. So, shortly after we met, Mary came to the Virgin Islands for a visit of several weeks. Later that winter she visited again. On both occasions Ginger was left with good friends in the States, but on Mary's third trip we invited Ginger to come along too and bring a friend. Ginger was cool to me the entire time and rude enough on one occasion to make me explode with anger.

Ten months after our first meeting, Mary and I decided to get married. At the time, I lived in New York City, Mary and Ginger in California, and we would have preferred to settle in one of those places. But Ginger pleaded with us to make our home in Arkansas, where she had grown up, where she was the adored first grandchild on both sides of her family, and where her father lived. For those reasons, we agreed to build a house there; Ginger and her father agreed that she would live with him during the months of the year when Mary and I might be cruising. But a year later, when our house was finished, Ginger and her father changed their minds about living together. Once again she became our full responsibility, and we tried to make plans that would suit everyone.

Our idea was to live in Arkansas in the fall and spring, and spend summers with Ginger on the boat. In the winter she had three weeks of vacation at Christmas and two in February, when she could also join us sailing. That left two months when she needed to be in school and Mary and I wanted to be on the boat. We knew we could make pleasant living arrangements for her.

But Ginger was outraged. From her point of view she was being left behind a lot of the time, and as she grew older and bolder, she reproached us for making her feel unloved, neglected, and abandoned. Although we may have been guilty of some ignorance and insensitivity, I don't think it was all as one-sided as Ginger's feelings told her. As I saw it, it was more often she who was unwilling to be with us. She adamantly refused to spend the first summer with us in Maine, which she imagined to be a cold and unfriendly place. Another summer we yielded to her request and stayed in Arkansas for a very hot July—but we saw little of Ginger. She spent almost all her time in town instead of inviting friends to our house by the lake.

It wasn't just summers that were a problem. For the first three or four years that we shared a home, it seemed to me that Ginger rarely looked at me or spoke to me. When I'd drive her to school because she'd missed the bus, I'd try to make conversation, with no response except for a muttered yes or no. Once or twice a year I'd explode. "Ginger," I remember saying one day, "in my seventy-five years, I've been acquainted with thousands of people, but not one of them has been as rude as you!" I thought I saw a faint smile of triumph.

As if I didn't have enough trouble just trying to be accepted, I compounded my problem by being critical of Ginger. At the table she would pick chicken into small pieces with her hands and then let her fingers dabble in the gravy. (Mary was sure she did this to taunt me.) She refused to wear her teeth-straightening headgear despite my insistence. She kept her room in utter chaos and every morning left her washcloth in a soaking wet ball on her washstand. Over and over I would explain that it couldn't possibly dry that way and would get mildewed. If she said, "Me and him were late for school," I would correct her grammar. What madness!

I often wanted Mary to reprove Ginger, but although she did

listen sympathetically, she naturally was reluctant to do anything to make Ginger think her mother was siding against her. Mary told friends that she felt her arms were being pulled out of their sockets by Ginger and me.

There are many more problems in stepfamilies than the ones I've focused on. In some cases both husband and wife in a new marriage have brought children into the family, and the two groups of kids have to learn to get along with each other as well as with their respective stepparents. Sometimes ex-spouses continue to be full of bitterness over visitation rights and money matters. A helpful book that deals with these and other difficulties that may arise is *How to Win as a Stepfamily* by Emily and John Visher (Dembner Books, 1982).

In my own case, time was a most important healing factor. Three or four years of painful relations between Ginger and me were followed by four or five years of gradual improvement. And Ginger's own development also eased our problem. She was moving away from a stage of almost complete dependence on her mother to an age when she desired independence. The older she got, the less of a threat I became.

In retrospect, though, we probably could have become friendlier sooner if I had had the sense and self-control to avoid criticizing her. All the experts who have written about the steprelationship agree that the stepparent should go slow in trying to become the disciplinarian. Assuming that role only makes the child say or think, "You are not my parent and I don't have to obey you!" This doesn't mean that a stepparent has to accept abuse—only that he or she should wait for acceptance before trying to take over the kind of *general* control and guidance that are a parent's responsibility.

Ginger is now twenty-two, and she and I are good friends most of the time. As a high school senior, she helped get me invited to speak at her commencement, a gesture of acceptance that pleased me enormously. She also refers to me occasionally as her dad, and although I have no wish to displace her father, the term of affection warms my heart.

I include here Ginger's version of our early years together.

He Stepped In and Took Over
by Ginger Councille

"One day, out of the blue, I had an instant second father. What had been missing from our family since I was seven years old was now replaced. The only problem was, my new father was a man I didn't know. I had only met him once when I was informed that he would be marrying my mother. The first fear that entered my mind was that our close little family of two was being invaded by a complete stranger. How would my new stepfather and I get along? Did I automatically have to accept him?

"I soon knew that my relationship with my stepfather, Dr. Benjamin Spock, would be like no other relationship I'd ever experienced—and it would be by far the most difficult. Once they were married I saw my mother, who was the closest person in the world to me, for only five months or so a year. I chose not to live with my real father in Arkansas, so while my mother and stepfather traveled and sailed, I lived with friends. It seemed to me that Ben and my mother didn't understand that I felt utterly unhappy and rejected —as I think any child would in this situation. I felt as if he had just stepped in and taken over.

"I never set out to make Ben feel unwanted or to be rude to him. Subconsciously, though, I probably meant to, because I found it hard to adjust simply to having him around. Ben has said, in several articles and speeches, that I never talked to him or looked at him for the first couple of years and that I would just ignore him in the morning before going to school. First of all, I'm not very talkative in the morning, and second, I honestly didn't have very much to say to Ben. For a long time, I just observed him.

"The first summer after they were married, my mother and Ben wanted to go to Maine. I had never been there and wanted them to stay in Arkansas. When they decided to go anyway, I felt as though my preferences didn't count at all. My mother would never have left me during the summer, or at any other time, if it hadn't been for Ben. I was compelled to compete with him for her attention, and I couldn't help taking that out on him.

"I never hated Ben. There were just so many differences between us that it had to affect our relationship. Since he is sixty years older than I and was raised in a puritanical environment, he has a more conservative outlook than I do. When I was thirteen or fourteen and loved to be on the telephone gossiping with my girlfriends and flirting with boys, I could tell that Ben thought I was silly. I always loved stuffed animals, but Ben, whose four sisters had never collected such things, looked down on this as babyish. And, of course, we had different tastes in music. I would be playing rock in my bedroom while he played classics and jazz in the living room. Occasionally one of us would turn up our own music to drown out the other's.

"My relationship with Ben has become much better over the years. As I got to know him, I realized that he wasn't an inconsiderate, devious man who was trying to steal my mother away from me. Gradually we started canoeing, sailing, and reading aloud together. Once when my mother and I were disagreeing about something that meant a great deal to me, Ben took my side. I was touched and realized that he really cared and really wanted the best for me.

"I remember the first time I gave Ben a Father's Day present. We both knew it meant that I now considered all three of us a family."

CHAPTER THREE

Divorce and the Consequences

▷ CHILDREN AND DIVORCE

▷ CAN ONE PARENT BE AS GOOD AS TWO?

▷ CUSTODY SOLUTIONS

▷ CHILDREN AND DIVORCE

How do you prepare children for a divorce, so that its effect will be as little harmful as possible? You have to realize that young children's sense of security is strongly tied to having a father as well as a mother and to having them both live in the same house. Just as soon as they hear that a divorce is possible they beg their parents to stay together. Even after the divorce has been a reality for months or even years, they're still hoping and pleading. So it's important that quarreling parents not use the threat of divorce in their battles unless and until they've made their decision. But once that decision has been made it's wise to be open with the children. When any serious crisis is looming but not being discussed with them, children know right away that *something* is wrong, and their morbid, anxious imaginations are apt to picture it as worse than the reality.

In the first place they are apt to assume, by some strange childhood logic, that they are to blame for the divorce. I suppose it's because they are used to being scolded for so many things that they take it for granted they are guilty till proved innocent.

Secondly, they think that the parent who leaves the home is disappearing for good and won't be their parent anymore. And if the departing parent actually does not keep contact by one means or another, the children may acquire a deep conviction that they are not worthy of love, which will handicap them for life. That's why it's so important for the parent who is leaving the home not only to promise visits but honor those promises as a sacred obligation or, if located far away, to keep in regular touch through letters, phone calls, birthday and Christmas presents, even valentines.

Thirdly, young children fear that if one parent departs—in their minds, deserts—the other one might do it next, leaving them orphans.

Finally, if they are persuaded by one parent that the other is a louse, they will be convinced that they are partly louse themselves, since they are made of both parents.

Even with the best of preparation, the parents can expect their children to show symptoms of being upset for at least two years. The symptoms are various and will depend on the children's personalities and ages: fears and bad dreams, clinging, weeping, demandingness, aggressiveness, quarrelsomeness, poorer schoolwork.

My advice to both the custodial and the noncustodial parents is to treat the children as far as possible as they did before the divorce. The mother who has not gone out to work before may, out of guilt, feel she must bring home presents often. But it's not possible to substitute presents for presence. Or the parents may be too submissive—in reading stories, playing games, accepting noncooperation and rudeness. The noncustodial parent may fall into an invariable Saturday visitation pattern of lunch at McDonald's, then a movie, as if this is the norm for all children. It's fine for the parents to do fun things with the children as long as it is fun for the parents too, and not too time-consuming. After that point, it is parental guilt. The children read it as such and are tempted to become more and more demanding. You can simply say, "I'm tired now and I want to read the paper."

The children should be encouraged to stick to their usual routines of outdoor play with others, bicycling, hobbies, limited television, homework, reading. It is also emotionally healthy for them to cooperate with housework, at both locations.

Can a mother be a father too? She can't, and she shouldn't feel bad about that. Grandfathers, uncles, coaches, camp counselors, scout masters, and the mother's men friends can fill in as father figures. She may worry that when a son grows large in adolescence she won't be able to control him. But physical power and punishment are not the way for a father to try to control a son either; it's done best by instilling respect and reasonableness and idealism.

What is important is that the mother not try to turn her son into a substitute husband by taking him into her bed or by discussing all her deepest concerns at length with him. And if she is bitter about the way her ex-husband behaved or has decided that all men are scoundrels, she should not try to convince her son—or her daughter—of this, though the temptation is great. It is important for boys and girls to grow up believing that men and women in general, and their parents in particular, are decent, well-intentioned people. Otherwise they will have the wrong self-image, the wrong image of the opposite sex, and the wrong image of marriage.

In many ways the mother, if she has custody, is the hardest hit by divorce and single parenthood. Many women who had never had a paying job before have testified that the question of whether they could support themselves and their children was the most frightening aspect of being single. (Mothers suing for divorce should always demand ample child support unless they are independently wealthy even though in a majority of cases it will prove difficult to collect. They shouldn't let pride stand in the way.) But they have also testified that when they'd proved to themselves that they could hold a good job and manage the children, it gave them a self-assurance and pride such as they'd never had before. However, in our society the mother will usually be handicapped by the fact that women in general earn only fifty-nine cents for work for which a man makes a dollar. So she has less for the children, less for herself, less for sitters and day care.

On top of a full day of work outside, the custodial parent must keep house, care for the children's ordinary needs, be extra sensitive to their special emotional needs arising from the divorce, and cope with their children's more demanding, less attractive behavior. This leaves little energy and little time for her (or his) social and romantic needs. (I once spent a long evening in discussion with a divorced parents' club, and a significant number of them said that, in view of the realities of their situations, they wished they had tried harder to make a success of their marriages, through understanding and counseling. I would interpret this to mean that some of them had persisted in going after a divorce because of anger and obstinacy and vengeance, feelings which evaporated later. (See the next section for a discussion on dating.)

Because they are not sure at first whether they can make a financial go of independence, considering that they aren't paid as well as men, some women move in with their parents, at least temporarily. Others have found it very satisfactory to form a cooperative household with another woman, usually another mother. This helps cut expenses, offers much-needed companionship, and makes it easier for one or the other to get out in the evening. Of course they should get to know each other very well before making such a commitment. Men might use the same arrangement.

So single parenthood is a tough challenge. But it can be maturing. This could be advantageous in a second marriage if a second marriage is desired. Or it could just make life more satisfying.

▷ CAN ONE PARENT BE AS GOOD AS TWO?

How do you succeed as a single parent? It's an important question these days because there are more and more such families. The largest number, of course, are headed by women who have been divorced or deserted or widowed. But in recent years some judges have been willing to award custody to suitable fathers. Then there are a relatively small but growing number of women who choose to raise a child—their own or adopted—without the benefit (or handicap, some of them would say) of a partner.

We can get clues about the best ways for single parents to raise their children if we think first of what children in two-parent families get from their fathers and mothers.

Children in general want a mother *and* a father, partly because they started out from infancy that way and developed a deep emotional dependence on both; this desire shows in how they beg divorced parents to get together again. Children also crave what other children have, whether it's a computer or a new style of doll or a nuclear family.

Back in the days when there were so-called orphanages, used mainly for neglected and abandoned children, you could see how children who had never known their parents still yearned for them. They would create them out of their imaginations and out of aspects of the various adults they did see and liked, such as staff people and visiting parents of other children. Such children would describe for you every detail of their imagined parents' appearance and tell how they visited frequently, what fine presents they brought, how they would soon remove their children from the institution to their fine homes.

So boys and girls in intact families use fathers *and* mothers to set crucial ideals that will guide them all their lives.

Up to now I've been talking as though children get their patterns and inspiration only from identification with or attachments to their own two parents. Parents are much the most important in intact families and in divorced families when visitation and other contacts (letters, gifts, phone calls) occur regularly, especially in the formative preschool years. But even in intact families, as children develop, learn about the world outside the family, and start to want to be independent of their parents, they come under the influence of teachers, group leaders, heroes; they form attachments to them and identify with them too.

And so a child whose parent is remote or out of contact altogether will instinctively turn, even in the early years, two to five, to substitutes—a grandparent, uncle, aunt, cousin, friend of the family, familiar tradesperson, who is *friendly* and *responsive,* to satisfy her need for the absent parent. (It's impossible to identify with someone who is indifferent to you.) I can still remember the four-year-old daughter of a colleague who had been two years on the staff of a military hospital unit in the Pacific during World War II and how she flung herself on me and took possession of me during a pediatric house call. There is no doubt—and many biographies attest to this—that children in single-parent families *can* grow up to be well-adjusted, successful people, because they can make do with live-apart or substitute parents.

What are some of the factors that make for success or lack of it? (I'll assume, for convenience in writing, that the children live mainly with their mother.) We can first discuss the situation when divorced fathers are within visiting distance and are happy to carry out their responsibilities to their children. Children can get a great deal from a live-apart father who visits with them regularly and keeps contact by other means—letters, gifts when gifts are expected, telephone calls. This is by far the most effective and relatively easy way for the mother to ensure that her children get the benefits of having a father—by encouraging these visits and contacts.

The best arrangement in one sense is when the parents share custody and responsibility and the children regularly spend a lot of time in both homes. Then the father doesn't feel so alienated. But joint custody requires a very cooperative attitude in both parents, for the children's sake. Joint custody works out badly if the two parents are antagonistic. Next best is frequent regular visitation, with the mother usually having custody. But too often this ends up with the father gradually neglecting his visiting rights and other contacts with his children because he feels that he no longer has any authority with or about the children. He says that the mother never asks—or takes—his advice about their care, education, and so on, and the children no longer ask his opinion or permission. They don't treat him like a father and this robs him of the sense of being one. He may feel that the mother takes advantage of his visits to scold him and that she punishes him by restricting his visits for such misdemeanors as coming late for the children or returning them late, for letting them eat junk food or stay up late and thereby catch colds, for not keeping up with the child support payments.

So an important responsibility of the mother is to foster the contacts by trying to ignore the father's faults, trying to be cordial or at least polite when he appears at her home, and asking for his opinion or advice occasionally (for example, about camp or medical or dental care).

If there is no contact at all between a child and father and no memory, the child is dependent on what the mother says about the father and on her attitude toward men in general. If she speaks about the father's good qualities and of his love for his children, and if she shows respect in general toward most men, her son will be able to make a positive identification with this image of his father that his mother paints. But if she always refers to her ex-husband as a louse, this will give the boy a poor model to identify with, since he will think of himself as half louse. And if she is bitter and scornful of all men—in her talk and in her behavior—she will give a sick image to her daughter as well as to her son. She may raise a daughter who is suspicious and cold toward males. Or she may raise a daughter who is fascinated with males but who links their attractiveness with unreliability; she is drawn unconsciously toward those who have wide streaks of meanness or unfaithfulness or incompetence in their makeup, or whatever else her mother has focused on.

"But," many a divorced woman will cry out, "he *was* a cruel person!" or a deceitful philanderer or an incompetent provider. This may express her feelings accurately but is aside from the point of trying to keep a good image in the children's minds—for *their* sake. To present the right picture to the children the mother can, with a great effort, think and speak about the qualities that made her fall in love in the first place and of how the father loved and was proud of the children in happier times.

The less a boy or girl have contact with their father, the more valuable it is that they have contacts with other friendly, responsive men. Can a mother create a relationship between her son or daughter and a substitute father figure? I'd say that she can set up possibilities but she can't make them click; clicking will depend on subtle matters of taste and personality that can't be controlled. If she sees that her child has responded to a relative, teacher, acquaintance, or neighbor, she can tell that person what a hit he has made and add that it pleases her especially because the child badly misses his absent father. If the person seems pleased but doesn't follow up, she can invite him to a meal—with his family if he has a family. Perhaps she can be more direct with a relative. Such steps should stimulate a teacher, group leader, or neighbor to at least show small acts of friendliness which may mean a lot to the child. (Throughout my youth and adulthood I've always owned a blue suit with a chalk stripe through identification with a kind, dashing teacher and coach who always wore one.) A mother can suggest to her child enrollment in the scouts, a gym class, a swimming class, or a Little League team, particularly if she has heard that the leader is unusually well liked. She can send the child to a summer camp.

What about the man (or the men) a mother has dates with? Of course such a man may become vitally important if marriage occurs. But that may be a long way off. Meanwhile there are several cautions.

Most children go on hoping for years that their mother and father will get back together again someday. So when their mother (or father) appears to be entering an intimate relationship with another person it seems like unfaithfulness. This is a reason for the parent to go slow as far as what the children see and hear. Sooner or later they should know that their mother has dinner engagements with men friends. But she can wait to invite a man to a meal at home, with the children, until she finds him a person she'd be proud to introduce to them. This is to avoid giving them the idea she's flitting from man to man. She can avoid even casual displays of physical affection until the children have gotten to know him and given indications of liking him. She shouldn't ask him to spend the night or reveal that she has spent the night out until after many months of increasing closeness, in which the children have participated, I'd suggest. These are precautions against the children getting the feeling she is promiscuous.

What I have said about a mother not showing evidence of promiscuity or too quick intimacy applies equally to a father. It's sensible to give this advice to both parents because it's a common reaction to the pains and humiliations and name-calling of a divorce for both parties to flaunt their affairs, as if to prove that they are attractive, despite their lack of success with each other.

If the mother is falling seriously in love and thinking of marriage, she should listen to what her children say about the man, tell them she's considering marriage and wants to hear their opinions, though she should not give them veto power over a marriage. Many children who enjoy the company of their mother's man friend may turn suspicious, jealous, and hostile when they realize that this person may be planning to become their stepfather. In fact it may take them several years to accept him as such. It's wise for the couple before and after the marriage to encourage the children to express their feelings toward their parent and toward the stepparent, provided they are not expressions of direct rudeness.

Several single mothers have phrased an anxious question to me in the same words: how can I be a good father as well as a good mother, especially to my boy? I think there are three misunderstandings here. One is that a mother *has* to be a father—in the sense, for instance, of teaching a boy how to throw a football or of talking to an adolescent about sex from a man's point of view. Another misunderstanding is that a boy *has* to learn such matters from his parent. The third is that women and men know entirely different things about life and are ignorant about the opposite sex. A mother doesn't need to become an athletic coach to her son. He can learn more comfortably from school coaches and other boys. She knows enough about sex from the male as well as the female viewpoint to talk to her son and answer his questions. Many mothers do a better job talking with their sons than fathers do, since a majority of men are notoriously shy and evasive at this job; mothers can also remember that most adolescents get their sex information not from parents anyway but from other kids and from literature—reputable and disreputable.

I've explained earlier that human males and females are not ignorant of each other's thoughts and feelings. There is a considerable amount of intuitive cross-knowledge between the sexes, more in some individuals, less in others, learned by identification with the parent of the opposite sex in early childhood. So mothers should not worry about trying to be fathers to their sons. They have other important contributions to make.

A mother should not remarry primarily to provide a father for her children; that should be incidental. She should remarry only if she loves the man deeply and is as confident as she can be that he'd make a good husband. Otherwise the marriage won't last. Then, sooner or later, he will probably be accepted as a good stepfather too.

▷ CUSTODY SOLUTIONS

In recent decades, as women have demanded jobs previously reserved for men, some men who have had the inclination have shown that they could nurture children as well as women. They've claimed and been granted custody in appropriate cases, by open minded judges. However a majority of divorcing fathers have no desire to have custody.

In the United States half of all marriages now end in divorce. What concerns me most is that one million more children each year are confronted with the breakup of their families. There are already in our country six million single-parent families with minor children. Though in the long run divorce may be the best solution for an unhappy marriage, close observers agree that with the usual decree—single-parent custody awarded to the mother in 90 percent of the cases—there is a misery for all concerned—children, fathers, *and* mothers—at least for a couple of years.

It was surprising to me to learn only a few years ago that prior to the twentieth century, custody customarily was awarded to fathers. Yet the laws of nearly all states, then and now, declare that there

shall be no prejudice in favor of mother or father in granting custody, that the determining factor should be the "best interests of
the child." In other words the strong bias of judges, first toward
fathers and later toward mothers, has been based on psychological
and sociological beliefs, not on the law. In the following discussion
I'll assume that custody has been awarded to the mother unless
otherwise specified.

Young children tend to show considerable regression right after
the divorce in toilet training, whining, crying, irritability, tantrums,
sleep problems, and aggression.

After a year the distress may be even worse, particularly if the
parents are still locked in conflict. Relations with their fathers are
apt to be improved, but relations with mothers may be worse.

In the middle years children tend to feel anger at one parent and
to end up siding with their mothers.

Divorce is painful to adolescent children too, but after a year
most of them no longer feel they have to take sides; they can
proceed with their own affairs.

The most significant fact brought out in studies is that children
of all ages tend to make a better adjustment, and the mothers
manage them more effectively, when children have frequent contact
with their father and the parents can cooperate with each other for
the children's benefit.

When custody is awarded to the mother, the father is, to a large
extent, divorced from his children as well as from his wife. In many
cases he is permitted to see his children only one or two days a
week or, in many cases, every other weekend. He may not be allowed to keep them overnight. Sometimes he may merely visit them
in the mother's home, not take them out.

Recently divorced fathers feel rejected, depressed, and homeless.
Some report that they've even lost some of their sense of identity.
They emphasize how painful it is to visit with their children because of the infrequency of those visits and the resulting sense of a
growing distance between themselves and their children.

The same feelings oppress mothers when custody has been
awarded to fathers.

Some fathers complain that they are being deliberately humiliated by their ex-wives, who, they feel, take a mean satisfaction in
being arbitrary and overbearing in respect to the conditions they
lay down for visiting. Often they forbid visits unless the child sup-

port is paid up. In some cases these complaints may be the fathers' excuse for poor performance in visitation and child support, rather than the truth.

Most mothers, despite having custody, are unhappy for at least the first two years after divorce. They feel anxious and angry and helpless. Two thirds must support themselves (half of nondivorced mothers do not work outside the home), and still they have to deal with a reduced standard of living. (It is calculated that it costs 25 percent more for the same number of people to maintain two residences. Child support payments are usually set low by judges, and even so they become delinquent in a great majority of cases.)

On coming home from the job, mothers have the housework to do, without the help or companionship of another adult. The children's needs, demands, disputes, and difficult behavior have to be coped with. And in most cases the children are distinctly less cooperative and more antagonistic than previously.

Most divorced mothers find their social life painfully restricted —by their jobs, by the need to be with their children, by the fact that their old friends are couples who think of entertaining in terms of inviting other couples, not single people, and by the meager opportunities, usually, to make new social contacts.

To summarize and emphasize at this point: The father's continued closeness to his children is of primary importance to them and to their adjustment. His cooperativeness with his ex-wife has been shown to be important to her sense of adequacy in dealing with the children and to her good relationship with them. Nevertheless most divorce judgments limit sharply the father's contact with his ex-wife and children. This makes him feel unneeded, unwanted, and uncomfortable and may cause him to decrease his visiting as the months and years go by. It's a tragic vicious circle. The situation is similarly bad for most of the mothers in the 10 percent of the cases when custody is awarded to the father.

I and many other professional observers agree that fathers can be just as involved and nurturing as mothers. Today 1.5 million single-parent families are headed by fathers because of the death or desertion of mothers as well as because of divorce. Fathers who have had custody of their children testify that this experience has decreased their previous preoccupation with discipline and has increased their sensitivity to their children's feelings and to the importance— and joy—of intimacy with them.

Joint custody—giving custody equally to both parents instead of one—is a relatively new legal procedure. To me the most important aspect by far is that both parents—for the sake of the children—will try to show respect for each other's opinions and to cooperate in all important decisions about the children, so that neither one will feel no longer a parent and so that the children will look up to both. But if there is considerable mistrust, antagonism, and resentment remaining, it is unlikely that joint custody will work; better then to grant custody to one parent, as was invariable in the past, with visitation rights to the other.

Some states include in joint custody an agreement that the children will divide their time equally between the two parents each week or at least in a one-third, two-thirds ratio. I can see a theoretical advantage in that both parents can feel equally close to the children. But this requires that the parents live in the same city, that both homes be close to the children's school, and that both homes be set up for the child. I feel that the joint responsibility, with neither parent feeling squeezed out, is by far the more important aspect of joint custody and that the time sharing is a separate issue that has to be decided on the basis of practicality.

When the spirit is generally cooperative but certain issues cannot be resolved, a regular counselor familiar with the situation and satisfactory to both parents can be called on.

I'm strongly in favor of joint custody for all parents who think they can summon the cooperation required. It will allow children to feel that they still have their father, because they will continue to live with him much of the time and because they know that he is still helping to make the decisions. The father will continue to feel that he is close to his children, that he is participating in their lives and is still partly responsible for their welfare. And though joint custody may confront the mother with frustrating compromises about the children's lives, it should compensate her in most cases by giving her free time and relief from the sole responsibility for all problems and all decisions.

I can see in theory the objections some professionals raise to children living split lives in two homes. But certainly by now we have evidence, not only from cases of joint custody, but also from all the families in which both parents work and preschool children spend all day in a day-care center or in the home of a care giver, that children can make a good adjustment to two homes when the plans are made with care and sensitivity to their needs.

I've always felt it's vitally important for the divorced father to see his children as often as possible. This is for the benefit of the children and for his sake, to maintain his sense of closeness and responsibility. Once made, it is critical that such plans not be cancelled. Better than excursions and treats, a divorced father ought to see his children in his home, where they should have beds and some of their toys, books, and clothes.

CHAPTER FOUR

The New Baby

▷ THE FIRST THREE MONTHS

▷ CRYING

▷ DOES A BABY CHANGE A
   MARRIAGE?

▷ EARLY PARENT-INFANT BONDING

▷ THE FIRST THREE MONTHS

The experience of most parents of the first three months of their first baby's life is a combination of exciting and nerve-racking. Which mood predominates will depend on the agreeableness of the baby and on the self-assurance of the parents.

Some babies are just naturally so relaxed that they never make a fuss even when they are hungry or cold or left by themselves for long periods. And the friendlier babies may be so beamingly responsive to any human attention that they evoke a warm response from the stoniest or meanest of adults. These babies are fortunate because all through life they'll find whatever kindness there is in everyone they deal with. They don't have *all* the advantages, though; for instance, they usually don't develop into the ambitious kind of people who turn the world around, if that is what their parents have in mind for them.

At the opposite extreme are the babies—more often boys, I think —who are hard to care for, sometimes hard to be in the same house with: the ones who fret a lot, the ones who always get tired and impatient quickly, the ones who are physically and emotionally tense, the colicky ones, the angry ones, the ones who stay awake most of the day or night or both and don't seem to be enjoying life. Most of these characters calm down and sweeten up as they get a little older—three months is often a dramatic turning point—but they can make their parents' lives miserable for a while.

Then I think of the occasional baby who is so deadpan that he doesn't give much delight to his parents. I've watched such babies with a bit of apprehension myself, wondering whether they might be constitutionally cool or unsociable. Of course they turn out later to have plenty of warmth and humor. But at the beginning they don't do their part in making friends or inspiring confidence in their parents.

A number of factors will influence how easily the early months will pass for the parents. For example, mothers and fathers who have great self-assurance can put up with a lot of difficult baby behavior and not be thrown off stride. But those brought up in a way that has always made them easily doubt themselves can be quite demoralized if they have a baby who's difficult.

And parents with considerable previous experience, because they took care of younger brothers and sisters or because they had practice as baby-sitters, can put up with more difficulty.

I think myself that those who have taken courses in child development but have had no practical experience in child care are apt to have a harder time. If their baby cries, they worry at a theoretical level whether it's because he needs more love or is spoiled—and there's no way to tell by looking at him.

It's a part of nature's scheme of things, I think, to fill new parents with quite a charge of anxiety to be sure the baby doesn't get neglected. After all, there are plenty of irresponsible individuals around, and they have just as many babies as the conscientious ones. The system works inefficiently, though, because the conscientious parents are the ones who feel the anxiety the most.

Doctors, nurses, and psychologists have come to realize that new parents worry intensely about an amazing variety of things in a baby: hiccups, burps, snores, sneezes, shudderings, tremblings, pallor, blueness, cold hands and feet, erections. A mother sneaks into her baby's room at night to be sure that he is still breathing and then nearly dies of fright because she can't see any movement of his chest. (Babies' breathing is mostly abdominal.)

If a baby cries a lot, inexperienced parents can't help becoming more and more anxious. It stands to reason, they feel, that something must be wrong. I know how ineffectual I've felt as a pediatrician, going through the routine examination of such a baby and then explaining that he is apparently in perfect health. Then *why* is he crying? To be able to tie to the condition an old label like colic —which doesn't really explain anything—is only slightly helpful. These parents may be partly reassured for a while, but then their doubts mount again and they want another examination. Anxiety like this wears the parents down.

Perhaps worse than anxiety are the depression and guilt that often accompany it. Coming in the early weeks, when so many new mothers have spells of blue feelings even with a perfectly behaved baby, a great deal of crying in the infant gives a focus to a mother's dread that she has harmed him through some fault of commission or omission. Consciously she may be worrying that he has had a birth injury or that she is not giving him the right diet. At the unconscious level, however, there often is guilt about sex that is left over from early childhood. My mother, in warning me in my childhood about the consequences of masturbation, said, "You do want to have normal children, don't you?" So when I was allowed in the delivery room a few minutes after our first son was born, I told my wife with great relief, "He has ten fingers and ten toes!"

Another reaction parents have in the early weeks is anger with the baby who cries a lot. Most people are horrified at the idea of being angry with a helpless infant. So if any such feeling starts to form, they quickly suppress it. But this doesn't eliminate the anger —it only gives it a different manifestation. It can be felt as guiltiness or compulsiveness or constant worrying or as depression. Perhaps most commonly the anger is felt as the tension that results from the effort to keep it repressed in the unconscious. This tension, when it lasts for days and weeks at a time, leads to emotional and physical fatigue and perhaps to irritability with everyone else but the baby.

I remember two mature, sensitive parents who were frantically tense after a month of their baby's constant crying with colic. When one of them impulsively admitted to the other how angry the baby made him feel, the other confessed the same hidden resentment. After some further discussion they felt much, much better.

There are several things new parents can do to maintain their equilibrium. Most important, I think, is to be thoughtful and co-operative with each other. The father should take equal responsibility with the mother for the baby's well-being.

This obviously doesn't mean that if the father is working at a full-time job and the mother is not working outside, he must give exactly as many bottles or change as many diapers as she. But it does mean that he should be fully involved—consulting with the mother and worrying with her, if worrying has to be done, and not hiding behind the newspaper as if the baby were mainly her concern. If the baby is bottle-fed, he could give the evening and 2 A.M. feedings. This is not because if he did otherwise he would be lazy —he may have an unusually arduous outside job. It is to show that he considers child care as important as his job and that he's supporting his wife during this time when she is taking on new and demanding responsibilities.

Psychological observations have shown that when a person is called on to give a lot more care and affection to others than he ever has given previously, he needs—for a while, at least—to receive more attention and love himself. The birth of a baby, especially the first-born, puts a heavy emotional drain on the mother in particular. Maybe this is only because in the past we've all assumed that the responsibility for baby care should be mostly the mother's. Whatever the cause, the mother needs the support, and the father has to be the principal supplier.

A grandmother may be almost as helpful as the husband if she lives nearby and if the mother gets along with her. In societies where the young family lives close to the grandparents and other relatives and where older people are assumed to be wise, the cooperative aspects of the relationship between the generations are uppermost; it is taken for granted that the grandmother is the new mother's best friend, confidante, adviser, helper, emotional support.

In the United States, by contrast, the rivalry between the generations and the young parents' need for independence are emphasized. Furthermore, it is assumed in most American families that older people are behind the times and therefore not so wise, so the usefulness of a grandmother when a baby is born often is *not* taken for granted.

If the new mother is a mature and secure person, she can turn to the grandmother and get enormous support from her. But if the mother has always felt criticized and belittled by the grandmother (no matter what the grandmother may have intended), she may not want her to be anywhere near, on the assumption that she will try to take over the baby and brush the mother aside.

Certainly the new mother needs to feel that the baby is hers and that she is learning to do the job well. So if she's in doubt about her own mother or her mother-in-law, for that matter, she should not ask her to help. Or if she has asked her to help and then finds that she is bossy or critical, she should explain tactfully that she now feels strong enough to get along by herself. Similarly, she should fire a baby nurse who belittles her.

I suggested in the previous section that parents—especially mothers—should get out of the house at least once a week in the early months. This is particularly important with the first child or with a fretful or colicky one. The parents may feel anxious or guilty about getting away. But if they make the break, they usually will find that they can enjoy themselves and will come home revived and relaxed. This will be good for them and for the baby. After they have been parents for a few years they will have made more of an adjustment from freedom to nonfreedom, and they probably won't have such an intense need to escape.

The first three months of the baby's life is a fruitful time for mother and father to try to develop the habit of talking out any kinds of worries, resentments, and tensions, of which there will be plenty in every family. If they can learn to be tactfully frank and try to understand each other's point of view, there will be much less chance that their marriage will be soured by quarreling and sulking over false or hidden issues. To put it more positively, they can take advantage of this turning point in their lives by learning a mutual openness that is one of the best guarantees of a strong and joyful marriage.

▷ CRYING

In any discussion among beginning parents a question that is most apt to come up is what to do about crying in infancy and how to avoid spoiling. But before talking about the management of crying babies, I think it's better to discuss some of the reasons why they cry.

A majority of babies do a considerable amount of crying during the early months of their lives. They cry for a variety of known (hunger, fatigue) and unknown causes. There's typical *colic,* with its symptoms of severe abdominal pain, distension, and passing of gas. This complaint comes at a regular time, most often in the evening, beginning at about two weeks of age and lasting about three months. Then there's what I call *periodic irritable crying,* which has the same timetable as colic but in which there is no distension or gas and the pain is questionable. There is a vaguer condition usually referred to as *fretfulness,* which may occur at any time of the day or night and last a shorter or longer period.

It's during the first three months that colic and periodic crying and fretfulness are quite common; no one knows why. The assumption I make is that the baby's focus on the outside world is relatively vague, compared to later on, and that this leaves her more sensitive to her inner feelings of hunger or abdominal discomfort or fatigue, which are sharper at this age because the digestive and nervous systems are immature and inexperienced. Some psychologists are inclined to blame the trauma of birth, though there is no correlation between the difficulty of birth and this later misery.

Unfortunately, there is as yet no sure, effective way of relieving colic or periodic crying or fretfulness. (Research funds go to the fatal diseases, no matter how rare, not to the everyday ones.)

I think that pacifiers work as well as anything. They cure nothing, but they comfort the baby enough—or at least seal the baby's mouth—so that the crying stops for the time being, though it may resume.

If the pacifier doesn't work, and you feel like holding or walking the baby, do it. You can also try, especially for colic, laying the baby prone on a hot-water bag, which is enveloped in a bath towel, across your knees. (The bag should not feel hot enough to your wrist to be painful.) Some parents have found that taking a crying baby on an automobile ride will do the trick (except when they are stopped by a red light).

I feel comfortable and reasonably correct in advising: just don't worry about spoiling during the first three months. It's very unlikely that spoiling is playing much or any part in the child's crying. Besides, you've got enough other things to worry about at this stage.

In many of the simpler parts of the world, babies are carried all day in slings on the mother's back or side while she works, and at night the baby lies close to the mother in bed. Yet there's no evidence or suspicion that such babies are spoiled. It's probable that the almost constant motion during the day and the sense of the mother's closeness day and night are what the baby's entire system was designed for and expects. Certainly that was just what the baby constantly experienced while in the womb. I'll contrast these early discomforts or tensions with an example of what I'd call spoiling in an older baby. The simplest is when a grandmother has come to visit for a couple of weeks and is so delighted with the baby that she plays with her every waking minute, carrying her around the house, showing her things, jouncing her on her knee, playing patty-cake, tickling her to make her laugh. By the time the grandmother leaves, the baby expects to be carried and amused all day and cries a lot for a couple of days if her parents don't give her this service. I call this simple spoiling because there is no particular pain or discomfort of the child's, nor any anxiety of the parents' to get it started.

▷ DOES A BABY CHANGE A MARRIAGE?

From one point of view it would be ideal, after the baby was born, if parents could go right on enjoying the same good times, keeping up all their interests and friendships, thinking of each other and taking care of each other just as much as ever. But of course a baby's care demands an enormous amount of time and effort— preparing and giving feedings, changing diapers and clothes, washing the laundry and washing the baby.

Much more thought-absorbing and energy-draining is the worry, or at least the preoccupation, especially at first. There are lots of unresolved questions. Am I making the formula correctly? What's that rash? Why is the baby crying now? Did I hear a cry or didn't I? Am I spoiling her? Does the thumbsucking indicate some deprivation or tension?

All this anxiety comes from the overwhelming sense of being responsible for the life and safety of another person for the first time—a tiny person who can't fend for herself, can't even explain what's bothering her. This anxiety doesn't arise just because parents are inexperienced and overconscientious. Sometimes the doctors may have been worried temporarily about a baby's condition in the newborn period. Or the baby may be one of those colicky or fretful types who are hell on first-time parents.

In addition, for all first-time parents, there's the loss of freedom: they can no longer go to a restaurant or a show on the spur of the moment, or visit friends, or shop, or stay up late on weekends and then sleep late in the morning. This loss of freedom causes not only regrets but also subtle resentment.

The problem isn't just that there's a variety of new strains. It's that the parents must abruptly make what is probably the most drastic shift they'll ever be faced with: from having been care receivers to becoming care givers.

Beginning parents can't be expected to pour out the huge amounts of altruistic and unqualified love that are necessary in the care of a first baby without feeling emotionally drained at the end of the day—as deflated as wrinkled balloons. It's the care of the first baby that actually trains parents gradually to be able to give, and give without a sense of strain and exhaustion. When the second child comes, the additional effort required is not as noticeable.

If one parent stays home to care for the baby, she will be the one, come evening, to feel that her emotional reservoir is depleted. The visible love and support of the parent who works outside the home can help to restore the parent at home.

Overconcern with the baby has various side effects: one is that it may make the parents boring to their childless friends. As a matter of fact, this can happen even when the parents have no worries about the baby but are simply delighted with her. It's hard to recapture friends who've been alienated on this score; once they've labeled you a "baby talker," they're disinclined to give you a second chance. (I still remember how we bored some of our childless friends fifty years ago.)

The relationship between the mother and father is affected too. When both parents are totally preoccupied with the baby, it steals attention and affection that should be flowing back and forth between the couple. They will sense the lack, whether unconsiously or consciously; they'll feel a flatness in their relationship, or they may even feel slightly depressed.

If one parent is far more preoccupied with the baby, it can eventually make the other really resentful, whether or not the cause of resentment is recognized. And at the same time, the preoccupied parent may feel that she is bearing the burden alone. Then it takes time to reverse the process and restore the old enthusiasm.

From the point of view of children, it's much better that they not become the focus of excessive attention. If the attention is expressed as anxious concern, the children eventually will absorb some of the anxiety and become anxious or fearful themselves. But even if the attention is wholly joyful, the children will become somewhat self-centered and self-conscious. They'll worry too much about whether people like them. They'll crave a little more attention than other people are ready to give. They'll get their feelings hurt more easily than the average child. These are attitudes that are common in first children and infrequent in subsequent children.

Even if parents don't become too preoccupied with their child but still give up too much of their independence and too many of their own pleasures for her, the mother and father can't help but resent this, consciously or unconsciously, in the long run. They may take it out on the child by being irritable or by scolding unnecessarily. (That was my mother's pattern.) At the least, they will expect too much from a child in the way of gratitude or perfection in behavior.

How much concern is too much? Babies need plenty of visible attention, appreciation, and affection—baby talk, smiles, ridiculous compliments, hugs, and carrying around. When there is something wrong with them, whether it's pain or only mysterious irritability, they need parents who are concerned enough to try to find the cause and apply a rememdy, or at least to comfort them.

My emphasis on the strains of baby care is only one side of the picture, though. Young people today usually don't decide to have a baby until they sense that they are about ready; that is to say until they feel eager to meet the challenge, until they yearn to have a child to cherish the way they were cherished themselves as children. So by the time the first two or three anxious months have passed, the strains are largely balanced by the gratifications.

I consider excessive concern to be a problem when there is no evident need to worry; excessive preoccupation is not being able to think of or talk about anything but the baby. Both conditions are caused by conscientiousness and inexperience, however, and are entirely understandable.

What can be done to prevent preoccupation—or, more positively, to preserve in the parents their joy in each other? It does little good just to tell beginning parents not to get too wrapped up in their child, just as it does little good to tell worriers not to worry. But I think it helps to use means that are almost mechanical. One of the best ways is for the two parents to go out together once or twice a week to visit friends (take the baby in a basket if there is no sitter), to see a movie or eat in a restaurant. If there are relatives, ask them to sit, or hire a sitter. If there isn't enough money for hired sitters, organize a sitting cooperative. In these cooperatives a group of parents sit for one another, taking turns and getting, by the end of the year, as much time as they've given.

The great thing about the early months is that babies adjust easily to being taken to other homes to sleep in the evening and to taking a bottle from someone other than the parents. If the baby is breast-fed, there is usually a four-hour interval between feedings, which gives the mother enough time to be on her own or with her husband.

Don't worry too much about going into debt for sitters, either by spending too much of the household money for them or by being under obligation to other parents. It's the first couple of months that are crucial in keeping a sensible degree of independence from a baby. If you can succeed then, the battle is won. You can begin paying off your debts after that.

If for one reason or another a couple can't arrange for babysitting, they can spell each other in the evenings, giving each parent at least one night out a week.

Conscientious parents may not feel right about taking so much time off-duty. It may make them feel irresponsible, like cuckoos, the birds that lay their eggs in other birds' nests. Or they may be bashful about imposing on relatives. Another difficulty is that new parents are apt to think and worry about the baby more when they are away than when they are at home. This is usually just a temporary stage and wears off as they become convinced that the baby can survive during their absence. But in any case, for the sake of their marital relationship and of the baby's future personality, I believe parents should encourage themselves to take time off.

Another mechanical trick is to train yourself not to talk about the baby when you are out with each other or with friends. At first you'll find your thoughts and conversations reverting to the baby every two minutes. But if you can discipline yourself to keep your lips sealed or if you can remind each other with a signal, you'll gradually learn not only not to talk but also not to think about the newcomer.

It's wise for both parents to keep up their hobbies, their reading, and their other recreational and cultural interests. Lack of time is not a good excuse.

Not everyone will agree with this philosophy. There are high-principled parents who believe with fervor that all babies deserve to be breast-fed for at least two years, that they should always be picked up immediately when they cry or even merely fuss, and that it's the parents' obligation to make every decision in the child's favor in the first two years. I can see why they take these positions but I still don't agree.

And what I've just been advising about not becoming obsessed with the baby may *seem* to be contradicted in the following section by observations on mother–baby closeness in other societies, and in other species. Obsession is an *anxious* preoccupation which blots out other interests and is commonest in the inexperienced, highly conscientious parent. I'll be describing the natural, unanxious closeness in simpler societies to show how far we have strayed from nature in our "scientific" culture, whether or not it would be practical to get back to some aspects of that closeness.

▷ EARLY PARENT-INFANT BONDING

Observations and experiments in the past forty years on the value of early closeness between mother and child in simple, non-industrial societies, in our own highly technical society, and among other animals, have shown how far we had strayed from what is natural. Before the 1940s, to protect babies from germs and to keep them under careful observation, they were all put, immediately after birth, in nurseries. There was a delay of many hours before the babies were brought to the mothers for the first time, in order to give them rest after their labors. Then the schedule for feeding —on breast or bottle—was rigidly kept to every four hours, except for the 2 A.M. feeding which was carried out in the nursery so as not to interfere with the mother's sleep. This meant that occasionally the baby was not ready to nurse, more often it meant that she had to wait much longer than she wished.

This rigid and carefully timed schedule was very different from the natural pattern: sleep for the first day or so; then very frequent waking for feedings for a few days and nights then a gradual spacing out to 7 or 8 feedings per 24 hours. This shifting frequency is well suited to the need for early stimulation of the breast milk supply. The fact that up until World War II private obstetrical patients stayed in the hospital for twelve days worked further against breast feeding, by delaying the natural flexibility that could be carried out at home. The fact that the baby in the nursery lived at a distance from the mother and that nurses took most of the care gave first-time mothers the feeling that they were much too dumb to be trusted with the baby, who seemed to be the nurses' baby.

In the 1940s came experiments with "rooming-in" in which the baby's crib is next to the mother's bed so that she can take care of him, become familiar with his sounds, his schedule of waking, and his BM's. And his father can visit with him and participate early in his care. (Rooming-in had been the usual pattern in America in earlier centuries and was still customary in some European countries.)

At about the same time came the revival of "natural childbirth" in which pregnant women are trained to cooperate with the contractions and relaxations of the uterus in labor, to do without anesthesia unless labor pains are distinctly distressing, and to be conscious at the triumph of birth.

Meanwhile various observations of animals showed that behavior patterns that once were assumed to be entirely due to inborn instinct were partially dependent on previous experience. For example, maternal behavior that rats normally show toward their first litter will not appear if paper ruffs are kept around their necks during the pregnancy. The ruffs prevent the rats from carrying out the normal pregnancy behavior of licking their changing abdomens and genitals. A new chimpanzee mother treats her first baby tenderly if she has a normal duration of labor. But if she has a sudden, precipitate delivery, she is frightened by the baby and climbs up the side of the cage to get away from it. Infant monkeys isolated from mothers and other monkeys from birth develop abnormally fearful and aggressive behavior when placed with other monkeys at puberty. These various distortions of animal behavior made observers look more carefully at how we have distorted the patterns of human behavior—in mothers and infants.

In the 1970s observations showed that if, within an hour of birth, babies are brought to their mothers for an hour's quiet visit, the mothers slowly and fondly feel their babies all over. They start by touching lightly the arms and legs and perhaps the face, with their fingertips. Eventually they get to the chest, abdomen, and back which they feel with their palms. Mothers given this opportunity show a greater inclination—at a month and at a year—to comfort their babies, look them in the eye and fondle them during feedings. And the babies feed better, develop more rapidly and have fewer infections.

Observations of Indian mothers and babies in Guatemala, where the mother goes back to work right after giving birth, carrying her baby in a sling, and breast feeds often, showed no signs of colic or fretfulness or even belching in the babies, though the mothers have never heard of bringing up a bubble.

But as we have shifted to more natural patterns of lying-in in some respects, we have acquired new, artificial methods in others, that bring, on balance, not only no benefit but new disadvantages. For instance the elaborate monitors that keep track of the baby's heart beat during labor have no basic advantage over the old fashioned stethoscope, and seem a little more scary to the mother.

Caesarean sections have increased drastically in number. In a great majority of cases, this is not because it is necessary for the safety of baby or mother but because of the much increased tendency of parents to sue the obstetrician if they ever find anything wrong with their child, making the obstetrician feel he must lean over backwards with precautions so that he can say at a trial that he has done everything conceivable. And he must carry a hugely expensive malpractice insurance policy, which must be ultimately paid for by his patients' fees.

So I now want to urge mothers more enthusiastically to breast feed if they have any such inclination: for more mothers have found that they can, and we have more evidence of the immunity to diseases conferred by breast milk. I would avoid the propping of bottles unless it's unavoidable, as in the case of twins who always wake and cry at the same moment. I think that a sling is better than a firm plastic seat for carrying the baby from place to place or when she is fretful. I suggest to mothers that they ask for natural childbirth, for an hour of close contact right after birth, and for rooming-in, because these will hasten the bonding of mother and baby.

I want to add here that, if you have not had the opportunity to use some or all of the more natural methods of childbirth, it doesn't mean that your child has been seriously or permanently deprived. Furthermore, we know that the great majority of American children who've experienced the artificial methods of the past turn out to be bright and warm-hearted. They may have been slightly delayed in bonding rather than deprived. What I am aiming for is to give parents in general the courage to lean in the direction of natural patterns and to be skeptical of highly artificial and technical methods unless and until they've been proved to confer real benefits.

CHAPTER FIVE

Sleep Problems

▷ TURNING NIGHT INTO DAY

▷ SLEEP AND SEPARATION ANXIETY
   AT TWO YEARS

▷ SLEEP PROBLEMS AFTER THREE
   YEARS

▷ THE FAMILY BED AND NUDITY

▷ TURNING NIGHT INTO DAY

A few babies are born all mixed up about the difference between day and night. During the night, off and on, they are wakeful and often fretful; they are eager to be fed. Then when dawn comes they fall into a deep sleep, during which vacuum cleaners, the shouts of children, the slamming of doors don't bother them at all. In fact, even when a parent deliberately tries to waken such a baby—picks her up, talks softly and then loudly, joggles her gently and then vigorously—she stays groggily asleep. Nobody knows why a few babies have this upside-down pattern at first, and nobody knows a solution for it.

I used to suggest to parents various ways to wake such babies up and keep them awake in the daytime, with the idea that then they would be so fatigued that they'd have to sleep more at night. You can try this. But usually nothing works. Even if you can wake up some of these babies and pop a bottle into their mouths to interest them, they're apt to go back to sleep promptly before they've taken a quarter ounce. The only comfort for parents is knowing that these babies outgrow their night wakefulness and fretfulness sometime between one and three months of age.

Chronic Resistance to Sleep, Going-to-Bed Type

This problem is one that I called chronic resistance to sleep when I wrote an article about it for a pediatrics journal in the mid 1940s. I said that I had never seen this type of sleep problem in earlier times, when pediatricians gave mothers rigid rules to follow in regard to such matters as infant feeding schedules ("Every four hours—not a minute early, not a minute late"), and rigid sleep schedules. It first appeared when pediatricians began to advise flexible feeding schedules adapted to each baby's needs. Some parents naturally made the assumption that infants should decide their own sleep schedules too. The trouble is that a few babies get the idea that night is the time for sociability and being walked.

Here's how the problem is apt to develop. A baby, usually one who has had a lot of colic or fretfulness in the evenings in the first three months, for which she was held and walked a great deal by her parents, then seems to outgrow her discomfort. But she doesn't outgrow her desire to be held and walked in the evenings. In fact, as she becomes four, five, six, and seven months old, her desire for it becomes even greater. Whereas she used to fall asleep finally by 7 or 8 P.M., she gradually learns to stay awake until 9, 10, or even 11 P.M.

If you ask her parents whether she doesn't get sleepy at these late hours, they'll tell you that her eyes keep closing and her head keeps drooping. But when the parent tiptoes over to her crib and ever so gently tips her into a horizontal position preparatory to laying her down, she immediately wakes with a start and sets up a loud crying that, her parent says, she'd keep up forever if she wasn't picked up and walked some more.

It is most often the highly conscientious, beginning parents, lacking confidence in themselves in their new role, who run into these going-to-bed problems. They can't think of anything to do but yield. Yet the more they give in, the more insistent some of these babies become.

There's a further complication that sets in here. When parents get the sense that their baby is overly demanding, they can't help resenting it, unconsciously. But to be angry at a "helpless little baby" seems brutal. So their guilt makes them quickly suppress all awareness of their resentment and give in more than ever. Perhaps, too, the baby senses their inner tension and this makes her more uneasy.

The treatment of this going-to-bed problem is relatively simple —once the parents are convinced that for the baby's happiness as well as their own, they have to be willing to decide certain basic matters of management, such as bedtime. They have to be convinced, though, that the baby will not cry forever if they decline to return to her room after saying good night. She'll probably cry hard for twenty or thirty minutes the first night, ten minutes the second night, and none after that.

I've urged parents, on putting such a baby to bed, to hug her and speak tenderly of their love to remind her and themselves that they haven't turned hard-hearted but are rescuing her from a painful condition. Then I suggest they add, in a friendly but firm tone, that she and they need their rest, so they aren't coming in anymore but will be right in the next room. (They can say the doctor told them, if this is easier.) The baby will not understand the words but she will get the message that they have turned a page and are not hesitant anymore.

If a parent, tortured with guilty thoughts that the baby's head might be caught between the slats of the crib or that she might be strangling, goes into her room in a quarter of an hour to make sure she is in no danger, the baby will assume she is about to be picked up at last. When she finds that she isn't she'll be truly enraged by this seeming deception and will redouble her crying. If the parent comes back for a peek every ten minutes, a baby will be able to keep crying indignantly all night long.

Waking-in-the-Middle-of-the-Night Type

There's a middle-of-the-night variation of this situation. The trouble is apt to start in the second half of the first year or the early part of the second year. How it starts sometimes gives us a clue as to what makes it continue and get worse. Here's an example: A baby of eight months wakes and cries hard and long for the first time. The parents try to wait it out for a few minutes, but eventually they pick her up and try to comfort her. The next day the doctor finds an ear infection or some other disease. The parents are frightened by the first real illness and feel guilty that they tried to ignore it. The second night—and the third and fourth and fifth—the baby stirs and perhaps whimpers briefly. The parents, who are now on the lookout, get up immediately and comfort her. Within a few days a pattern may be established. Probably the baby had always stirred, made a few sounds and shifted position several times each night, just as older children and adults do, but the parents had slept through because they had no reason to be concerned.

There are several factors, I think, that contribute to the problem. One is the parents' heightened alertness. Behind this are their feelings, however slight, of anxiety and guilt left over from the discovery of the infection. I suspect that these feelings engender a slight anxiety in the baby too. "If they act worried and come to me so quickly," the baby might feel, "perhaps there really is something to be frightened about," for infants and children are acutely sensitive to their parents' feelings. Furthermore, as the nights go by and the parents get up to comfort her, the baby gets an increasing sense of her power to control them.

Gradually over the weeks and months, as the wakeful periods increase, the parents come to resent this power that the baby exercises over them, and they would like to resist giving in. But they can't admit to themselves how resentful they feel. And they don't have enough self-confidence to know they would be doing the right thing if they decline to go back into her room. So they keep giving in. The baby, I think, feels both their resentment and their guilt about letting her cry, and this combination encourages her to become more insistent.

In half the cases of waking in the middle of the night, there is nothing as dramatic as an ear infection or other disease to account for it, and I've often had to fall back on teething as a possible explanation. Certainly some babies are miserable in the daytime as their teeth come closer to erupting, beginning around five or six months, and especially with the first molars at about a year. At night you can see some of them wincing and whimpering in their sleep. But the situation can become as difficult as in the cases starting with an infection, if the parents are too quick to respond to the baby's slightest whimper by picking her up, taking her into the living room, amusing her for longer and longer periods, and perhaps feeding her. And there is further tension as they later find themselves becoming resentful but unable to stand up to her demands.

The best proof that parental guilt and hesitancy can prolong this kind of trouble can be seen in how swiftly the Going-to-Bed and the Waking-in-the-Middle-of-the-Night types of sleep problems yield if the parents can be encouraged to stay out of the baby's room despite the crying. This usually takes up to thirty minutes of hard crying the first night and ten minutes the second night. By the third or fourth night, there is usually no crying at all.

To overcome an established habit of middle-of-the-night waking and crying sometimes takes a little longer than two nights, especially if the baby is older and more determined. But the principle is the same: don't go back into her room after she has been put to bed for the night.

If you are living with the grandparents or in an apartment and you fear that the baby's crying will bother others, explain to them that you are doing this on doctor's orders and that it will take only a few nights.

If the baby has been sleeping in the same room with you, it will probably be necessary to find another place for her to be after you retire—in the living room, kitchen, or hallway if there is no extra bedroom. If a baby who has become accustomed to being picked up at night sees the parents pretending to remain asleep, she will feel challenged to cry louder and louder and for as long as is necessary to get them up. If there is no other possible solution, parents can try a screen between her bed and theirs.

There is a telephone-in clinic in Los Angeles that deals with common problems of infants and small children. They are often consulted about sleep problems such as the ones I'm discussing here. They say it isn't necessary to let the baby cry even for thirty minutes. They recommend that the parent sit by the baby's crib (not pick the baby up), in the dark, occasionally murmuring reassurances. They say this will end the problem in a week or so. This method is easier in one sense on parent and baby, and I suggest that parents us it. (I have had no opportunity to try it myself.) If it doesn't work, they can shift to the method I've described.

I was very hesitant at first to give this advice about not going in, because it would sound heartless and difficult to parents. But when one mother after another reported back that the crying lasted for only thirty minutes the first night and ten minutes the second, that the baby became so much better rested and happier in the daytime, and that the parents, after months of fatigue and tension, were at last able to relax and enjoy the baby again, I felt I was on the right track. Besides, nothing else had worked.

But I found to my dismay that I had gotten the reputation among a few parents and physicians of recommending—as a general policy —that parents always let a baby cry rather than give comfort, for fear of spoiling. *Not true!* I've always advised that if a baby cried unexpectedly, the parents should of course, comfort her and try to find the cause. Illness, teething, bad dream? The advice that I've been discussing—of not going back into a baby's room—applies to a very specific and uncommon problem, the baby who has been resisting sleep for weeks and months and has baffled and frustrated and exhausted the parents.

But I should admit that I've advised inexperienced parents not to hurry to pick up their young baby when she occasionally whimpers in her sleep, but to wait a few minutes to see whether she will settle down again. This is to encourage her to sleep through the night and until a civilized hour in the morning, as soon as she is ready for that. But I've always added that if she really wakes up and cries steadily, the parent will have to go to her. I'd try first sitting by her crib, murmuring reassurances or singing in the dark. If that doesn't work, hold her in her dark room. If possible, avoid lights, walking, and feeding (if she's outgrown night feedings). I've also pointed out that some infants cannot slip quietly from fatigue into sleep but must always go through a brief period of fretfulness or hard crying first. There is no easy way to avoid this transitional crying.

▷ SLEEP AND SEPARATION ANXIETY AT TWO YEARS

From age one and a half to three a child is, by nature, very aware of his dependence on his parents and particularly on the parent or parent substitute who takes on the major share of his care—most commonly the mother. Here are some dramatic examples of what may happen if he is separated from her.

If the mother departs abruptly for a week—to take care of an ailing relative, for example—or starts a full-time job, leaving the child in the care of an unfamiliar person, his anxiety may be acute. But usually it does not show itself in a recognizable form during the mother's absence. In fact, the substitute may report that the child has been an angel the whole time. Eventually the mother can figure out that the too-perfect behavior was an expression of suppressed anxiety; the child was too upset to try to face what had hit him. He didn't (in most cases) even dare ask the substitute the fearful question that was on his mind: "Where's Mommy?"

The fact that anxiety was the child's true feeling becomes clear later, when the mother returns. The child rushes to her, won't let her out of his sight, follows her from room to room, cries if she does slip out of sight, clings if she tries to leave the house.

The child turns hostile toward the parent substitute, with whom he had gotten along so well, and won't let the substitute near him or do anything for him.

The most dramatic scene occurs at bedtime. When the parent tries to put the child in his crib, he clings with a grip like steel and cries in terror. If the parent can succeed in prying him loose and starting for the door, the child may unhesitatingly vault over the crib railing, even though he has never climbed out before. He lands on the floor in a heap, picks himself up, and races after the parent. If he doesn't dare climb out of his crib, he may sit up all night long, half asleep, half awake.

For weeks the child follows the mother like a shadow and tries to keep her from leaving the house or even the room.

Back in the 1930s a few nursery schools took two-year-olds. But most of them gave up this practice, mainly because so many of these children developed anxiety about separation from the parent. Some two-year-olds, from the first day of school, wouldn't allow the parents who had brought them to leave. Others made an apparently good adjustment for several days. Then such a child would get mildly hurt in a minor accident or scuffle, wail and demand his parent, and might keep right on crying inconsolably for hours— until the parent could get to school. The next day the child would refuse to be left at school. He might even refuse to leave home.

In England many years ago, detailed observations were made of the behavior of a two-year-old girl who was hospitalized for a few days for repair of an umbilical hernia. (It was an interesting contrast in surgical traditions that in America at that time the commonest operation by far was for removal of tonsils and adenoids and in Britain it was for repair of umbilical hernias. Nowadays both operations are only occasionally considered necessary.) The child was depressed and inactive most of the time. But when a nurse spoke to her or another child cried, she cried for her mother. When her parents visited, she was friendly to her father but cool to her mother for an increasing number of minutes on each subsequent day.

This rejection of the mother was observed frequently in other young children who had to spend long periods in convalescent hospitals. In fact, the period of coldness grew longer with each weekly visit until it persisted throughout the entire visiting period —as if the child had forgotten altogether who his mother was. But the fact that these children remained cordial to their fathers showed it was not a loss of memory. The children were punishing the parent to whom they had been closer, as if to say, "I trusted you most of all and yet you abandoned me."

The depth of the resentment on the part of these children showed in another way after they returned home. They would continue to pretend not to know the mother for several days. But when this pretense finally broke down, a child would attack the mother with such harsh, bitter words that she would be shocked.

I have brought up these relatively severe examples to make it clear to skeptical people that there really is such a thing as separation anxiety in small children and that it can have a severe impact.

There also are mild expressions of separation anxiety that frequently show up at bedtime in children between one and three quarters and two and a half years of age. A child who previously has always gone to bed willingly (it inspires me to see how eagerly most one-year-olds snuggle down) begins to try to hold his parent at his bedside. The commonest of gambits are "Want to go peepee" or "Want a drink of water," even though he did one and had the other only a couple of minutes before.

Since this is at an age when parents may be trying to get cooperation in toilet training, they find it almost impossible to turn down their child's request to use the bathroom. The child will alternately use "peepee" and "drink of water" until the parents are quite sure that these are emotional not physical needs.

In another variation, the child allows the parent to leave him and then, five or ten minutes later, turns up in the room where the parents are, all full of charm and seductiveness. A child who in the daytime is too impatient to sit in a parent's lap for five seconds now clings there all by himself and stays. He compliments his mother on her dress or his father on his tie. If he is finally hustled off to bed, he reappears in a few minutes, as innocent-looking as if he had never heard of bedtime. I've been consulted about cases in which the child climbed out of bed twenty times a night, despite increasing parental disapproval and anger.

It takes a long time, in my experience, to ease the anxiety of the child who has been made severely panicky. If it was the mother's absence on a trip that caused the upset, she should avoid another trip like the plague if at all possible. And it's best even to avoid daytime separations for several weeks afterward if possible. If she has to go shopping, better to take the child with her.

It's wise to keep the child consciously aware of what it is he's afraid of; every time he cries out or grabs his mother when he thinks she's leaving him, she can say understandingly, "You are scared because you think Mommy is going away to Florida again, the way she did before. But Mommy is not going away again. Mommy is going to stay with Bobby." Otherwise the child's main worry may get repressed and disguised as a phobia—a fear of a certain room or of a certain object—in which form it may last indefinitely.

At bedtime the mother may have to sit by the child's crib every night for a number of weeks until he is fast asleep. If she tries to sneak out before he's really asleep, the child may become alarmed and then remain more wakeful than ever. It may take two hours for the child to fall asleep the first few nights. But after he becomes reassured, his wakefulness may last only twenty or thirty minutes a night. It doesn't work to have the child lie on the same bed with the mother; her slightest move to leave will wake him. It does no harm for the mother to keep a low light on so that she can read during her long sittings.

Can the parents leave the house in the evening, once the child is sound asleep? If the child is at all likely to waken, it will usually stir his anxiety to a high pitch to find his parent gone again, so it is not wise. If he never wakes in the night after falling asleep, there is no harm, provided the sitter is someone he knows well.

I have been referring to the mother in all these examples because it is usually she whose absence is most upsetting. But if the father or grandmother or a sitter is the principal care giver, then that person's absence could create the panic.

The best treatment of the mild bedtime anxiety, I think, is for the parents to be friendly but firm: "One drink of water, one peepee is enough." And, "When people go to bed they are meant to stay there." If the child reappears, he shouldn't be allowed to stay and be charming. The parents should promptly, firmly, lead him right back to bed. They don't need to be angry or even cross—that might increase his anxiety—but just very definite and consistent. The parents' certainty says that there is no need for worry.

To put it the other way around, it is parental hesitancy that seems to the child to substantiate his fears. He feels that if they are hesitant about leaving him, there must be a real danger. And it is parental hesitancy that encourages him to see if he can get around the rules.

Separation anxiety, once it has been aroused, raises problems of treatment. But more important is the question of prevention. Should a mother leave town to care for her ailing mother? Is this as good a time as any for her to go to work? Should she go on a business trip with her husband? Or on that two-week vacation with him that her parents have offered to pay for?

The first child, who usually is an only child until he is two or three years old, is often more susceptible to separation anxiety than subsequent children. In most cases his family consists of himself and his mother, who are together all day long, and his father, who appears only in the evening. So most of his social and emotional existence revolves around his mother. If she suddenly goes away to visit or to work, it leaves an enormous gap. A second or third child whose mother goes away still has the older child there to maintain a substantial part of his security. So precautions are more important with a first child—or with any child who for some reason seems particularly dependent on the parents.

If the father can stay at home longer in the morning and come home earlier in the afternoon while the mother is away, this will help to lessen anxiety. If there is a regular sitter who has been around a lot during a small child's waking hours and who has really participated in his care, this too will be an effective preventive.

Suppose there has been no regular sitter and the mother *has* to take a job or go away for a while. In that case, I feel, every effort should be made not only to find a naturally comforting substitute but also to have that substitute participate gradually in the child's care for at least a week before the mother leaves. A two-week period would be safer.

After the child has accepted a substitute's participation (not just her presence), then the mother should begin to go out on errands of increasing length without the child, to accustom him to her absence and to the fact that she does always come home eventually.

If there's a question about the urgency of the mother's going to work, I'd advise her to try to avoid sudden or full-time involvement in a job until the child is about three years old. There are several compromises. It may be possible for father and mother to stagger their work hours so that one or the other will always be at home or so that the child will be cared for by a sitter for only a few hours each day. Or the mother may be satisfied temporarily with a quarter-time job, then a half-time job, gradually increasing to full time. What I'm arguing against is a parent who has been a full-time parent for a first child under three suddenly becoming a full-time worker outside.

As for vacations without the child or the mother's accompanying the father on a business trip, I'd advise against it up till about the age of three in the case of a first child or of a very dependent one.

Up till then, it might be best to take the child along, though of course the vacation won't be nearly as much of a vacation. If parents do go on a trip, it's better for a child who is being left to be cared for in his own home if that's at all possible. Around the age of two, children are sometimes made insecure by a move even when with their parents.

I don't mean to be as arbitrary as I sound. I don't want to say flatly that a mother can't go to work full-time or can't go on a vacation if her child under three has been almost entirely cared for by her. Parents have done these things apparently successfully; on the other hand, children who have older brothers or sisters or who have regular sitters sometimes get upset too.

The most important advice I can give to parents is that from their baby's early infancy they accustom him to care—for several waking hours every week, if possible—by at least one regular sitter or relative, so that he won't think it's the end of the world if his closer parent has to leave him.

If he gets used to one sitter, this won't completely solve the problem if that particular sitter can't care for him on a full-time basis when his parent leaves. He will still have quite an adjustment to make. But he will be readier to make that adjustment if he has learned not to depend on his mother exclusively.

If a mother is as eager to have a career as her husband—and she has every right to be—then together they should work out appropriate arrangements. From before the baby's birth—preferably from the time they plan to marry—they should decide how they will coordinate their careers and dovetail their working hours so that they can share equally in the care of the child, with or without the part-time help of a regular sitter.

Separation anxiety is not a strange and inexplicable phenomenon. It is a part of human nature. It is a part of animal nature in all those species in which the young stick close to the mother for a number of weeks or months. There is a critical period in the early life of each of these animal species—cattle, horses, sheep, goats—during which the young creature becomes *imprinted* with his mother's appearance and smell and sounds. She in turn becomes imprinted with his image.

After that, whenever the young animal is separated from his mother he becomes anxious and cries with the cry of his species, which is meant to make his mother respond. If a human being is there during the critical period instead of the animal's mother, the young creature becomes attached to that human being. This is the reality behind the nursery rhyme, "Mary Had a Little Lamb."

A child is meant to acquire a strong dependence on his principal care giver. But in our species this dependence can be, and in other societies usually is, attached to other relatives and neighbors as well, but to a more limited degree. This dilution of the dependence is valuable in helping the child to become adjusted first to the extended family and then to the wider society. It also relieves the parents of the feeling of oppression that comes from the sense that a child is like a leech. So the dilution of the dependence is doubly valuable.

▷ SLEEP PROBLEMS AFTER THREE YEARS

Arguments about Bedtime

The commonest situation that bothers parents, I think, is when children, told to go to bed, keep arguing that it isn't bedtime yet or that they were allowed to stay up later last night or that their friends don't have to go to bed so early or that they have to prepare something to take to school. Or they beg plaintively to watch just one more television program. They may give dozens of other reasons—you know them as well as I do.

Part of the cause of this problem is that all children are lawyers. They'll argue immediately and persistently for any privilege or object they want, despite what the rules say, if they think there is the slightest possibility of winning.

A more important cause is vacillation in the parents. Children will double and redouble their onslaught if parents hesitate for a tenth of a second before turning their requests down—if, for example, a parent feels sorry for a child because the child has been sick lately, or if the parent feels slightly guilty over having been cross with this child an hour before, or if this is the kind of parent who always feels uneasy about turning a child down even when the parent is quite sure it would be wrong to give this privilege or object.

Whatever prompts a child—let's say it's a girl—to want to stay up or causes the parent to fail to be definite about sending her to bed, the progress of each episode is much the same. Even after the child has given up arguing, she still keeps stalling. She hangs around the television set a little longer. Or she putters over some private object. Or she says, "I'm *going!* " But she doesn't go. The parents, however, instead of paying attention to her nonperformance, resume reading or watching television or chatting with each other. It's a cold war that never ceases and that is never decided.

You might think I'm implying that parents should be harsh watchdogs at bedtime. Not at all. The parents can remain friendly and soft-voiced; it works much better that way. They simply have to keep paying attention to the child for two minutes or so, until she goes off to bed. Actually it works better for a while, when stalling has been a chronic problem, for one parent to get up and accompany the child to her bedroom or get her started or to say good night. Or the parent may promise, after seeing to it that the child is really going, to come up and read a story to her when she is ready for bed. It's a good idea for the father to take over this obstinate problem at night, if he has been away most of the day. The mother's discipline may have worn thin by this hour.

Then there has to be reasonable consistency. The parents have to call bedtime at the same time every night. If they want to make an exception on rare occasions—the Fourth of July, for example—it's better for them to announce the exception themselves, rather than wait to be pestered, or at least to grant a request right away if they are going to, otherwise not at all. In other words, it is better not to give in just because a child has finally worn you down with endless pleas and arguments.

This degree of consistency is not obligatory in families in which the children are generally cooperative with parents' rules. I'm giving advice here for families in which the children are never satisfied or convinced about the hour for bed.

Of course some parents let their children stay up until the children are tired enough to take themselves to bed. I'm not lenient enough to recommend that, especially with television having such an appeal. But if you are going to be concerned about your children's sleep, you must be consistent. You can't let them decide on bedtime half the nights and you the other half—not without endless argument.

A very different kind of sleep problem is the following. Suppose a girl between three and six years of age wants her door left open all evening. This is often not because she is afraid of the dark, but because she wants to keep track of her parents. When they retire to their bedroom she seems to be wide awake and asks that they leave their bedroom door open. If an hour later they stealthily close their door for a little privacy, the child is instantly awake and asks them again to leave it open.

Wakefulness Out of Rivalry

Another variation of this problem is when the child keeps getting up during the night, climbing into her parents' bed and snuggling down between them. Sometimes the parents resist this at first and carry the child back to her bed. But when she reappears every half hour, they finally give up out of fatigue and sleeplessness and let her stay. A father laughingly said to me recently about his four-year-old son, who crawled into his parents' bed in their seashore cottage every weekend when the father came to join them, "He's the world's greatest birth control device."

The father spoke more meaningfully than he realized. Children in the three-to-six-year-old period are in the first stages of sexual development. A boy forms a romantic attachment to his mother. By the age of four he may declare that he is going to marry her when he grows up. Gradually he comes to realize that his mother's marriage to his father makes his own plan impossible, and he becomes increasingly rivalrous with his father. But the idea of a bitter rivalry with a man so much larger and stronger than himself is frightening, and eventually he supresses these thoughts into his unconscious mind, where they continue to exist in disguised form.

In a similar way a girl falls in love with her father and then gradually becomes aware that she is a small, weak rival of her mother. But in her unconscious mind she does not give up hope of winning her father somehow, someday.

When a girl keeps track of her parents all evening and then insists that they leave their bedroom door and her door open all night, or when she keeps crawling into her parents' bed, she may be trying unconsciously to keep the parents apart—physically as well as figuratively.

But do children of three, four, and five really know what goes on between parents? Some have been told; others haven't. But all of them have enough possessive sexual instinct, however vague, to want to get between the parents in some sense.

The wish becomes an action in only a minority of cases, depending on circumstances. If a father is a traveling salesman and a mother lets her small son sleep in the double bed or his father's single bed while the father is away, the boy's wish is encouraged mightily, and he may become more openly competitive toward his father. If a mother is too seductive in her manner with her son, or a father with his daughter, it may bring the rivalry more into the open.

Sometimes very considerate modern parents, after learning about little children's frustration when they find they can't have the parent of the opposite sex for themselves, are too polite—even submissive—to the rivalrous child, carefully refraining from any embraces in front of the child or even allowing a very demanding child to forbid them to talk with each other. This kind of kowtowing to a child's unrealistic demands is no favor in the long run; it gives him the idea that his wishes have a much higher priority than his parents' and that he really can reserve his mother for himself.

I think it is helpful for parents to know about children's sexual and romantic striving at this early age because it explains various kinds of behavior that would be baffling otherwise. But there is no need—in fact, there is even harm—in parents' yielding to children's wishes or encouraging them in any way to think they can replace one of their parents in the affections of the other. To encourage false hopes only leads them up blind alleys that are difficult to get out of later.

Actually children usually sense it when they are demanding more than their due or trying to function at a stage of development that is beyond them. Then it is a comfort to them to be told—in a kindly but firm tone—that what they are asking is impossible.

Human beings of all ages feel more comfortable when they have to respect the rights of others and keep their own place.

I think that whenever a child crawls into the parents' bed, she (or he) should be taken back promptly to her own—just as often as she does it. If this makes no impression on her, the parents may have to lock their own door. A child who demands that the parents leave their door open should simply be told that they want their privacy. A child can understand that. The parents don't need to be rude or cross. The can say it kindly and matter-of-factly.

It can be very helpful, when a child of this age is demanding that the parents' door be left open or that they not embrace or that they stop talking to each other for the parents to be more specific and explain to a girl that she wants Daddy all to herself (or that a boy wants Mommy all to himself), that it makes her cross when Daddy talks with Mommy (or kisses her or is in bed with her, as the case may be). But, the parent continues, Mommy and Daddy love each other and they want to do these things sometimes. They also love the child and want to talk with her and kiss her sometimes too. This all may sound too self-evident to an adult. But it can be enlightening and calming to a small child tortured by a blind jealousy that she (or he) doesn't understand at all.

I don't want to leave the impression that the only reason children climb into their parents' bed at night is to come between them. Children may be wakened by bad dreams and seek out their parents' bed for safety and comfort.

Fears of the Dark and of Monsters

The third kind of problem I'm thinking of is when a child (let's say a boy) doesn't want to go to bed because he's afraid of the dark. Or he may be more specific, fearing that there's a lion under his bed or that a kidnapper will come in his window or that a shadow on his wall is some kind of creature out to get him. Fears such as these are particularly common in the five-and-six-year-old period. They are often related to the child's rivalry with the parent and fear of his resentment.

The possessive romantic attachment to the parent of the opposite sex is valuable in setting children's romantic ideals, which will guide them toward good marriages when they grow up, and it helps them mature in other ways too. But it would never do if this attachment became so deep and so long lasting that the individuals, when they grew up, could never break away and marry people their own age. A few individuals do get stuck in the three-year-old pattern, and they remain mother's boys or daddy's girls throughout life.

But in most children the attachment, after doing its job, is gradually broken. The boy gives up his quest for his mother's undivided love because he's afraid that his father is becoming as jealous of him as he is of his father—and his father could win easily, he figures, if it came to a real fight.

This fear, we believe, is the main element in the nightmares that are so common in the five-to-seven-year-old period. Boys characteristically dream of giants and gorillas who are chasing them; girls more often dream of witches. It is the commonest factor in the bedtime fear of the dark and of scary monsters.

There are additional factors that contribute to the phobias and bad dreams of this age period—that stir up and intensify the child's underlying fears. One is frightening television programs, especially in the evening. I believe that programs that are violent and upsetting are bad for children whether or not the children show anxiety, but there is a strong additional reason why such programs certainly should be banned for the child who already has bedtime fears. (It is an interesting sidelight on human nature that many of the children—and adults—who are upset by scary programs also beg to see them.) Scary storybooks should come under the same ban.

Roughhousing with a father in the evening can easily get small children overexcited, though they love it. To the boy's unconscious it makes too vivid the potential aggressiveness of his father. To the girl's unconscious it may have a sexual significance that is too exciting in itself and that then arouses fear of the mother's rivalry.

It may sound as though I'm being a killjoy in implying that this excitement should be eliminated. But children get plenty of excitement out of living their normal lives and listening to their own imagination. They don't need deliberate stimulation from parents or from television networks.

In discussing what to do generally for the child with bedtime fears and nightmares, we should distinguish between the child for whom this is the only problem and the one who seems to have a number of maladjustments.

Getting advice from a child guidance clinic or a family social agency for the child who has fears (or problems of any kind) is never a mistake and it's always helpful. I would say it is particularly important when a child is fearful and timid in many respects and shows other symptoms of tension, such as stuttering, bed-wetting, or poor social adjustment. On the other hand, in the case of the child who has bedtime fears or nightmares but who does well in school, is sociable with other children, and is reasonably easy for the parents to manage, consultation can be postponed to see whether further maturing will relieve the fears.

As for handling fears of the dark and of monsters in the bedroom, parents can of course reassure a boy (or girl) that there is nothing real to be afraid of in his room, that such fears come from other worries. (These worries are too complex, I think, for the parents to try to interpret to the child.) They can encourage him to be grown up and go to his room by himself. If he hasn't the courage, they can accompany him. If he wants a dim light in his room during the night, I'd cheerfully allow it. This is preferable to a bright light, which encourages playing and reading and wakefulness.

It is sometimes hard to wake a young child who is having nightmares. A boy (or girl) may appear awake but may still be seeing his tormentors. It usually helps to take him into a well-lighted room and to keep talking reassuringly until he is awake and calm.

In the olden days parents used to try to scold or shame their children out of their symptoms of tension and immaturity. Then later, when the causes of some of these anxieties became known, parents—and teachers—leaned in the opposite direction. They tried to be completely understanding and to remove all external obligations from the child because of his internal tensions. Now we realize that this sometimes encourages a child to stay immature and to hang on to his symptoms. So we remind him from time to time that it is no fun to be frightened—or, in other cases, to be a thumb sucker or a bed wetter—and tell him we are sure that someday he will be able to break these habits and become a big boy.

Incidentally, if you think these explanations—about rivalry and fear of the parents' wrath—are preposterous and morbid, you don't have to accept them; you can be a fine parent without them.

▷ THE FAMILY BED AND NUDITY

Several years ago a book titled *The Family Bed: An Age-Old Concept in Childrearing* endorsed the idea of children's sleeping with their parents. In the book the author, a Minneapolis housewife, Tine Thevenin, points out that families always slept together in primitive cultures, and they did so in the early days of the settlement of this country. Even before Thevenin's book came out, many American families had been drifting in the direction of family-bed coziness as part of the get-back-to-nature movement of the sixties and seventies.

Is there anything wrong about this? Child therapists report that some children become sexually overstimulated by sleeping with their parents. Others, who simply sleep in the same room as their parents, are troubled by the sight and sound of intercourse, with its —to children—appearance of violence. It is also true that once a child—especially one who is afraid of sleeping alone—gets used to sleeping in the family bed, the parents will have a devil of a time getting him out. I've known a couple of twelve-year-olds who were still there.

Children between the ages of three and six are attracted both physically and spiritually to their parent of the opposite sex. There is nothing abnormal about children's desire to see and touch their parents, and their declaring their intention to marry them. These desires are held in check by two factors. The first is the child's unconscious fear of rivalry with the parent of the same sex. The second influence is the parents' sense of what is appropriate, which keeps them from letting their children go too far.

Good parents spontaneously hug and kiss their children and respond happily when their children hug and kiss them in return. But there is a difference between this relatively brief show of affection and prolonged nighttime contact in bed.

What's the harm? If it becomes a regular pattern, it may lead to an intense relationship that the child may find hard to dissolve later, when it is time to fall in love with a contemporary.

But I've come around in recent years to the idea that it's good for young children to climb into their parents' bed in the *morning* (particularly on Saturdays and Sundays) for a cozy, leisurely family get-together. One good reason for this is that our Anglo-Saxon–influenced culture has inhibited physical demonstrations of affection between males. My own sons reproached me for this when they got the perspective and courage in adulthood to do so.

A few parents may shrink from having children in their beds, even briefly, because they worry about sexual arousal—both theirs and their children's. If the child should become too focused on the parent's body and too persistent in caressing the parent, it's not necessary, or wise, to act as if the child is doing something wrong.

Instead, you can change position casually or distract the child. If all else fails, simply get out of bed as if to start the day's work. On the other hand, if the parent is very uneasy with close physical contact (perhaps as a result of his own strict upbringing), it would probably be better not to allow the child in bed at all. The child will undoubtedly sense the parent's fear of contact and will be more bothered by that than by the absence of a Sunday morning get-together in bed.

While we're on the subject of sexual curiosity and contact between parent and child, I would like to comment on the increasing numbers of people in this country who have become casual nudists, in the sense of not covering up at home when their children are around. Is this beneficial or disturbing?

Of course, all this is a matter of custom. The amount of clothing worn in different societies varies greatly, from the Arab veiling of face and body to the most minimal bathing suits of sophisticated Westerners. Common sense tells us that total body covering won't eliminate the excitement of looking at members of the opposite sex and that nudity in a society where everyone is nude won't keep everyone excited.

Parents should take into account their underlying intention in going nude. Most of us have some impulse to show off our bodies, dressed or undressed, especially when young and attractive. An exhibitionist has that trait to an exaggerated degree. An exhibitionistic parent, without necessarily being aware of it, may use his or her body to dazzle children as well as other adults. Another parent will have no noticeable exhibitionistic impulses at all. The effect of parental nudity on children would be different in those two cases.

Parental nudity may not only stimulate a child of the opposite sex but also antagonize a child of the same sex. For example, one of my sons at the age of four got into the habit of "shaving" himself (with a bladeless razor) while I shaved, nude, in the mornings. After a few weeks of this he began to make grabbing gestures—half joking, half fierce—toward my genitals. I realized that I was bothering my son with my nudity, because it stirred up rivalry, and I began wearing underpants when shaving.

Millions of parents are casual nudists at home and obviously this is not doing appreciable harm to large numbers of children or we would hear about it from child guidance clinics. Yet I don't feel we can entirely ignore therapists who say that parental nudity can be disturbing to some children.

If I were a father or mother of small children and modest by inclination, I'd stay that way. If I much preferred to go nude, I wouldn't feel compelled to reform for my child's sake unless I saw that the child became silly, excited, or preoccupied with my body when I was nude. In that case, I'd keep some clothes on.

CHAPTER SIX

Discipline

▷ LOVE IS THE BASIC INGREDIENT

Most of the time that I was in the Navy during World War II, I was a psychiatrist in charge of a ward full of what were then called psychopaths. (Today they are called sociopaths.) They are individuals who are irresponsible, demanding, and impulsive and who never learn from experience. In the Navy they won't attend to business or obey the regulations. They often overstay their leaves or are absent without leave. Repeated punishments have no beneficial effect. After a number of offenses of increasing seriousness, it becomes painfully apparent that they will never be useful in the Navy, that they will only be nuisances, so eventually they are given less-than-honorable discharges.

Since they had all committed recent offenses, my patients were kept in a prison ward for the several weeks it took to compile their psychiatric histories and get their discharge papers processed in Washington. In most cases it became clear, even from the skimpy information these sociopaths could recall from their childhood, how their characters went wrong. They simply were never loved in their earliest years. They never felt they really belonged to their parents. And so they never developed any sense of responsibility—to their parents or to anyone else. A common story would be that the father deserted the family, the mother had to go to work and so turned over her children to some other woman, who gave them little attention or affection. Or the mother died and the father farmed them out to an indifferent care giver. Some of them were neglected even in their own homes.

Characteristically, such unloved children do poorly in school. They don't have any impulse to please or cooperate with the teacher. (Loved children start out wanting to please their parents and then automatically expand their horizons and want to please their teachers and other people.) Furthermore, these children have no interest to give to schoolwork, for it is loving parents who introduce their children to objects and ideas and endow these with meaning.

Unloved school children spend considerable time playing truant or showing off to other children in the classroom or sitting in the principal's outer office, waiting to be reprimanded. On the average, they fall a couple of years behind in their school placement but are really further back than that. By the time they are fourteen or fifteen years old, they often are tired of being scolded in school, ashamed of being with smaller children, and aggressive enough to quit school for good.

I was interested in the stories my Navy patients told about how they left home. A common story went as follows: The father tells his son to carry out some chore. The son, perhaps sixteen years old now, is at a rebellious-enough age to refuse. The father angrily insists; the son angrily refuses again. The father doubles up his fist to hit his son. But the son is faster, and before he knows what he is doing, he knocks his father down. He realizes that it won't be comfortable to stay at home any longer, so he goes to the nearest town and looks for a job.

But sociopaths are not any better at jobs than they are at school. They want to earn good money, but they can't really get interested in any job, and they have no impulse to please the boss. So they are wretched workers. They soon get fired or they quit just before being fired. They have various excuses: "The boss was always riding me," "They didn't pay me enough." It's rare for a sociopath to hold a job for longer than a few weeks.

The Navy—or the Army or the Air Force—is an even less suitable place for a sociopath than a civilian business. The rules are more arbitrary and much stricter—for instance, you can't leave the base unless you get permission. Your superiors, on the average, take less interest in you as a person. So the sociopath is repeatedly and constantly in trouble. I'd ask, "Jenkins, why did you go over the hill?" And he would answer with great indignation, "I asked for leave and they wouldn't give it to me!"

Most chronic criminals in civilian life are sociopaths too. The ones who commit petty crimes—like "borrowing" cars that don't belong to them—were merely neglected in childhood. They want possessions and money. But since they don't know how to earn them, they steal them.

The ones who commit crimes of violence, in addition to having been neglected, usually were treated cruelly in childhood. They are sent back to prison every time they are caught, for longer and longer sentences. But this doesn't make them feel ashamed, because they have no sense of having let anybody down and they have no desire to please. So punishment does no good; it only makes them more resentful.

All this description of the sociopath is only to make one simple, important point: punishment has no good effect on the adult or child who hasn't been loved. The pain of punishment is not a sufficient deterrent. Punishment has an effect on people who've been loved, mainly because it represents a temporary loss of approval and love, which leaves them feeling out in the cold, miserable.

When children have been well loved by their parents, this engenders a responding love in them that makes them want to become grown-ups like their parents and—most of the time—makes them want to please their parents. This is really the main leverage parents have in controlling or motivating their children. If parents don't have this reciprocal tie with their children, they are helpless. There is no way to make children do anything, once they become truly defiant, as can be seen in child guidance clinics or juvenile court.

It's in the first couple of years of life that the largest part of this process—in which the parents' love arouses the responding love in children—is carried out. It's in that period that such issues as whether the individual is going to grow up to be a warm person or a detached one, trusting or mistrustful, optimistic or pessimistic, are mainly determined. Various other specific traits—such as occupational interests or mannerisms—develop later in life, but the fundamental ones are laid down early.

Some people think of love as meaning simply the expression of physical and emotional affection. Parental love has more sides than that. It's wanting the children to grow up to be responsible citizens and successful individuals. It's reminding them every day, if only in the kindliest manner, how to behave to become that kind of person.

There are many other aspects to managing and motivating children—the example set by the parents, the sincerity of the parents, their consistency, their self-assurance, their respect for their children, their manner of punishing, if any. But the parents' love for their children and the responding love of their children for them is by far the most important.

In the following three sections I want to look into three different controversial issues in child management: lenient versus strict; authoritarian versus democratic; imposed versus inner discipline. I'll describe extreme opposite positions on each issue, to clarify the differences, though of course no parent takes a totally one-sided view. Then I'll try to clarify my own position.

▷ LENIENT VERSUS STRICT

First I'd like to focus on that frequently argued question of strictness versus "permissiveness," a word with various interpretations. If by *permissive* you mean lenient but sensible and effective ways of handling children, I'm all for it and would gladly use the word without quotes. But most people nowadays use it in a disparaging way to indicate a foolishly kowtowing, submissive parental manner, which may produce demanding, spoiled children. So I'll use *leniency* instead.

Some parents who incline toward strictness assume that their approach is a guarantee of good behavior in their children and that leniency will surely produce undisciplined, rude offspring. Both of these beliefs are mistaken—or at best only partly true. It all depends on the spirit or unconscious motives behind these parental approaches.

What determines the methods and attitudes of parents most of all in dealing with their children is the manner in which they themselves were brought up. If the parents were taught, for instance, that cordiality to others under all circumstances or instant obedience or telling the whole truth at all times are essential (as I was taught but no longer believe quite so absolutely), they will be inclined to emphasize the same values to their children—unless the parents themselves have rebelled against certain of the things they were taught.

When parents are strict because of unusually high standards—in regard, for instance, to politeness, punctuality, personal appearance, helpfulness, neatness of room—but are basically kind and loving (which lots of parents are), the combination will tend to produce similar high standards and strictness in their children when they grow up, without necessarily cramping their spirit in any important way. That is to say, the children don't have to turn out to be uptight or hostile individuals because of a strict upbringing, as some people would have you believe. I've known plenty of people who were strictly but lovingly brought up and who have been delightful friends and creative workers.

On the other hand, there are parents called strict who are really overbearing—they have an inner need to be bossing and controlling even when their children are behaving properly. The children are apt to be meek, at least until they become parents themselves.

And there are the harsh, hostile parents who are always belittling or shouting or hitting at their children, who are either cowed or, if they dare fight back, obnoxious.

Many domineering and harsh parents assume that the main determinant of good behavior in children is fear. They forget all about the power of love, of the wish to imitate, to achieve, to please, to take responsibility, to grow up. To my mind, these factors are infinitely stronger than fear in making children—or adults—perform well. Most parents who rely on fear came to do so back in their own childhood, when they became convinced by *their* parents' attitude that human beings, including themselves, cannot be trusted to have good intentions and to do the right thing simply because they would prefer to.

I've been pointing out that strictness isn't a single parental attitude or method. It springs from different motives and different feelings. It is these other motives and attitudes—not strictness itself —that determines whether children turn out responsible or delinquent, loving or hostile, cooperative or disagreeable.

In a similar way, a lenient approach—in which the parents don't worry about table manners, interrupting, messy rooms, unwashed hands, the fine points of politeness as long as there is no deliberate unkindness—may work well or poorly, depending on the spirit in which it is used. I've known, professionally and personally, hundreds of children who were brought up without punishment, without threats, with very few scoldings or even stern looks. Their parents clearly respected them and spoke to them politely. Of course, the parents had to give them a lot of guidance, as all good parents do. Yet despite the lack of strictness, these children were what any person would call "good." They were generally cooperative with their parents and teachers. They carried out their responsibilities. They did at least reasonably well in school. They had good friends. They were kind. They didn't whine or nag. The ones I have known as grown-ups had become good citizens and good workers.

Then can you say that leniency is the preferred approach? You can't, for leniency can go astray when used by parents who are too hesitant, too guilty, and too submissive toward their children, perhaps because they've *always* been submissive, or because they're afraid their children won't love them if they don't always give in, or because they feel so badly about all the abuse that children have suffered in past generations, or because they don't want their children to resent them the way they sometimes resented their parents' severity in childhood. For whatever reason, such parents don't ask for respect; they allow their children to be uncooperative or inconsiderate or demanding or rude. In exaggerated cases such children when frustrated may shout at their parents, "I hate you," or, "You stink," without any parental reproach, as if the parents feel they deserve the abuse.

There has been a pernicious psychological theory in circulation for nearly a century, often untrue or only partly true, to the effect that unfortunate behavior in a child is simply the parents' fault. This hits conscientious parents particularly hard. It ignores the fact that the roots of behavior are incredibly complex and that most parents do the best they know how.

I recall a mother's saying with shame that her adolescent son's disagreeable, insulting behavior proved that she must have failed to meet his basic needs. I thought to myself that one of his basic needs was to have a mother who asked for respect. A vicious circle gets going in these families: The parent takes the full blame for the child's bad behavior and reacts by becoming more guilty and submissive. The parent's acceptance of the abuse makes the child feel guilty—at the unconscious level—because any child knows somehow that a parent shouldn't be treated this way. Then the child instinctively acts worse, as if to say, "How badly do I have to behave before you will control me in the way that I sense I need to be controlled?"

A father may manage two of his children competently and be submissive only to a third. Some unconscious factor is perhaps at work. The third child may remind the father of a brother whom he used to resent, for which he was made to feel guilty.

So I conclude again that the issue of leniency versus strictness is not a vital one. It's the spirit in which they are carried out that is crucial. Strictness in parents who love and respect their children can be successful and nonoppressive. Strictness in parents who are overbearing or hostile can rear children who are meek or aggressive, or they may be meek in childhood and turn aggressive in adulthood. Leniency in parents who are apologetic and submissive to their children may produce children who are on the rude, demanding side.

But leniency in self-respecting parents can make for an ideal family. Their affectionate, democratic attitude inspires loving feelings in the children, a pride in being treated in a grown up way, a desire to please. And if a child brought up in this spirit gets out of the wrong side of his bed one morning and starts to be a bit rude or uncooperative, his self-respecting parent promptly, firmly but *kindly* says, "It makes me unhappy when you speak to me that way. I need you to help me." This very gentle reproach from the parent won't work at first if parent and child have been used to noisy recriminations; but it will be effective if mutual respect has been the general spirit of the family.

▷ AUTHORITARIAN VERSUS DEMOCRATIC

Next I want to contrast authoritarian and democratic disciplines. *Mistrustful* might be a more explanatory word than *authoritarian,* I think. Parents with this slant tend to be stern because they assume that children, if left to themselves, will be more inclined to be naughty than good; that they won't be polite or cooperative or generous or industrious or honest because they prefer to be, but because they fear disapproval and punishment. So only vigilance and frequent correction will keep them on the right track. These parents feel that they can't often let their children make their own decisions, even in adolescence. They say such things as:

"I'll be listening to hear whether you're doing your practicing."

"Do your chores now or you're not going to the game." (You may have to threaten punishment like this if a child has been repeatedly irresponsible about his work, but it doesn't build long-term responsibility.)

"Do it because I say so!" (This is a natural command for *any* parent to use very occasionally, I think, when exasperated by a child who knows perfectly well why you've made a request but asks why just to be argumentative; however, it's certainly not a good way to get cooperation every day.)

I remember a new mother of the authoritarian disposition who, when her baby was brought to her the very first time in the hospital, sucking her thumb, said immediately in a cross tone, "You bad girl!"

Authoritarian parents are indignant when schools have a policy of promoting children even though they haven't come up to a satisfactory grade level in all their subjects, because they assume that pupils will stop trying to learn if they find that they'll be promoted anyway—this despite definite proof that such children make more academic progress when advanced than when held back.

Just as children absorb other parental anxieties—whether about thunder and lightning or snakes—so they accept their parents' fears that they have predominantly bad intentions and must be strictly held down. They accept this mistrustful picture of themselves even though they may resent the parental severity at the same time. Then when they grow up, most of them assume that their law-abiding behavior is due to their stern upbringing and unhesitatingly apply the same to their own children.

Of course, some of those brought up in a stern manner revolt against it and resolve to bring up their children differently, to one degree or another. But it is difficult to change—in a thoroughgoing way—from having been a mistrusted child to being a trusting parent.

Parents with the opposite attitude from authoritarian might be labeled *democratic* or trusting in the sense that they think of children as being as well-intentioned and worthy of respect as themselves. Even though they realize that children require an enormous amount of firm guidance because of their inexperience, these parents are inclined to let their children share in decision making—within reason. They see children as predominantly eager, hardworking, honest, original, creative, wanting most of the time to please, striving to become more mature and responsible. They respect their children's feelings, their dignity, and their individuality.

Children who grow up in a family atmosphere based largely on mutual love and respect acquire a trust in themselves as dependable citizens and a trust in most other people as being well motivated too. When they have children of their own they naturally expect them to turn out well. They tend to favor childrearing methods and educational philosophies that give children as much independence and scope for initiative and creativity as is sensible.

Of course, no parent is totally authoritarian or totally democratic in spirit. We all are strung along the scale somewhere between the extremes. Each one will be more authoritarian in one situation, more democratic in another, and each of us varies somewhat from time to time.

In the nation as a whole, as well as in different groups or localities, the pendulum swings first one way and then the other. The direction depends on such factors as an overall sense of economic security and civil tranquillity, which favors the democratic attitude, or domestic and international crises, during which people and leaders demand stern measures.

If parents who are inclined toward the authoritarian spirit also are hostile people, always on the edge of anger with their children —because of anxiety about not being able to control them or because of other tensions—the children are apt to develop too much hostility in their characters also. Whether they become distinctly disagreeable on the surface or whether the anger has been effectively subdued, it still will be an important part of their nature. If the parents are quite comfortable in their authoritarianism, the children may perhaps be less flexible, more conformist than average in their basic personalities, but still friendly people.

Parents who take to a democratic philosophy may have considerable trouble making the system work if they are timid about leading their children—if, for instance, they are afraid to be definite about cooperation, considerateness, bedtime or chores. From an early age children are acutely aware of who, if anyone, has the upper hand in various family situations—are aware of whether they have parents who'll give them anything they demand or who can be seduced into yielding or who can be bullied with temper tantrums or reproachful shouts of "I hate you!" I've known a few infants who became obnoxious tyrants by eight months of age because their parents were afraid to be firm about anything. Parents in one family may be quite firm about denying their children soft drinks and candy, for example, but may always yield when the children resist being sent to bed. So the children don't argue about sweets but never go to bed without prolonged wrangling. In another family it may be the opposite.

I myself lean quite far toward the democratic side, which, I feel, fosters such qualities as flexibility, reasonableness, initiative, and self-discipline. But, of course, I also believe that parents may have to be slightly authoritarian in the end in deciding that babies must be put to bed at a certain time even though they may protest, that children shouldn't be allowed to eat junk food, that teenagers can't stay out all night, that parents have the right to be spoken to with respect.

But before exercising a veto, parents can listen sympathetically to their children's requests, discuss the issues in a democratic rather than an overbearing manner, and demonstrate in their discussions that they are trying to advance the welfare of the whole family and are not just being arbitrarily restrictive. And parents can show a sense of humor. They can encourage discussion of the feelings involved including the children's resentment of the parents—as long as this is expressed nonabusively. These attitudes in a family discussion usually bring the children around to cooperative agreement. But not always. Then parents have to exercise the right (at least I'd call it a right) to a unilateral decision—not expressed angrily, which would suggest they're unsure or guilty—but matter-of-factly.

Being a democratic parent doesn't mean that you need to get involved in endless discussion of every little issue that comes up. If children discover that their parents are too timid to bring a discussion to a sensible conclusion, they may make the whole family miserable, including themselves.

▷ IMPOSED VERSUS INNER DISCIPLINE

Long ago, experiments were carried out by a group of psychologists to clarify the differences in the effects of authoritarian and democratic styles of discipline on boys of ten or twelve years of age. The experimenters set up after-school activity clubs and invited boys to join.

In the authoritarian part of the experiment the leader called the boys to order at their first session and announced, for example, that they were going to build small end tables. He proceeded—then and at later stages—to dictate what the steps would be, what supplies and tools would be necessary, how they were to be procured and used, and what each individual's or committee's job would be. Except for planned absences, he stayed right on top of the group at all times, directing and correcting and reprimanding. He brushed aside all suggestions from the boys, who soon stopped making any.

The democratic part of the experiment was conducted entirely differently. The leader told the group of boys that this was to be their club and they were to decide what their project would be. Different members suggested various projects. Some of these were voted down because they appealed to few individuals. A suggestion to build a real plane in which a boy could fly, for instance, might have great appeal at first. But further discussion—of such practical questions as the great expense or whether parents would ever permit flights in such a craft—would eventually lead to the abandonment of the idea.

The leader was very much a part of this group. If disruptive behavior occurred, he controlled it by reasoning. He sometimes guided the discussion by raising a pertinent question that had not occurred to the boys. But he carefully left most of the suggestions, arguments, and decision making to them. If they decided on a course of action about which he had raised doubts, such as borrowing tools from a professional carpenter, he let them go ahead—as long as this course was not harmful to anyone—to discover for themselves that a sensible carpenter couldn't afford such trust and generosity.

Just as methods differed dramatically in the two parts of the experiment, so did results. If, for instance, the boys in the democratically run group, after consideration of many proposals, decided to build birdhouses, discussions followed, primarily among the boys themselves but with occasional guidance from the adult leader. They talked about where to find plans and which to select; the best sequence of steps in the actual building; which jobs would need a committee to carry them out, which should be assigned to one person, and which should be left to the individual builders. As decisions were gradually made and carried out and as the boys got to know each other's capabilities, they themselves made the assignments of particular responsibilities to individuals and committees. As a result of all this, each boy came to feel that he had some special responsibility to the group.

Which approach produced articles at the faster rate? The authoritarian method was *much* faster. It also created neater results. But whenever the authoritarian leader left the room, most of the boys stopped work and horsed around. Some of them, in their roughhousing, were mean to the more submissive members of the group or they abused the end tables they were working on. Obviously they felt that the project, which had been dictated throughout by the leader, was his more than it was theirs and that they were entitled to drop it when he wasn't around. And obviously some were so resentful of the leader's domination that they took it out on other boys or on their work.

On the other hand, when the democratic leader left the room the work went on almost as efficiently as when he was present. The boys knew that the project was theirs in every sense. They knew pretty well what the next steps were to be. They were aware of each one's particular responsibility to the group. And they were eager to get on with their jobs.

Up to now I've left out a third aspect of the experiment—a group in which the adult was really no leader at all. This part of the experiment was named after the French expression *laissez faire,* meaning "let happen what may." The job of the leader was just to be there. He was allowed to give assistance when specifically asked for it, but that was all; he was to offer no leadership whatsoever. In this group the boys just fooled around. They never accomplished anything or even decided anything. From time to time some of the more mature boys urged the group to get organized and choose a project. The others would agree, for the moment. But the boy leaders didn't have sufficient leadership qualities to achieve and maintain group discipline.

I'm glad that the experiment included *laissez faire,* because some people (they are of the authoritarian philosophy) assume that there are only two ways of leading children, whether by teachers, parents, or anyone else. One is to boss and correct them constantly, and this, they believe, produces good behavior and constructive activity. The other is to let them do exactly as they please, and this produces poor behavior. But as the experiment showed, there is a big difference between democratic leadership, which is concerned with fostering social skills and self-discipline as well as with getting things done, and *laissez faire,* which is no leadership at all.

The experiment demonstrated clearly that authoritarian leadership can get jobs accomplished and can teach manual skills. (In school it can teach simple academic skills such as spelling or multiplication tables to children who are well motivated and ready.) But it does not teach cooperation—quite the opposite. In addition, the discipline it produces is imposed from the outside and collapses when the leader goes away, whereas democratic leadership builds self-discipline, which lasts under most conditions because it comes from within.

This good result comes from being trusted with increasing responsibilities by a friendly leader and from learning from experience that one can carry out responsibilities. Out of this grows self-trust, pride, initiative, and resourcefulness, which gradually become part of a child's character. These are qualities that make for good citizenship. They are also what make students at later stages —in high school, college, and professional school—take responsibility for their own learning as opposed to merely submitting to daily assignments. In later life these are the qualities that motivate people to carry out the tasks of their chosen occupations—not just adequately enough for them to get by, but for the sake of doing a job well. They can see how their jobs, at home or outside, can be done better and better, and they take satisfaction in improving. They perceive the requirements for the next higher job and, consciously or unconsciously, prepare themselves for it.

Children who are led democratically, at home and in school, also are learning—for now and for their future lives—how to function well in groups, whether in the family or on the job or in community projects. They are learning how to really listen to the suggestions of others, how to make their own suggestions in a persuasive and tactful manner, how to recognize and appreciate the particular capabilities of other individuals and help get them assigned to the right jobs, how to accept the leadership of someone else and how to be a leader—not a leader who dominates or nags, but one who inspires the group.

Some parents who themselves attended authoritarian schools where children sat in rows, kept silent until called on to recite, were never asked for comments or contributions, and had no relationship to one another in class (except for secret teasing or note passing) are upset when they visit classrooms where children are gathered in informal subgroups. They see that the children move about to get materials or to consult the teacher or each other, are asked for their ideas and encouraged to discuss them freely, work cooperatively in groups on certain projects, often without immediate supervision, help to decide which child is to be given a special responsibility such as going to the library for additional information. To authoritarian parents this atmosphere seems too "free," almost chaotic.

But nowadays teachers in good schools are deliberately encouraging spontaneity, independent thinking, self-learning, self-discipline, cooperation, appreciation of others—qualities and capacities that are just as important as the three Rs. In the long run, they are a lot more important than learning to sit as quietly as a mouse to please a teacher.

If children are to profit fully from acquiring initiative and responsibility during their school years, it is wise for parents to begin fostering these attitudes during the preschool years—even when the children are only one or two years of age. For if children in their early years at home have learned that the way to get along with their parents is simply not to "get into things," not to ask questions or argue, just do what they're told, whether or not they understand why, to "be good" when their parents are watching and to save all their other impulses until the parents are out of sight, then it will be very hard for even the best of teachers to encourage curiosity, self-motivation, and self-discipline in the school years. The basic patterns are set.

How do you, as a parent, establish a democratic kind of leadership when your daughter is a year old? Obviously not by holding family meetings daily under *Robert's Rules of Order.* You let her explore and experiment freely as long as her safety and the safety of your precious possessions are not threatened. You do not shout, "No! No!" or slap her every time she tries something. You remove breakables temporarily while you teach her a few prohibitions at a time. You let her play with spoons, eggbeaters, and cartons, climb up on hassocks and couches, and make some decisions for herself.

When she is two or three years old you try to answer sensibly all sincere questions. (Sometimes a small child falls into an obsessive habit of saying, "Why?" to every statement of the parent without paying the slightest attention to the answer, and there is no point in giving answers to such whys.) You encourage your small daughter to fall into the habit of helping, whether in raking leaves, setting the table or clearing it—all this on her own initiative. Don't stop her because at this stage she is more of a nuisance than a help and then at a later stage direct her to do such chores as obligations.

When a child is four or five or six years old it's not too early, if the parents are discussing alternatives for an outing or a vacation, to ask her to express her preference. If her preference makes sense, then the child has had a part in making a family decision. If it is quite impractical, you can explain politely why. It's wise when a child of preschool or school age asks for help, in making a toy work or in understanding a homework assignment, to ask her first for her suggestions, which indicates to her that children often have as good solutions as adults do. (Parents shouldn't *do* their children's homework, in any case.)

If you give an allowance or pay for chores, let children spend the money as they wish (except for junk food or anything else potentially harmful) so that they can learn money management by trial and error. And let your children help to choose their own clothes, within sensible limits, even if you think their taste often leaves a lot to be desired.

When a child is creating a game or a project of her own invention and is clearly off on a mistaken course, the parent should resist the impulse to volunteer criticism and advice, at least until asked for help. (That was the hardest part for me as a parent. I was always too eager to suggest a better or more complicated way to build something.)

It's a valuable aspect of democratic leadership, when children are to be assigned ongoing as well as temporary jobs, if parents can ask the children to participate in the assignment. "Who do you all think could do this job best?" "Who doesn't have a job at the lake?" "Who would like to volunteer?" In this way children see that chores are not just a form of parental oppression. And they develop some sense of obligation to the whole group in doing their share.

▷ MY OWN POSITION ON DISCIPLINE

Since 1968 I have been hounded and haunted by the accusations of those who say that I advocate permissive child rearing. And other people have claimed that I subsequently renounced my "permissive" philosophy and turned strict. If "permissive" means allowing children to have and do and say almost anything they want (which is what most people think it means), then I never had such a philosophy. In fact, I believe the opposite; I'm bothered—really bothered—when children are allowed to be demanding or uncooperative.

When my sons are interviewed, they make it clear that I was a rather strict parent. And people who stop me in the street to say, "Thank you for helping me raise two fine children," often add, "And I don't see that your book is permissive!" Since *Baby and Child Care* came out forty-two years ago no one who has actually used the book has claimed to me that it advocates permissiveness. In reality it emphasizes the opposite; it urges parents to give their children firm, clear leadership and to ask for cooperation and politeness in return.

The original accusation of permissiveness came two weeks after I was indicted by the Lyndon Johnson administration for my activities in opposition to the Vietnam war. It took the form of a sermon by the Reverend Norman Vincent Peale, Jr., in which he said that the irresponsibility, lack of discipline, lack of patriotism that he objected to in young people (referring to their refusal to kill and be killed in a war they considered contrary to the principles and best interests of our country) was caused by my having advised their parents to give them "instant gratification" when they were babies.

Those two words proved to me that the Reverend Peale had not read *Baby and Child Care,* for there's nothing in it that even remotely advocates instant gratification. He had simply projected his notion onto me because, like the youthful resisters, I too was an opponent of the war.

His accusation was eagerly taken up by conservative newspaper editorial writers and columnists all over the country who supported the war, who were troubled by the attitude of the young, and who were eager for an explanation of it. His accusation was spread most widely by Spiro Agnew. Remember him? He had to resign the vice presidency because he was caught still demanding graft from road contractors in Maryland where he had previously been governor. Fortunately no one can accuse me of having raised Agnew. He grew up before my book appeared.

Then, a dozen years ago, there was a report that I had disavowed my previous philosophy, a report that resulted indirectly from a *Redbook* press release. It called attention to a forthcoming column in which I discussed half a dozen different reasons for some parents' hesitance to be firm with their children. The release singled out only one of the reasons: that professionals (including myself) who write advice for parents give those parents with little self-confidence the impression that only an expert knows how to rear children properly. The headline of the press release read: "Why are there so many bratty children? Dr. Spock blames the experts."

The newspaper editors and newscasters who were under the impression that I was permissive interpreted the press release to mean that I had now turned my back on that philosophy because it produced spoiled children. This brought me endless requests for interviews from publications all over the world wanting to know why I'd recanted. I denied that I had ever been permissive or that I had changed my mind. But it's impossible to counter an incorrect report. I'm still asked the same old questions almost every week of my life. You can see why I'm touchy.

Of course, I have changed many things in *Baby and Child Care* in the forty-two years since it was published. But my basic philosophy about the discipline and management of children has not changed, and I'll explain it in several ways to try to make it as clear as possible.

Children themselves work hard to grow up, to be more mature, to become more responsible people. From infancy they explore and experiment and practice skills for hours on end. In the three-to-six-year-old period they watch their admired parents constantly and practice being like them.

It has only been in the twentieth century, through studies of child development, that we have come to realize how well-intentioned and self-motivated children are. In Europe and America in the past they were generally not respected. They were treated like slaves (though not considered to be as valuable), or as second- or third-class citizens. Teachers felt free to hit them, employers of child labor abused and exploited them, parents and clergymen assumed they were born with an inclination to be bad and could be redeemed only by constant vigilance, correction, and punishment.

Children deserve to be respected, I feel, because they are, on the average, as idealistic as adults, as truthful, as original and creative, as loving, as loyal. Parents can show respect for their children in various ways—by speaking to them politely, giving them explanations when asked for them, listening to their stories with interest, granting reasonable requests, sympathizing with their feelings of grief or anger or guilt, and asking courteously for their help with routine and special chores.

I also believe that it is important for parents to show, in all their interactions with their children, that they respect themselves too and ask for respect from their children. I don't mean that parents should constantly preach to them. I am speaking of simple actions. A mother should not, for example, allow a cranky nine- or ten-month-old baby to pull her hair or let a teething baby bite her arm. She shouldn't get disagreeable or bite back, but she should draw away if she sees the lunge coming. When a one-year-old starts developing a pattern of screeching when she wants something, the mother can lean over and say very quietly and seriously that she doesn't like screeches and then distract the child temporarily to another plaything, to show that screeches don't get the desired object. When a four-year-old first experiments with calling his parent a "stinker" or shouts, "I hate you," the parent should immediately show concern and should say quietly, "That makes me very unhappy." When an older child speaks rudely or refuses to cooperate, the parent might take his hand and say earnestly, "I know how cross you feel with me sometimes; I know that you don't always want to do what I ask; but in this family everybody has to help, even when he may not want to."

I keep mentioning the serious and quiet manner of speaking to emphasize that when parents just shout or scold or slap a child, they give up their position as mature moral guides. They descend to the angry child's level; it's only a question then of who can shout louder or longer.

The realization in the twentieth century that children have a strong inner drive to develop and mature and that it is possible to raise them with an emphasis on mutual respect instead of correction and punishment has produced three different reactions in parents.

Some have welcomed this new philosophy and have treated their children in a friendlier, more trusting spirit. At the same time they have been able to preserve their own self-respect and elicit the respect of their children. This approach can be labeled as mutual respect. It can and does produce children who are cooperative, flexible, polite, and warmhearted.

Other parents are overawed by the evidence of their children's good intentions. They are so aware of their own lack of expert knowledge, so distressed about the way children were abused in the past that they've guiltily elevated their own children above themselves, morally speaking. Such parents tend to submit to quite a bit of punishment from their children, accepting rudeness and lack of cooperation, giving them more possessions and privileges than is sensible. This is my idea of overpermissiveness. It produces children who are strong at arguing and demanding, weak in politeness and cooperation. (It also gives the concept of respect for children a bad name.)

A third group of parents are deeply convinced—perhaps by the way in which they themselves were raised—that children will be lazy, destructive, disobedient, and evil unless they are kept on the straight and narrow by constant warnings and punishments. These parents are greatly alarmed by professionals and by other parents who put their faith mainly in love and understanding, who believe in making school interesting, and who lean toward leniency at home as well as in the juvenile courts. They see "all hell breaking loose" if children are treated "softly." Such disciplinary attitudes may produce children with either a tendency toward meekness or toward aggressiveness, and with less-than-average warmth and flexibility.

These are the extremes, of course. Most parents, although they lean to one style of child rearing, show traces of others, especially during times of doubt or stress. I myself believe strongly in a philosophy of mutual respect.

But no matter how well-intentioned children may be, they start out with no experience at all and with impulsive natures. They need lots of supervision and clear guidance. Babies should gradually be taught what "no" means. A two- or three-year-old must learn not to cross a street unless a parent is holding her hand. The school bus must be boarded on time. For adolescents, careful parents set an hour for coming home.

In order to be happy members of a family, children need to feel they have obligations toward it. They should be expected to be polite. They should put their toys away (with parental help during the early years); they should help in preparing meals and washing dishes, take care of their rooms, rake leaves, take out the trash—all according to their ages and abilities as well as their parents' wishes. At the same time, it shouldn't be necessary for the parent to be overbearing or disagreeable or punitive. If an adult friend is staying with you and you need her help in preparing supper, you don't shout irritably at her, "Turn that television off and set the table immediately!" At the office or shop, the manager who is not satisfied with the way a new worker is doing his job doesn't rush in and give him a swat on the behind. He or she explains what change in performance is needed—more than once, if necessary. Ideally, the same should be true of the way we handle our children. Unfortunately, the fact is that most of us do go at our children impatiently and disagreeably at times, which sets their teeth on edge and provokes them to be uncooperative.

There are many reasons for our losing our patience so easily. We are apt to jump on our children unnecessarily because of the excessively tense, complicated society we live in, as discussed in Chapter One. But the most powerful reason, I think, is that most of us were treated impatiently in our own childhood. You can hear four- and five-year-olds scolding and spanking their dolls in exactly the same manner as they themselves are being disciplined, and this spirit will tend to persist into adulthood. I don't mean that we all are doomed to follow the example of our parents in all details, but the urge to do so is strong and automatic.

▷ PUNISHMENT

I get frustrated when once in a while I arrive in a city to give a talk and a young, unmarried male reporter sent to interview me asks solemnly, "Doctor, do you believe in physical punishment?" When I back away from an immediate no reply, saying that there are a number of other factors in discipline that come first and are more important, he becomes somewhat disapproving and asks, "So you believe in letting children do as they like?"

This view—that you either punish a child physically or you raise a spoiled one—is fairly common, held oftenest by males and most especially by childless people. (Most parents are compelled by experience to give up such oversimplified ideas.)

I remember having been spanked only once or twice when I was a child. It was done gravely by my father—on the recommendation of my mother—with the back of a hairbrush to the palm of my hand. I can still recall the awful fear and guilt that hung over me between the time when my mother pronounced the sentence and the hour when my father came home from work and carried it out.

But for all the rest of my childhood I was held firmly in line by my mother's stern rulings and even sterner disapproval. She didn't just disapprove of an act. Her facial expression was intended to convey withdrawal of love—for the time being, anyway—and the substitution of condemnation and some anger. It's what I call moral discipline, used in an unnecessarily severe form in my mother's case, its purpose being to make the child feel guilty. For guilt in its simplest childhood form is anxiety about losing the parents' love, with all that love implies at this dependent stage of life. As children mature, the fear of losing their parents' approval is increasingly transformed into fear of reproaches from their own conscience or from society.

Anyway, my mother's six children rarely, if ever, needed any form of overt punishment—spanking, deprivation of privileges and possessions, or isolation. A warning or a scolding was painful and effective enough. Generally we got into trouble not by disobeying —we didn't dare—but only by doing something about which there was no previous rule or by quarreling among ourselves. (Constant quarreling can be a natural outlet for children who frequently are disapproved of and scolded.) All six of us grew up with a more severe conscience and a greater sense of guilt than was necessary or healthy.

Of course a moderate amount of conscience is a regular and necessary component in the disciplining of the child and in the building of good character in the adult. It is the reverse side of the coin that represents the child's pleasure in love from his parents and the wish to please them. An ideal amount of conscience produces a gentle reminder when there is temptation to misbehave; it should not be so great as to produce a constant sense of oppression.

Is punishment—physical or otherwise—necessary? Many of the highly conscientious, psychology-oriented parents who chose me as a pediatrician in New York felt—as I did—that punishment was seldom, if ever, necessary. We felt that children would learn to behave responsibly because their parents loved them and showed respect for them as human beings; because their parents taught them and reasoned with them; and also because children loved and admired their parents, wanted to be like them, and wanted to please them.

Yet a considerable majority of American parents not only spank their children when upset by their behavior but also consider spanking an essential element in upbringing. It's mostly parents who themselves were given fairly regular punishment, including spankings, who tend to think of punishment as natural and necessary. Some of them would feel powerless and resentful if told by an authoritarian psychologist or teacher that they must not punish. And parents have to raise their children according to their own basic convictions. On the other hand, most parents who were raised without physical punishment tend to think of punishment in terms of adults imposing their will arbitrarily, just because they are bigger.

In earlier decades—and in earlier editions of *Baby and Child Care* —I avoided a flat statement of disapproval of physical punishment. I contented myself with the statement that I didn't think it was necessary. This was because of my belief that it's disturbing to parents when a professional person appears to imply that he knows better than they. What made me go against my own rule was my growing concern over the sky-high and ever-rising figures for murders within the family, wife abuse, and child abuse in America, and our government's enthusiasm for the nuclear arms race and for an aggressive foreign policy. It's not that physical punishment creates these alarming conditions by itself, but it certainly plays a role in our acceptance of violence. If we are ever to turn toward a kindlier society and a safer world, a revulsion against the physical punishment of children would be a good place to start. My other reasons for advising against physical punishment are, in brief, that it teaches that might makes right, that it encourages some children to be bullies, and most fundamentally, that to the degree that it results in good behavior it's because of the fear of pain. I have a strong belief that the best reason for behaving well is that you like people, want to get along with them, want them to like you.

Since I believe in depending as much as possible on love and on reasoning with children, I can't get too concerned about just which nonphysical punishments are better than others. But it's easy to list some obvious generalities: The child should know ahead of time what the rules are and the punishments for breaking them. The punishment should be appropriate to the misbehavior. A favorite toy can be taken away for a day or two, an allowance can be docked, a child can be sent to her room.

But I think it's important to add that punishment will have a good, permanent effect only if in her heart the child knows and respects the parents' fairness (children rarely admit openly that punishment is justified), and if the child learns to be a bit more responsible with each incident.

Threats have a positive value if they are reasonable and usually are carried out. (Perhaps *warning* is a better word than *threat* in these circumstances; *threat* has a belligerent sound.) There are a few parents who shout threats all day, seldom follow through, and seldom really intend to. These parents expect children to misbehave all the time and expect—subconsciously, at least—not to be able to control them (probably as a result of their own childhood experiences). So their constant empty threats really have the sole purpose of venting their own frustrations. Their children are learning only to ignore threats and to have little belief in their parents' sincerity.

Warnings, in my opinion, are second-best to the kind of discipline or relationship in which the parent explains, in a manner that shows respect for the child and gains respect from the child, what is harmful about an action (or lack of action). The parent can ask in a trusting tone for the child's cooperation. Warnings should come only when this mutual respect has temporarily broken down.

Another trouble with warnings is that they sound like dares, especially to a child under the age of three. For a child this young, who has not yet developed a respect for authority based on confidence in her parents' wisdom and good intentions, a warning carries the clear implication that the child may decide to disobey if she is willing to take the consequences. In other words, a warning gives a child a choice: to be meek and obey or to be independent and disobey. And since impulsiveness and the drive to be independent are strong in a child this age, the cards are stacked against the parent. So it is better to give a child this young the feeling that there really is only one right way to do things.

Consistency is often emphasized as a necessary factor in good discipline. For instance, if half the time a mother corrects her child for interrupting adult conversations but the other half appears not to notice, the child will continue to interrupt. If a father refuses to buy his daughter soda on four outings but gives in to her pleadings on the fifth, she will learn that requests and demands and whining are worth trying at every opportunity.

Consistency doesn't have to be absolute, but the parents' control will be better if it is they who suggest the exception or if they agree immediately without an argument to the child's special request. What I'm saying is that I would avoid like the plague giving in out of exhaustion just because a child won't stop nagging.

Some mothers and fathers assume that they must stand together on all rules and standards if these are to be respected. I don't think that this degree of consistency is necessary. Children show themselves to be perceptive and flexible in adapting to the somewhat different standards of father and mother—in neatness, for example, or quietness or helpfulness. They also can adapt to requirements at school that are quite different from those at home. However, parental discipline and good family relationships are corrupted if parents who have serious disagreements and conflicts between themselves allow a child to play one parent against the other. This will compound the parents' own problems and, even more serious, will train the child to grow up to be an individual who manipulates and poisons other people's relationships.

In summary, I'd say that the questions of punishment, threats, and consistency, about which many parents worry, all are issues of secondary importance. For the most part they will take care of themselves as long as parents and child love and respect each other.

▷ DO YOU MEAN IT?

Whether you really mean what you say to children is probably more important than any other factor except love in your success in their management.

Parents assume, of course, that when they ask a child to do something or to stop doing something, they mean it. And this is true of a majority of parents, most of the time. You mean what you say when you tell your three-year-old *never* to cross the street again without holding your hand or *never, never* to play with matches again. But child guidance clinic work or observation of parents in action shows that most parents have one or two areas in which their control is unsatisfactory because they don't quite mean what they say. And a few of them hardly ever mean what they say.

You could put it the other way around and make an even more startling statement: any behavior that parents truly want from their children they can get.

I'm thinking of two different ways in which parents don't mean what they say. One is when they are not sure they are right—a very common situation with conscientious parents these days. The other is when parents consciously want their children to behave a certain way but are undermined by the deeply ingrained patterns by which they themselves were raised.

One simple, common example of unsatisfactory control is when a parent says, "It's your bedtime; go take your bath." But the child makes no move and the parent appears not to notice. Half an hour later the parent says, "It's past your bedtime. Go take your bath." Again the child appears not to have heard and the parent seems to drop the matter. This goes on and on. Another common example is when a parent says, "You've watched enough television now," but makes no effort to see that the child turns the set off.

You may think that this sort of noncompliance on the part of a child is inconsequential. But it isn't. It creates a chronically balky child and nervous exhaustion for the parents. Parents should see that their requests are carried out reasonably soon, especially when experience shows that a child will procrastinate.

These small examples reflect some of the reasons for many parents' difficulties. They may be vacillating about sending a child to bed because they remember themselves as children, hating to go to bed and putting up a long argument each night. They don't want to repeat that struggle every night for years with their own children, and they don't want their children to become resentful of them as they remember being resentful of their parents. In a sense, they feel guilty in advance over the possible hostility they may be stirring up in their children.

I'd say that *all* children resent their parents at times—good parents as well as poor parents. So there's no point trying to avoid this altogether. Children resent most, of course, the parent who is grossly unfair or mean or unloving. They also resent the parent who is permissive one day or one hour and strict the next, depending on the mood she or he is in. (Adults working in an office or shop are similarly uneasy with and suspicious of a boss who frequently changes the rules.) Furthermore, parents who submit to their children's constant pushing and unreasonable demands inevitably will have to take a stand sooner or later. So in the end there is exactly the kind of unpleasantness the parents were trying to avoid in the first place.

To turn it around, children resent least the parents who are very sure and consistent about what's permissible and who can turn down unreasonable requests promptly and cheerfully. When children sense their parents' sureness about issues, they don't argue or work themselves up to a state of resentment.

Parents who as children were regularly made to feel incompetent or naughty may lack in adulthood confidence in their ability to make wise decisions in important or unimportant matters.

It's certainly a problem for parents who have high standards for their children to know how and how much to limit television viewing. In a a general way they feel that all the violence and vulgarity is bad, and they don't like the idea of their children sitting for hours and passively accepting entertainment instead of inventing their own play, preferably outdoors. (I agree with them in these concerns.) But in view of the fact that their children crave television and that most other children are allowed to watch to their heart's content, parents don't know where to set the limits. One day when they are self-confident they may be strict, and the next, when they have less conviction and are feeling more guilt, they may be lenient. Hesitancy, guilt, and vacillation are noticed instantly by children, and this encourages them to argue and push.

If as parents we are much more affluent than our parents were, say, or our circumstances are otherwise different, then we have no inner guide and are thrown back on our general common sense, our general self-confidence, or on what we've read or heard, none of which are as helpful as inner conviction.

A more general reason for hesitancy is when parents feel guilt—consciously or unconsciously—in relation to one particular child. Even if they think they should be firm about this or that matter of discipline, their feelings of guilt keep making them give in, in the end. A son may remind his mother of her older brother who often made life miserable for her, and she may feel guilty because of her anger. Or a boy may remind his father of a younger brother who got under his skin because he seemed to be the favorite of the parents.

A divorced mother sometimes feels chronically guilty toward a child because she decided to go to work while the child was very young, before she had resolved in her own mind—by herself or with professional counseling—her conflicting feelings about it. (In an intact family with a small child, when the wife decides she must go to work it is usually she who feels the conflict, and if it is not clarified and resolved, it is she who feels the guilt, I don't think that this is right; the father should have an equal sense of responsibility toward the children and perhaps at least should *consider* changing his hours of work so that *he* can care for them during some of his wife's working hours.)

A more extreme example of lack of control—you've seen this fairly often on the street or in the supermarket—is when a parent constantly and irritably yells at a child to "stop that" or makes dire threats of all kinds without the slightest sign of follow-through or of meaning any of it. It is just a continuous venting of irritation—and it may be coming partly from marital conflict or other troubles. In any case, such a parent has no expectation or trust that the child will obey or even that the child has any good intentions. And the child, chronically antagonized, retaliates with endless petty provocations that are carefully graduated so as not to bring down severe punishment. It is like the sparring exercises that boxers in training use, in which they trade jabs monotonously but carefully avoid any decisive action.

You can be sure that a parent with this problem was yelled at in a similar way throughout childhood and learned then to assume that a parent rarely means it and has little effective control, and that a child has no inner motivation to cooperate in a way a parent can count on.

Parents who have considerable difficulty making their children behave can usually get help from a period of regular consultations with a counselor in a family social agency or with a private counselor.

A quite different type of "not meaning it" may be detected in the families of children who develop delinquent behavior (a catchall term that covers every kind of misbehavior that the law takes cognizance of). The parents ostensibly want the child to be "good." But they themselves have strong impulses, usually suppressed into their unconscious minds, to commit illegal or disapproved acts, and they can enjoy them vicariously when committed by their child. So they manage, in one subtle way or another, to let the child know that they won't crack down very hard.

A father brings a boy of ten years to a child guidance clinic complaining that he keeps running away. The boy is extremely bold and ingenious for a child so young; he manages to cover hundreds —sometimes thousands—of miles on his trips by begging and lying. What is most significant is that the father beams with pride when he describes his son's supposedly forbidden behavior—and in the boy's presence.

A girl is brought to the clinic because of shoplifting. Careful questioning reveals that the mother's first question to her daughter, after the child had stolen some pens, was, "Did anyone see you?" Without meaning to, she was telling her daughter that it wasn't wrong to steal as long as she wasn't caught.

A potent factor that interferes with parental self-assurance in child care in the United States is our lack of consensus about how children should be reared. Should they be treated strictly or leniently? Will giving them a lot of possessions spoil children, or is it valuable in making them feel equal to their friends? Is religious training essential or should the choice be left to them? Should children have duties to the family? When they complain about their teachers, should a parent sympathize or take the attitude that the teacher is right? Should the emphasis be on service to others or on getting ahead? Should they be permitted or forbidden to fight with other children? Is punishment necessary or harmful? These are very common questions among American parents. But in many other parts of the world there are no such choices. The traditions in each society are long established and universally believed in.

Our American lack of consensus comes partly from the fact that we are a composite nation made up of the children of immigrants who had different traditions in their various native countries but who were impatient with some of them; it comes partly from our excessive mobility, which keeps young parents from comfortably absorbing the beliefs and methods of their own parents; it comes partly from the disparity of views of all the professional people in the child-rearing field, who, with the best of intentions, shower parents with advice that seems to vary from expert to expert and from decade to decade. (A dozen new books on child rearing, new magazines, each year!) So parents have many choices and no assurance about which one will be best for their family. We take this freedom of choice for granted and consider it an advantage—which in some ways it is—but it is also a handicap.

Any discussion of whether you mean what you say brings up the matter of how consistent you have to be. A few extremely conscientious parents worry a lot about whether they are being fair in setting certain rules, and then worry just as much about whether they are being 100 percent consistent in applying them. Absolute consistency isn't necessary as long as you are generally consistent and—more important—as long as you are definite, cheerfully definite, whether you are granting an exception or turning down a plea.

I say be "cheerfully definite" because it's not just parental hesitancy that makes children argue and whine; it's the irritable tone in the father's or mother's voice. That tone says, "It makes me cross when you keep asking for things because it puts me in a quandary, and half the time I give in when I don't want to." That irritable tone in the parent's voice also antagonizes the child (as it would antagonize another adult) and makes the child want to keep up the needling, quite apart from the hope of gaining some concession. The cheerful tone says, "I'd like to please you, but I can't. There's no doubt in my mind."

▷ ARGUMENTS WITH CHILDREN

When a parent has had to refuse a daughter's request for a possession or a privilege—no new bike (or coat) because it's expensive and the old one is serviceable still; no soda or candy on the way home from school because it's junk food and hard on the teeth; no sleeping at a friend's house because the school theme hasn't been written as promised or the special home chore hasn't been done—then it's natural for the child to protest and to show how resentful she feels. And it's good for the parent to reply—if it can be done sympathetically, not tauntingly—that he or she knows how angry the child is and feels sorry to have to say no.

If the child persists in arguing or asking why (she knows why, of course), it's all right for the parent to explain the reason once more, matter-of-factly, as if the reason speaks for itself. (When parents become angry at such times, it usually means that they feel a little uncertain or guilty about their refusal and can stick to their guns only if they work themselves into a state of noisy indignation.) If the child wants to go on arguing, it can lead only to endless repetitions and rising tempers, and it's sensible for parents to point this out and then go about their other business.

But when a child later comes back with what she considers an entirely new angle, I think parents have to listen again even though the final answer may be the same no. In other words, parents should always be ready to listen to reason and to reopen a discussion—especially after tempers have cooled. But they still can decline to get hung up in endless, meaningless, repetitive argument.

It's not only permissible but also valuable for a parent to admit it if she or he has been at fault. This doesn't decrease the child's respect; it increases it.

If a child gets angry enough to shout, "I hate you!" I myself would be inclined to say, "I know this makes you angry with me. But I still don't want you to speak like that to me. It's unkind and makes me unhappy."

My point is that parents should not meekly accept verbal abuse as if it is deserved. Parents, I feel, should protest—for their own sakes as well as for the child's sake—even if the protest is ineffective at the moment and the child repeats the offensive remark. The second time, parents can walk away, as if they have no further point to make. It's wise, if possible, for parents not to descend to the child's level of temper and scream back, for that way they lose a lot of their value as leaders and models.

There is another type of meaningless discussion, which occurs in families in which the parents are excessively conscientious and are afraid to exert any leadership. The parent says, "I'd like you to wear your snow pants to kindergarten today." The child says, "Why?" though she knows perfectly well. The parent says, "Because it's very cold." The child says, "But why do I have to?" The parent says, "You wouldn't want to shiver all the way to school and back." The child says, "Yes, I would!" The parent says, "You might catch a cold." The child says, "No, I wouldn't," or, "I don't care."

This sort of thing can go on hour after hour. It wears the parents down. And it doesn't help the child learn to make decisions, only to make a nuisance of herself. It doesn't teach her respect for her parents' reasonableness; it shows her only that her parents are afraid to be definite. This compels her to argue every point compulsively, even though she has no real interest in what she's saying. In other words, it's a bore for her too. And it's a bore for all the friends of the family.

The parents needn't say, "We're older and we have the authority." They have only to say, "I think you're arguing for the sake of arguing."

The only point of such discussions with a child is to clarify the reasons for the parents'—or the children's—requests, to give the children the feeling that their good sense and their cooperativeness are appreciated and confidence that their wishes will be considered.

But full consideration shouldn't mean that the children, after hearing their parents' concerns, can override them if they wish—at least not until they are eighteen or twenty years old. Parents' experience and responsibility have to count for something, and parents shouldn't be afraid to use their veto after the final argument has been heard.

Actually, if children have been listened to—about their requests and about the responsiblities assigned them—and if their wishes have been granted as far as has been sensible, and if they have found reason to trust their parents' fairness, they will not argue interminably or threaten to rebel outright.

One of the biggest obstacles to successful family conversation is that most good parents feel a compulsion to be on the lookout for disapproved behavior in their children and are quick to criticize. If a boy reports that his teacher was mean, a parent is apt to say instantly, "What did *you* do to make her angry?" A parent may promptly reproach a daughter for losing her gloves without waiting to hear her story, for getting a lower-than-usual grade in class, for giving her mother a headache ("too much arguing"), or for catching a cold ("You didn't wear your rubbers yesterday"). So it is not surprising that when a parent asks, "What did you do in school today?" a child's immediate and strong impulse is to clam up, on the assumption that the parent will be likely to find something to criticize in anything the child reports.

Yet if an adult friend of the mother mentions unkindness on the part of an acquaintance or that she has lost her gloves or caught a cold, the mother wouldn't think of pouncing on her in an accusatory way. We automatically give our friends the benefit of the doubt and sympathize with them. That's being a friend. Why can't we be equally friendly with our children—at least to start with? We could say to the boy who felt treated meanly, "That must have made you angry" or "sad." It's time enough to gently point out a child's fault when the evidence of fault has become clear. Often it is not necessary to speak reproachfully if the child feels bad already. Parents might even join the child in searching for a lost object in order to show their concern.

Why are we so instantly critical of our children? It isn't because we don't love them. It isn't because we don't want to be their friends as well as their parents. We can say, correctly, that it is our responsibility as parents to train them in good morals and good habits. But we usually haven't tried other approaches that might work better than criticism. The real reason, I think, is that most of us were constantly watched and scolded as children, and this built up a powerful compulsion to do the same when we became parents.

We squelch communication with our children not only by being too critical to allow a conversation to start; we often don't listen when they do feel like telling us something. Perhaps we grunt "uh-huh" occasionally, but it's clear that we aren't paying attention or responding to the dramatic turns in the story. Children retaliate by appearing deaf when their parents are talking to them or calling them.

One further suggestion. Instead of assuming that family discussions inevitably will be concerned with family matters, unpleasant or pleasant, we ought to expand our horizons and devote at least half the time at meals and other family gatherings to nonfamily subjects—the news of the day (world and neighborhood), gossip, movies, television happenings, events in the music and entertainment fields, good books and stories and even jokes.

The parents, by their example, can teach the older children to be tolerant of what younger children contribute, including what they consider jokes.

▷ TAKING CHILDREN OUT

Taking children to museums, exhibitions, zoos, fairs, sports events, factories, dairies, circuses, amusement parks, and beaches can be enormously rewarding, both to the children and to their parents. Children's curiosity and their desire to master new experiences are intense. They talk about new events in their lives and reenact them in their play for days and weeks afterward. This is how they learn and mature.

New experiences for children are exciting for parents too, because they can share in their children's delight and can relive the best days of their own childhood. Children keep parents young and lively. When excursions go well, the love and companionship between children and parents are heightened.

But there can be strains that turn excursions sour. New experiences are more tiring than familiar ones, particularly for small children. It's hard for parents to make allowances for this.

Most adults, when visiting a museum or zoo, would like to see it all, at least briefly, to make sure they haven't missed anything especially appealing. But they can protect themselves by quickly ignoring what doesn't interest them. Young children can't be that selective. At a zoo, every animal engages their intense interest. Therefore it's wise for parents to plan in advance to see only part of any exhibition, perhaps not more than one and a half hours' worth, when they take along preschool children.

In this same connection it also is wise—though difficult—for parents to let children go at their own pace. The typical scene at the zoo, for instance, is for the adults, having seen enough of the elephants, to press on, calling back to the child, "Come on—hurry up. We want to see the giraffe over here." But the child is still lost in wonder at the elephant's trunk or eating habits or huge BMs. So aim to follow the child rather than pull her.

Adults also tend to keep talking at the child about what impresses them, rather than letting the child find her own interests and then ask questions about them.

The food and drink and souvenir concessions were always the greatest problems for me in my relationship with my sons. Children who have the meagerest appetite at home become ravenous when they see hot dogs, ice cream, candy, and soda pop at a ball game. Even when the game is over, you are leaving the grandstand, and the child will be able to raid the refrigerator at home within fifteen minutes, he insists that this drink or this bag of popcorn is essential to ward off death from thirst or hunger and that the stuff at home won't do. The souvenirs, which irritate me because of their trashiness, inappropriateness, and expensiveness, fill children with longing.

The solution I arrived at was to give them a fixed sum of money at the start, for all souvenirs, rides, and food and let them do the balancing of their own desires. That was better than having to argue about each request. This system works really well. In fact, in that situation many children shift from being spendthrifts to misers.

As for junk foods, I feel so strongly today about the deteriorating diet of Americans and the accumulating evidence of its many ill effects that I would flatly, matter-of-factly, cheerfully forbid all of them at home as well as away from home. Take along a bag of fruit and a container of fruit juice on excursions. The children will scorn these things, but they'll eat them if they are really hungry and drink them if they are really thirsty. Even if these provisions are not touched, they are valuable in protecting the parents from accusations of cruelty.

Sporting events are a dubious investment with young children, at least until experience shows that they are able to appreciate them. They tend to lose interest in the game quickly and to focus on the unusual characters near them in the grandstand or on the wares being sold. It is better to realize this and leave them at home than to let them spoil the fun for you. Or take them at first only to inexpensive events.

Taking children on a day's fishing expedition also can be frustrating, if you expect them to fish. A few of them, from a relatively young age, have the quiet concentration required for fishing. But most children want to be active and creative. They soon begin to throw stones into the stream or drag a twig on a string behind the boat or build a dam across a brook. These activities are all right if they don't bother you.

A good idea for many outings is to bring friends along for children of school age and perhaps adult friends for the parents too. Then the generations can split up in their activities from time to time, instead of getting on each other's nerves.

Before taking school-age children to a special exhibit or on a trip to, say, Washington, D.C., it's an excellent idea to organize some library research in advance. Each child who is old enough can be assigned to or can choose some aspect of the subject to read up on and then report to the family on what he or she has learned and wants to see. It is most important for the parents to participate in the research and reporting, for that shows it is a grown-ups' activity, not a chore. Such advance study, even if it is quite skimpy and informal, usually will quadruple the interest in the project and the value derived from it.

I suppose that before discussing restaurant behavior, we should raise the question whether it is sensible to take young children out to eat, except, of course, when it is obligatory—while traveling, for example. Babies bang the highchair tray with a spoon and make a terrible mess, which may bother the parents or the staff. Small children want to play with the unfamiliar ice in the water glasses, which eventually leads to spilling part or all. They become restless and want to get down and wander around; this means that a parent has to keep chasing them, which is no pleasure, or has to let them bother other guests or the waiters.

A lot depends on whether the children are the restless kind or are quiet observers. If they are restless, it then depends on whether this spoils the parents' enjoyment or whether the parents are the type who aren't bothered at all when their children are messing up the place or bothering the other customers. A lot depends too on whether the parents have trained their children to be reasonably obedient and considerate or whether they've always allowed them —or even encouraged them—to be out of control. (This is basically the parents' choice.)

For myself, I think children should be trained, from the age of about eighteen months, to stay at the table in a restaurant without making a shambles of the place. Very important, with babies and small children, is to bring along crackers or other snacks for a child to eat before the restaurant food comes and a small toy to play with after the appetite is gone.

One problem for which I never found a solution was ordering for my children and grandchildren in a restaurant. Often they insisted on choosing one of the more expensive dishes, despite our efforts to sell them on something reasonable, and I never had the nerve to flatly refuse them in public. I wouldn't have minded the expense so much if they had eaten the food when it came. But in the half-hour delay they *always* stuffed themselves on the unfamiliar rolls or crackers, washed down with ice water, and then had no appetite for the steak, lobster, or shrimp. They would just stare at it coldly. But when dessert time came, they would suddenly regain their appetite.

I would try the next time to get them to learn from the past experience. I'd remind them of the untouched main dish and urge them to order the child's plate or hamburger or chicken. But they'd decline flatly. Then I'd urge them to omit the rolls, but they would whine pitifully with hunger and I would grumpily give in. It was my fault that I was not firm. Children accept what their parents insist on.

When I was a child I was much more docile than my descendants, and the rules were strict. We *never* ate in a restaurant. In the move to Maine from Connecticut each summer, we went by train from New Haven to Boston and there drove over the cobblestone streets in a two-horse carriage to the Eastern Steamship wharves for the overnight trip to Portland or Rockland or Bath. We children yearned to eat supper in the white-paneled "dining saloon." But my mother always had brought along the familiar homemade sandwiches, which we ate in our cabins. (On community picnics I always thought other people's sandwiches were more delicious.)

Once my father took me with him on a steamboat trip in the spring to inspect a summer cottage he thought he might rent, and I was delighted to find that we would eat supper in the saloon with the other passengers. But my father, obeying my mother's rule that strange food was potentially too upsetting for children, ordered me milk toast, an invalid's food consisting of crisp, buttered, salted toast in a bowl of hot milk. The waiter smiled condescendingly and said, "We call that tombstone stew," referring, I think, to the shape of the pieces of toast, but perhaps also to the suitability of the dish for toothless, feeble ancients.

Only once do I remember cutting loose dietetically in childhood. Mansfield Horner's parents invited me to go ice-skating with them on Whitney Lake, not far from where we lived, on a bitterly cold Sunday. At the dark end of the afternoon, when I was numb with cold, the Horners invited me to join them in hot dogs—the first I had ever seen—which came steaming out of a vendor's pot and were slathered with sauerkraut and mustard. I knew I would be breaking all the family laws to eat one, but I couldn't resist, and I never tasted anything so good in my life.

Taking children to visit friends and relatives brings up special questions because of the expectations and feelings of these people and your desire to keep their good will.

I get quite a few letters from grandparents complaining bitterly that their grandchildren wreck the place on each occasion and that the children's parents don't seem to notice or to care. In some such cases I'd suspect that—subconsciously, at least—the parents know how upset the grandparents are becoming and take a secret pleasure in letting their children get away with what they themselves could never do.

At the opposite extreme are the hosts who enjoy letting the children run free and are bothered by conscientious parents who constantly warn and curb their children when there really is no need. I suggest that the parents keep tuned to the hosts' feelings and set their controls accordingly.

CHAPTER SEVEN

Stages of Childhood

▷ WEANING AND COMFORTERS

A *number of years ago I wrote a column for* Redbook *discussing two related topics: the resistance of many bottle-fed babies to be weaned to the cup in the second half of the first year compared to the apparent willingness of many breast-fed babies at the same age; and the relationship of this contrast to my ideas on the meaning of comforters such as "security blankets," cuddly stuffed animals, and thumb sucking. My explanation was that the bottle had become a precious comforter too in the second half of the first year and that's why a lot of babies fight against giving it up.*

But my casually expressed assumption that a good portion of breast-fed babies appear ready to give up the breast between six and twelve months provoked several indignant letters from mothers. They stated that all babies are entitled to nurse at the breast for two full years and that it is harmful to deprive them of this right. So I later wrote another column replying to such mothers and explaining my position.

It seems to me that these two positions—not only on the advisable age for weaning from the breast but on other aspects of emotional development—are still hotly debated and are just as worthy of discussion today. So here's the first article:

What's a good age to wean from breast or bottle to cup? There's no agreement today.

In the first half of this century there was a great itch in some families to hurry babies along in all possible respects: Get them off the 2 A.M. feeding by two weeks, whether they were ready or not. Start solids by a month. Wean to the cup by a year, even if it meant a hard battle. "Break" a child of thumb sucking as soon as the "habit" developed. Some parents tried to bowel-train by six months.

This anxious pushing attitude has persisted in some families into the 1980s, but now it is focused not on infancy but on advancing preschool children's readiness for the three Rs and later on filling their after-school hours and summer vacations with additional educational, cultural, and athletic training courses.

At the same time there has been another movement in the opposite direction that shows itself particularly in regard to weaning. I know parents who are not only content but also rather proud that their children are still on breast or bottle beyond their second birthday.

Partly this represents a back-to-nature philosophy that is evident also in very relaxed attitudes toward toilet training, table manners, sleep schedules. Parents with this philosophy point out that in many of the nonindustrial parts of the world, children are nursed at breast until two or three years of age, and sometimes longer.

In general, I'm in favor of doing what seems to be the most natural thing. But I'm not sure that breast feeding until two years or later is natural in the sense of being what most babies themselves want. Anthropologists point out that in many of the simple societies where breast feeding is prolonged, parents believe that it is their best method—in fact, their only method—of birth control (though actually it is not at all reliable). And this is why they continue breast feeding as long as possible.

Another reason I think for the interest in prolonged breast feeding and other tolerant procedures is that some young parents have always had an impulse to lean in the opposite direction from their own parents—whether in child care or interior decoration or artistic tastes or social customs—if they can find any reasonable justification for doing so. This comes from the natural rivalry between successive generations. Such competitiveness accounts in part not only for the pendulum swings in all styles but also for many of the advances that occur in science, technology, music, painting, and other arts, advances that are created frequently by persons just on the threshold of adulthood.

When I was a child at the beginning of the century it was the young progressive parents who, along with the pediatricians, were advocating—in a crusading spirit—strict infant feeding schedules; early toilet training; large, rigorous doses of fresh air; an end to such shameful indulgences as pacifiers; and the energetic conditioning of young children to try to mold them into whatever kind of person the parents had in mind, whether musician, athlete, or scientist.

When I was starting my pediatric practice, in the 1930s, I had a special interest in its psychological aspects, which had led me to take psychiatric and psychoanalytic training. I saw many cases of conflict created by the anxiety of parents to get their babies weaned from bottle to cup before the age of one year (as if their children otherwise would be emotionally and intellectually retarded) and the resistance of babies to be weaned at this age. (There were very few breast-fed babies in those days, but those few impressed me by their lack of resistance to moving to the cup.)

I strongly recommended that babies be given sips of milk from the cup by four or five months of age; I felt that this would get around the later resistance to weaning, because all babies accept sips at that age. But many babies foiled me, and their parents, by turning firmly against milk in the cup at a later age—seven, eight, nine months—and remaining adamant until a year and a quarter or later, some until two years. I assumed that most bottle-fed babies needed that kind of sucking until a year or later. But I couldn't explain why the breast-fed babies seemed quite willing to give up breast for cup *before* the age of one.

After puzzling for years, I finally realized that the babies who were allowed to hold and drink their bottle in bed (rather than in their mother's lap) after they were six months old were the ones who developed an intense attachment to their bottle that made them reject the cup. They perceived the cup as a threat to the continued use of the precious bottle. So I advised parents who wanted to get on with weaning to continue to give the baby the bottle themselves, in their laps, even though babies become quite capable of holding their own bottles by the second half of the first year and enjoy doing it.

It took several more years before I was able to fit other pieces of the puzzle together. I came to several conclusions about the favorite old "security blanket" or cuddly toy (I call them all *comforters*). Some children must have a comforter to stroke while sucking their thumb at bedtime or when upset. It reminds them of the security and bliss they felt in their first five months when they were lying in their mother's arms, nursing at the bottle or breast, and at the same time touching the soft material of the blanket they were wrapped in or touching their mother's clothing or skin.

Then at five or six months they begin to feel the urge to do things for themselves—sit up, stand, hold the bottle and other objects. This beginning sense of autonomy or independence from the parent is insistent and exciting and precious. But there is a problem. When babies are tired or unhappy they want again to be blissfully soothed by sucking or stroking. Yet they can't abide to give up their tiny bit of independence. So stroking the comforter and sucking the thumb seem to be the happy compromise, I believe. It gives them a feeling of security without having to be enveloped again in the mother's arms, without being submerged in her personality again, as was true in the early months. They have the comforting aspects of the mother without the surrender to her.

The next step in my reasoning was that the bottle that's taken in bed after six months also becomes a mother substitute, endowed now with this new emotional significance. That's why the baby now becomes *more* dependent on it. But the breast—or the bottle that continues to be taken in the mother's arms after six months—can't become a mother substitute, because the mother is right there with both her security-giving and her enveloping aspects. So the baby doesn't need a substitute, can't use a substitute. And the independence-seeking side of the baby encourages the giving up of the bottle or breast, for weaning to a cup.

When I was able to think of the first impulse to self-weaning as a development that begins in the last half of the first year rather than in the second year, I began to notice that many breast-fed babies show less dependence on the breast as early as five or six months. Before that, they nurse intensely until satisfied. They sometimes cry with frustration when interrupted. After five or six months of age they nurse for a few minutes, then release the nipple, grin and coo at the mother, play with their own or her clothing. They may have to be nudged by the mother before they resume nursing. And a few babies refuse to go on with the breast at all, after seven, eight, or nine months.

I used to say that babies who interrupt their nursing to socialize were showing the first faint signs of boredom with the breast. But mothers objected strongly to the word "boredom," feeling that it insulted them and grossly minimized their babies' continued devotion to the breast. It was the wrong word. I was only trying to explain dramatically that the avidity for the breast was decreasing. To get this idea across is necessary to my concept that many babies are increasingly ready for weaning in the last half of the first year, that it isn't necessary to go into the second year—with breast or bottle.

Why did I think it was important to have discovered this early readiness for weaning from the breast? I wanted to make breast feeding—a full program of breast feeding—seem not too long-drawn-out, not too arduous, not too confining to mothers. For in earlier times the relatively few mothers who were interested were apt to ask anxiously, "How long do I need to nurse? Will three months be enough?" I reasoned that if they were ready to devote three months to breast feeding, six months would not seem too much more.

Of course I could and did say that any duration of breast feeding

—one month, three months—was valuable, valuable physically for the baby, valuable emotionally for mother and baby. But I was trying to encourage the mothers who were half-inclined to do so to carry on the breast feeding for six or seven months and then wean to the cup directly without bothering with the bottle at all.

If a mother has no set idea ahead of time and asks me today how long she should breast-feed, I say, "You will have given your baby all the physical advantages (easy digestibility and purity of milk, immunity to many germs) and all the emotional advantages (mutual closeness and an early conviction on your part that you are a successful mother) by nursing for at least a full half year. After that you can wean gradually at any time when you are ready, and when you notice clues that the baby is ready, allowing time for the breasts to adjust to the decreases in demand and causing no abrupt change for the baby in this intimate relationship. You simply offer formula or milk in the cup at every meal and drop the breast feedings one at a time—at weekly intervals, for instance. You can drop the six P.M. feeding last, because that's usually the one that the baby appreciates most, when tired and regressed.

Some parents ask, "Why not wean from breast to bottle instead of to cup?" If you are weaning from breast *before* five or six months, I think you should wean to the bottle, because most babies show the need to suck until that age. But why bother with bottles when weaning from breast in the second half of the year, if I am right in believing that babies don't really need to suck for sucking's sake after that?

I believe now that the pacifiers and thumbs—and not only the bottles—that some babies demand beyond six, eight, or ten months are for security when tired or frustrated, not for sucking satisfaction itself.

Why not go on breast feeding into or through the second year? I happen to think it is slightly preferable to wean by a year, for several reasons, as I will explain. But some parents and physicians disagree emphatically. The subject is a controversial one. So I would never want to argue with a woman who wanted to nurse till eighteen months or two years or even longer.

I think it's a sound psychological principle to encourage children to graduate from phase to phase when they show readiness. If children are encouraged to lag behind in one aspect of development, this may in certain cases contribute to a more general slowing of emotional maturation. Take an example from another area.

When parents show delight in a child's baby talk long after baby-hood is over, it may encourage the child to remain babyish, passive, and dependent in other respects.

I've had the impression that in the case of some children, the prolonging of breast feeding beyond a year may increase rather than decrease the dependence on it, at least for a number of months. Theoretically, this may slow down the child's progress in gaining independence from the mother. Some of these reasons apply equally to weaning from the bottle.

Many women who have breast-fed have told me that they were more dependent emotionally on the breast feeding than their babies were. What they said more exactly was: "The baby gave up the breast with no regrets at all. But I felt a great loss. I felt rejected." I believe that this is a normal as well as a common reaction. I also think mothers should take it into account in deciding when to wean.

But in general children's needs are always changing as they move from phase to phase, and they should be met more or less on time to have the maximum benefit. In the case of breast feeding, a moth-er's reluctance to wean may go on indefinitely, so her disappoint-ment might as well come at the time that is ideal for the baby.

Dentists have recently added another reason for getting on with weaning, or in any case for not letting babies over a year old go to sleep—either at night or naptime—with a mouthful of milk. This most usually concerns the baby who is given a bottle to finish in bed. In a few susceptible children this leads to a rapid decay of the teeth. Decay is caused by lactic acid, which is formed by bacteria that live on sugar and starches that remain in the mouth for ex-tended periods. The susceptibility varies greatly in different individ-uals depending on such circumstances as inheritance, maternal diet during pregnancy, flouride content of the teeth, and other factors.

Again, most of the reasons I've given for weaning by the age of a year don't *prove* that it is better; they only explain my conclusion.

▷ CRITICISM OF MY IDEAS ON WEANING

Here is my second article on weaning from the breast and other steps in development, written after I had received several letters critical of my first article.

In this section I want to take up again the question of the appropriate age for weaning but also the broader issues concerning the satisfaction of babies' basic needs. These were raised by those readers of my earlier column who were upset at the idea of weaning by the age of one year.

One mother wrote, "As for the need to wean from bottle or breast at such an early age, I totally disagree. You are undermining the basic trust of the child. Erik Erikson's theory of basic trust versus mistrust is generally accepted by psychologically oriented parents, and wisely so. More basic trust is instilled when a mother breastfeeds and, as often as possible, answers to the personal needs of her child throughout the early years. There are enough taboos for a small child without the parents' imposing arbitrary rules in order not to 'spoil' her. The theory that it presumably helps a child's development to compel specific advances 'when the child is ready' is a gross presumption, I think. It does not help a person climb a ladder if the bottom rungs are removed beneath him."

A similar protest was expressed by another mother: "You seem to feel that the child who is forced to nurse past the age of one is forced into extended dependency."

In my article I had merely said that children are presumably helped to advance on all fronts in their development if they are *encouraged* to make specific advances; in saying this, I was expressing a generalization about child development. For parents have often told me how their small children, having got over one hump in their development, then leaped forward in other areas of development. I didn't mean that this is an absolute law or that a child who stays on bottle or breast until one and a half or two years of age will necessarily be slowed in any other respect. I am afraid that I made the connection with weaning sound too specific and that I made some parents who had weaned late feel criticized and defensive, which wasn't my idea at all. I certainly don't believe in compelling or forcing a baby to do anything, and I didn't use those words.

Another mother raised the issues of dependency and security in these words: "Other experts write that the child who has problems in later life is the one who was not allowed to be dependent long enough. (Ask those who work with juvenile offenders.) Let's have equal time for other professionals, who view children as human beings with strong needs: educators Miles Newton and James Hymes, anthropologists Ashley Montagu and Margaret Mead—who has studied children in other societies, children who aren't forced to be weaned early, left with strangers, or allowed to cry alone at night."

Another mother was upset because she claimed that I said in *Baby and Child Care* that every baby should be left by his parents two evenings a week. "What's so wrong with a mother's staying with her baby, with her being 'wrapped up' in her child? Isn't that what good parenting is really all about? We have so much child abuse and neglect in this country. Parents need to be told to give maturely of themselves, not that 'it's vital that both parents keep up their hobbies, their reading, and their other recreational and cultural interests.' Then why have a baby at all? People in the United States need to be told how to grow up, not how to stay young."

I agree with most of what these mothers say about the importance of giving children what they need in the way of love, nurturing, and security at each stage of development. Infants in the first half year, specifically, need a lot of sucking as well as calories, fondling, play, and parental responsiveness to their appeals and to their developmental advances. And in the first two and a half years they require continuous contact with the people who are their main care givers; changes in care givers should be made only very gradually. These are only examples of children's many needs.

But equally important is the child's need to advance and to gain independence, a need that manifests itself in dozens of ways at each stage of development. Correspondingly there is the need for parents to relinquish control when the child is ready. Professional people to whom the parents turn for help when they are in trouble are made aware of problems for both parent and child that may not occur to many other parents.

When I suggested, in *Baby and Child Care,* that beginning parents with a colicky or fretful baby try to take a couple of nights off a week, together or separately, it was not to encourage irresponsibility but to try to prevent the parents from becoming physically and emotionally exhausted. This sometimes happens (and usually to the mother) when a baby's crying lasts four hours a night for three months and the two parents, tense and distressed, sit and take it. Even in cases in which there is no misery in the baby, I think it's sensible for highly conscientious, first-time parents to take a little time off and keep up with friends and interests, if possible. Otherwise some of them become totally obsessed with the baby, as I've sometimes seen, which means strains on the baby as well as on the parents and sometimes on the parents' relatives and friends. This excessive preoccupation doesn't often occur with a second or third baby, or when more casual parents have a first baby.

I've known six- or eight-month-old babies whose inexperienced parents had been so accommodating to their wishes that the babies gradually had learned to stay awake until 9, 10, or 11 P.M., insisting on being held and walked all those long hours. It was an exhausting experience for both the babies and the parents. And it could have been prevented had the parents sensed—or been advised—that it's all right to put an infant to bed after the 6 P.M. feeding even if she cries for a few minutes in protest or from fatigue.

There can be other problems of dependence and independence. I remember children who wanted to get hold of their spoons and feed themselves at about a year of age but whose parents refused to let them for fear of the mess. At two and three years of age when the parents *wanted* them to feed themselves, these children were insisting on being spoon-fed because they had long since passed the period when it seemed exciting to them to feed themselves; they now demanded to be fed as their rightful privilege.

There are children who are still talking "cute" baby talk at five years of age (I don't mean mispronunciation of only certain words) because their parents found it so appealing at two years that they continued to echo it back to their children, instead of using a more grown-up pronunciation.

I've been told by several parents about children who climbed into the parents' bed at night at two years of age because they were uneasy about being alone—and who were still going into their parents' bed and absolutely refusing to budge at ten years of age. That's why I said, in *Baby and Child Care,* that it's wiser to take night wanderers promptly back to their own beds, even though I realize that many of the small children who climb into their parents' beds will not develop a permanent need to do this.

There are occasional children who are still calling for their parents to wipe them after bowel movements at six years of age because their parents failed to sense that they were able to take over this function by three years of age.

There are parents who are still doing most of the homework of children in high school because they can't believe that their children are able to work it out for themselves.

These examples, although they are not common, show that it isn't quite enough to say that parents need only to respect their babies' dependent needs and not push them prematurely. Parents *should* respect these needs when they are genuine. But babies have a whole set of other needs that have to do with gaining skills and autonomy. Parents' attitudes may play a large role in the balance between their children's needs for dependence and independence. Parents can satisfy the dependent needs and still be on the lookout for signs of readiness to move forward.

▷ MORE ON COMFORTERS

The degree of attachment to a "security blanket" or other comforter varies greatly. Some children become so dependent that they are desperate if it is lost; they can't go to sleep without it. At the other extreme are those who've never had a real comforter. In between there is every gradation of attachment. Some children shift from one object to another. The dependence usually decreases as children get to be three, four, and five years of age. But a few have a secret comforter that they don't want other children to know about well into the school years, and I heard of women who took their teddy bears into the hospital when they had a baby.

It's typical for small children to suck their thumbs while they stroke the woolly toy or the fuzz or the silk binding of the blanket. (A few stroke an ear lobe or twist a lock of their hair.) I'll use the word *comforter* to include this wide variety of objects.

Some children want to hold the comforters right under their noses so that they can smell them. One mother who cut a tattered security blanket into small pieces to ensure its longer survival noticed that her child sniffed all the remaining pieces before selecting one, trying to find the one with the most aged aroma. Usually children won't tolerate the washing or dry cleaning of a comforter; they want it to stay gray and grimy—just the way they are used to it.

Young children characteristically want their comforter to stroke and their thumb to suck at those times of day when they are tired or frustrated. Bedtime at night or after lunch is the commonest occasion. Other situations are after getting hurt, after being treated badly by another child, after being deprived or scolded by a parent. Psychiatrists call these times of regression—when a child doesn't feel up to coping with life at the level of his or her age and so slips back to a more infantile level. (Even the mature adult may slip into babyish ways when sick or discouraged.)

I believe the thumb and the bottle in bed become comforters, at the end of the day and at other times of regression, after the middle of the first year. (In the first four or five months of life thumb sucking expresses, I believe, only the sucking need that hasn't been satisfied at breast or bottle, and it occurs before and after nursing. After six months it takes the place mainly at times of regression.)

Most psychologists and psychoanalysts have assumed that during the early months of life babies have no way of realizing that they are separate individuals. A good part of the time when they're awake they are in their mothers' arms, being nursed at breast or bottle, which is obviously their most intense satisfaction. As they gain a little control over their fingers, many of them can be seen to be gently stroking the blanket that envelops them, or the mother's skin or clothing. (This may be likened to the instinct in puppies and kittens to massage their mother's teats, which is believed to facilitate the "letting down" of the milk.)

During these early months babies have no deep worries. They wake when hungry, cry automatically, soon get picked up, cuddled, cooed to, and fed—all by the familiar, beloved mother. Then off to sleep again. Everything is taken care of without effort on their part. This is the most totally secure stage of human existence, and in most families all the security comes, in different ways, from the mother. Though she is not always visible, the cry always brings her, and young babies presumably don't think of her as being separate from them.

This stage of intensely close relationship in which the baby is still almost a part of the mother is sometimes called *symbiotic,* meaning that their lives are intertwined.

This spell of total symbiotic security begins to be broken in the middle of the first year as babies' instincts stimulate them to sit up, to use their hands, to resist too much cuddling. You can see how important this tiny bit of independence is to them by the fierceness with which, after they have learned to sit, they fight against being laid down. Though they have to be pushed down a dozen times a day—for diaper changing, bathing, and other ministrations—they protest vigorously and loudly every single time, as if they had never heard of such an outrage.

I suspect that they get their mental sense of separateness—and their striving for more—from finding themselves struggling for physical independence. In other words, the physical instinct comes first and the child becomes conscious of it secondarily.

But along with the sense of separateness—particularly separateness from the mother—comes an awareness of loss and anxiety when she is not there. It's in the last half of the first year that a baby may begin to fret and cry whenever the mother leaves the room. This sense of dependence and loss is also shown by babies over six months who have been separated from their mothers—by prolonged hospitalization, for example. They go into a real depression, never smiling, crying much of the time.

I believe that it is infants' mild feeling of anxiety about separateness from the mother at times of regression during the day that makes them want a comforter (or two comforters, such as thumb and blanket) to remind them of the complete security and pleasure of the early months.

If human infants were different, they might turn back and become one with their mothers again. But it is clear that they refuse to give up the small step of autonomy they've achieved. So they prefer the comforter, which is motherly in its associations and in its ability to give security but which is still not the mother because it doesn't threaten to envelop them and infantilize them. Babies and young children control their comforter—not the other way around. It's amazing to see how brutally one- or two-year-old children may occasionally treat their precious comforter, slamming it against the furniture when irritated.

I think that bottles and thumbs become mother-substitute comforters after the age of five or six months. It's interesting to learn from psychologists who've observed babies who have been in institutions and emotionally neglected from birth—who've known no mothering—that these babies don't suck their thumbs. I think that pacifiers become comforters after five or six months.

There are certain rhythmic habits that a fair number of babies acquire toward the end of the first year and use at times of regression—rocking, head rolling, head banging, and what I call jouncing (bouncing the buttocks against the heels from a hands-and-knees position). I think these probably are—at least in part—comforting actions by which children recall the rocking or joggling they received in their mothers' arms in the earliest months.

The use of a pacifier from birth is the best way I know to avoid thumb sucking, especially for the baby who shows from the first a need for more sucking than breast or bottle provides. But to prevent the pacifier from becoming a comforter that will be demanded for many months, it's wise to see whether the baby at three or four months, when the sucking need usually becomes progressively weaker, can give up the pacifier for good. In most cases this can be accomplished easily, without unhappiness for the baby and without provoking thumb sucking.

There are two common problems with the use of pacifiers. There are many beginning parents who don't like the looks of them and therefore decline to start them before the baby becomes attached to the thumb; then it's hard to get the baby to make the switch. And some parents who do start the pacifier, soon after birth or later, themselves get so dependent on it to keep the baby contented under all circumstances that they are unwilling to let the baby give it up at two, three, or four months, when most infants show they are quite willing to do so.

Once thumb sucking becomes really established, it usually goes on till three, four, or five years of age, occasionally longer. I know of no remedy. Nagging prolongs the habit. As the child gets to be three or older it is sound for the parents to say occasionally (once a month, for example), "I know that you want to stop. Someday you will be a big girl and you will stop." This encourages the child without belittling or irritating her.

There is no way that I know of to determine in advance which babies will become intensely dependent on a stroking comforter or to prevent this from happening. You can't deprive a baby of soft toys, of blankets, clothes, or ear lobes.

I have a few suggestions that may help a little if you find that your one-year-old is just becoming really dependent on a certain object as comforter to stroke: buy a duplicate toy or blanket, if it still can be purchased, so that you will have a substitute to offer while the first one is being cleaned. You can wash and dry a blanket comforter over night; a stuffed animal takes longer. Be careful not to offer a dry-cleaned article until all cleaning odor is gone.

A couple of mothers I've known have kept their children from dragging a blanket around all day long by insisting from the start of the dependence that the blanket must stay in the crib, where the child can go to stroke it when the need arises. It's probably impossible to confine the comforter to the bed once the child has become accustomed to carrying it around.

For head rolling (rolling the head from side to side), I know of no solution. But it is not a bothersome symptom. It occurs only in bed and it makes no noise.

Head banging—banging the head rhythmically against the head of the bed—looks as if it is painful to the child, but it isn't. It looks as if it might damage the brain, yet it doesn't. But it makes a racket that bothers the parents. The sound can be almost eliminated by taping a firm, flat pillow or cushion to the head of the bed.

Jouncing rattles the crib and inches it across the room until the head of the crib is close to the wall. Then each jounce bangs the head of the crib against the wall with a noise that can be heard several rooms away. In an apartment house it can be heard in the next apartment. The crib can be held in place away from a wall by placing it on a rug that's tacked to the floor or that has a foam-rubber padding under it.

The reason I have gone into such detailed explanation of various comforters—the sucking kinds, the stroking kinds, the rhythmic kinds—is that the main frustration for parents, I think, is not being able to understand comforters. Once their meaning is clear, they become merely minor nuisances. Yet they are of great importance to babies and children.

▷ HOW TO MANAGE ONE-YEAR-OLDS

Managing a child less than a year old is relatively easy, for several reasons. Babies that young aren't walking yet. They aren't intensely exploring their surroundings. They usually can be kept in their pens for at least moderate periods of time. As a result of these factors they don't "get into everything," as they will later.

Management during the second year is a much trickier matter. Now children begin to sense that they are separate individuals. They assert their wishes and their rights on very slight provocation. They balk at foods that they were willing to eat before. When their parents make a suggestion, they say, "No!" on principle, even when it is something they enjoy doing—going outdoors to play, taking an automobile ride, or going to visit a friend. It's not that they really reject the proposal; they just don't want to be pushed around.

One-year-olds haven't acquired much respect for their parents' authority yet. Even when they've learned what their parents disapprove of, it doesn't mean that they know how to obey. They'll do something they know is forbidden, say, "No! No!" or even slap their own hands, and promptly do the forbidden thing again.

They've learned the sequence, all right—certain acts will be followed by disapproval—but they haven't caught the real meaning of obedience.

The opinionatedness, the obstinacy, the willfulness of the one-year-old can be intensely upsetting to some parents. They fear, when defied over some small issue, that this tiny whippersnapper has successfully flouted their authority, that they have lost face and control.

I remember well the K. family, whose first child was one of my patients when I started practice in 1933 in Manhattan. The mother was frantic when she telephoned me about her son, who was then about fifteen months old. She said that he defied her all the time, especially by twirling the knobs on the radio (there was no television then). He was a "real devil," she said, and she begged me to make a house visit. I was glad to go, even though the family lived far away in Brooklyn, first because I was eager in those Depression days to earn five dollars in any legitimate way. Also I wanted to learn how so young a child could be a fiend.

While his mother, almost in tears, was pouring out her indignant story, the devil himself came toddling into the room. He stopped in his tracks and gazed at me in the way a one-year-old typically regards a stranger. His mother shook her finger at him and said angrily, "Now, don't you touch the radio," though he hadn't even glanced in that direction. He stood motionless, looking her right in the eye, for what seemed a full minute. Then he began a slow, slow side step toward the radio. "See what I mean?" his mother cried.

Mrs. K. believed that a parent must always and obviously be on top. She thought that the slightest disobedience, or even independence, was dangerous.

Quite a few people have this authoritarian attitude—bosses as well as parents—though most of them aren't as panicky as Mrs. K. The attitude is a leftover from their own childhood. *Their* parents acted that way, convincing them that children naturally will run riot unless kept under strict control. To put it another way, these parents were taught as children to mistrust their own ability to behave reasonably except under strict domination. So they assume in adulthood that their own children can't be trusted either.

Mrs. K. was an extreme example because she had such a degree of anxiety that she saw crises before they existed and brought them on through her panic. You may assume her behavior was so extreme that we can't learn anything from it. But I consider her case particularly valuable because it shows so clearly how anxiety about children's untrustworthiness and about the parents' ability to control them compels authoritarian parents to be so overbearing.

Of course, there is a certain amount of hostility in such people too that encourages them to be aggressive. But it is touched off each time by anxiety. The hostility was built into their personalities in childhood as a result of having been dominated unpleasantly by their parents. They couldn't express the hostility in childhood because they were too afraid of their parents, but it comes out later when they are parents themselves.

Most people, by contrast, were raised by parents who had sufficient confidence in their ability to lead, and sufficient confidence in the reasonableness of their children, to be able to use a light, friendly touch in asking for their cooperation. (If such people are employers, they assume in the same way that most of their employees are well-intentioned too and need only to be treated kindly and have their duties clearly explained in order to give a satisfactory performance.)

But one-year-olds are in a special category because of their inexperience in the business of cooperation and because of their newfound determination to make up their own minds and do things for themselves.

In other words, I'd say that the key word in managing one-year-olds is tact. As the responsible adult, of course, you must keep reasonable control of a situation—for your child's safety, for your child's sound upbringing, and for your own comfort. But it isn't necessary to be overbearing or unpleasant. You are much smarter than the child. You can find various ways to make things turn out the way you want them to while letting your child—let's say it's a girl—feel independent and practice her independence. Let's take some examples.

When you take your daughter out for a stroll, she may well want to go up the walk to each individual house along the way. And if there are front steps, she'll want to climb all of them, perhaps several times. Steps are always irresistible at this age. If you keep calling, "Come along," the chances are great that your child won't respond positively. Both her curiosity and her desire for independence will work against you.

You have two alternatives. You can allow her to make all her side excursions and expect to take half an hour to go one block. Even so, you will need to keep moving slowly along the block—without calling to her—in order to make any progress at all. When she feels that you are getting too far away, she will follow. Children at this age keep track of their parents most of the time and don't want to let them out of their sight. It's the same instinct that makes ducklings and lambs follow their mothers. But if you need to get somewhere quickly, take your child in her stroller or in your car. In the market put her in the shopping cart, of course.

If you want your one-year-old to come indoors or into the kitchen for lunch, you can take her hand and lead her, in an automatic sort of way, or you can pick her up and carry her, talking about something pleasant all the while. Certainly don't ask her whether she wants to come to lunch. There is too much chance that her independence will make her say no. If it's time to dress her or undress her or to put on her outdoor playsuit, just do what needs to be done while chatting to distract her.

When your child has reached the age of one, the time also has come to put most of the breakable and dangerous things in the house out of her reach. Cigarettes, matches, fragile ashtrays, vases, and tippy table lamps can be put on the tops of bookcases or in the attic for a while. Drain cleaners, furniture polish, cleaning fluid, insect sprays, turpentine, paint thinner, plant sprays, and every other substance that is not absolutely harmless *must* be put on high shelves. Roach powders and tablets and rat poisons should be thrown out or locked away. Medicines should never be left where small children can reach them or climb up to them. All pills, tablets, and capsules should be in childproof containers—including aspirins, the commonest poison ingested by children. Put safety plugs in unused electric outlets.

Some parents worry that if everything is put out of reach, their children will never learn about prohibitions. But it's almost impossible to put *everything* out of reach. Some lamps and tablecloths must be left in place, and children can be taught gradually not to pull them down. Some electric cords, too, have to remain, and children must be kept from chewing them.

How do you inhibit one-year-olds? Just to say, "No, no" is not enough at first; that's not sufficiently compelling. You have to combine your no with the brisk removal of the object, or, if the object is not removable, the brisk removal of the child to another part of the room. If the child obstinately goes back, put the child in the playpen or in another room. (Gates in certain doorways and at the head and foot of the stairs are a great convenience and an important safety measure.) Remember you can say firmly, "No, no," whenever it is called for, but it is a mistake to get angry. The child can accept the lesson better if you don't get irritable. I don't think physical punishment is necessary or particularly effective. Prompt, firm removal is the most convincing method. After a while the child learns that you mean what you say, and then "No, no" becomes a sufficient reminder.

It's possible to prohibit a child from touching certain things only if there are plenty of other objects that she or he can play with. Put old magazines within reach of the child—to look at and to tear. Small children love to tear paper. On the other hand, stack books in the lower shelves of your bookcase so tightly that the child can't pull them out. Put pots and pans, lids and strainers, eggbeaters and stirring spoons on the lower shelves of the cupboards in the kitchen, within easy reach. Have a few cartons on the floor so your child can put utensils and toys in them. Putting objects in containers, taking them out, putting them in again, is endlessly fascinating to children at this age.

They also find cartons and carts delightful to push around. As a matter of fact, cartons are better than carts because they can be moved sideways when they meet with obstructions, whereas carts want to go in a straight line, which frustrates small children.

Simplified and sturdy toy cars, trucks, and planes made of wood or durable plastic also begin to appeal to children between one and two years old. All toys need to be indestructible, because the tiny fingers of one-year-olds are capable of dismembering almost anything.

Distraction is the most effective way of getting your one-year-old's mind off a forbidden object or a forbidden action. Have a few objects on hand such as a ring of keys, a piece of chain, a bell.

I remember, when my first son was a year old, trying to find out how long I could keep him distracted with the same object. I used two cuff links, the kind with metal buttons connected by a loose link. I handed him one of them, which he examined carefully and manipulated. While he was doing this, I handed him the other. He dropped the first and examined the second. I picked up the first and handed it to him and he dropped the second. After fifteen or twenty minutes I became bored with the test, but he was just as keen as ever to give his attention to the one I had just handed him.

There is no need to fear that you will fail to manage your one-year-old just because you are inexperienced and because children at that age are willful and inexperienced at minding. Remember that independence and assertiveness are not bad attitudes. You *want* your children to have these attitudes; otherwise they'd turn into zombies. Your agreeableness will keep your children cooperative in spirit most of the time, and your cleverness and tact will take care of the other times.

▷ HOW MUCH CONSCIENCE

In the stern family in which I grew up, there was no allowance made for psychological or human explanations of naughty or unwise behavior. Every issue was somehow a matter of morality or health. Food had nothing to do with pleasure: even for our parents, eating was for reasons of health. Anything remotely to do with sex was sinful except when sanctified by marriage and the desire for children. Touching the genitals was a high crime against which my mother was particularly vigilant. Plays, movies, novels, "cheap" magazines were suspect.

I remember that when I was a teenager, my mother's great friend Patty Foote once suggested that they take their oldest sons to see the movie *Dr. Jekyll and Mr. Hyde,* starring Lionel Barrymore. At a certain point Barrymore lecherously kissed the bare shoulder of a woman wearing an off-the-shoulder dress. My mother rose, crying loudly, "Benny, we're going home!" To make sure that I agreed, she grabbed me by the hair and pulled me to my feet and out into the lobby. Nearby patrons stared and I was ashamed to be part of the scene.

Friendships were allowed only when the person had the same strict ethical standards as we. Otherwise they were to be given the cold shoulder.

Even such health matters as fresh air, plenty of sleep, cleanliness of the house—all of great importance to my mother—had a moral overtone. To pay attention to them was good; to neglect them was slightly degenerate.

All the six Spocks of my generation assumed that our mother could detect guilt accurately and immediately, so there seemed no advantage whatsoever in lying. If you lied, you would be punished for lying as well as for the original crime.

Of course my mother did not have magical powers of detecting wrongdoing, as I came to realize when I had children of my own.

She had implanted such a deep sense of guilt in us that we betrayed our minutest sins by a hangdog expression even before she questioned us. So she knew immediately when we were uneasy and had only to fix us with her piercing eyes and demand a full confession and we told all.

The result was that my brother, sisters, and I developed an unusually harsh conscience that has plagued and often handicapped us. We are always ready to consider ourselves guilty until proven innocent.

It was not until I'd grown into an adult, had my psychiatric and psychoanalytic training and then had turned around and tried to help parents manage their children that I realized that the heavy moralistic method by which I was controlled was not the best and only way to manage a child.

In the first place, it's not mentally healthy for people to be saddled with such a heavy conscience. Some of them become compulsive neurotics; they may, for instance, spend a great deal of their lives having to wash their hands repeatedly or having to add up a column of figures again and again, in order to do penance for their real or imagined sins.

A more general disturbance occurs in a person who, because of an overbearing conscience, becomes excessively cautious, rigid, or restricted. He is afraid to do anything outside his narrow daily pattern or to let himself feel his emotions or to think any fresh thoughts, out of anxiety that these might get him off the straight and narrow path and lead him into some kind of trouble. These people are pathetic.

There is another important disturbance that often results from too much guilt. A person may constantly fail to straighten out his relationships with his spouse or with the people he works among when these become strained. This is because he doesn't know how to analyze the trouble in terms of his own upset feelings and those of the other person. In his mind everything comes down to the simple question of whether he was innocent and the other person guilty or vice versa. Needless to say, he tries to fight off any admission that he was to blame and tries to pin all the fault on the other person. The other individual responds to such an accusation by claiming innocence and by trying to toss the blame back again. So they don't make any progress in resolving the dispute. They don't come to understand each other—or themselves—any better.

A person with less guilt and more maturity is apt to be able to explain, after a misunderstanding or a fight, what it was that hurt his feelings or caused a misinterpretation. When the other person then explains what he had meant or why he did what he did, the first is not only mollified but usually sees more clearly how his own weak points or his oversensitivity may have caused the trouble. He becomes aware enough of some particular personality quirk of the other individual so that he is less likely to make the same mistake at some other time.

To understand another person better usually leads to trusting him, liking him, respecting him a bit more. The second individual also takes at least a small forward step in understanding himself and the other.

How do you bring up a child without giving him an excess sense of guilt? One general answer—in early childhood—is to keep him from doing wrong, rather than letting him do the naughty thing and then shaming him. I think of the situation shown in that drawing by Dorothea Fox in *Baby and Child Care* in which a one-year-old is toying with the lamp cord and his mother is saying, "No! No!" from across the room. A one-year-old has very little respect for authority and he is developing a strong urge to assert his independence. So his inclination is to defy his mother.

Much better, in the early months of teaching taboos, is first to remove some of the easily removable temptations so that there won't be too many prohibitions at once. Then in regard to such items as lamp cords and hot stoves that can't be dispensed with, you become cheerfully masterful. Move right in close with a distracting plaything. Don't leave him with the first temptation still in the front of his mind and with the impulse to assert himself still strong in his heart.

Some parents worry that if they use a lot of baby-proofing and distraction during the second year of life, their child never will learn that certain things are forbidden. I agree that removing objects doesn't teach anything; you'll be returning these gradually, however, as the child becomes better able to respond to a no and to reasoning, and he will learn about these taboos then.

But distraction does teach. If a child is consistently distracted or blocked or removed in relation to a specific temptation, he certainly learns—by conditioned reflex—that it is prohibited.

It's very important to be cheerful or at least casual at the time you are blocking and distracting a child. When you are irritable or antagonistic, you arouse a corresponding hostility in him that is apt to defeat your purpose.

Why is it that we parents tend to fall into a cross, accusatory, or shaming tone in warning or correcting a child? One reason is that this was the tone with which many of us were admonished in our own childhood. We still recall unconsciously our antagonism toward our parents when they were controlling us. We assume unconsciously that our children resent us at similar moments and would like to disobey. We recall unconsciously all the times we've failed to manage them effectively and we dread a repetition. What our tone signals to our children, then, is our antagonism and our lack of self-confidence, both of which provoke them to resist us.

Highly conscientious parents, sensing their own liability to antagonism and wanting to counteract it, may lean over backward to be pleasant. In reacting in this way they may be too gentle, too hesitant, in making their wishes known to a child. Or their subtle submissiveness may encourage him to make trouble. I don't think that unadulterated pleasantness in a firm parent will spur a child to be balky. But if the pleasantness is partly a cover for a guilty hesitancy, a child—even at twelve months of age—can detect it instantly and will take advantage of it. This is the toughest aspect of raising children for overconscientious parents.

As your child grows older you rely mainly on other approaches. The simplest is positive suggestion. Rather than say, "It's naughty to cross the street," or, "You'll get run over," or, "I'll spank you if you do it," you explain, "You always take Mommy's hand and wait for the green light to cross the street," "We wash our hands after lunch so that we won't make the sofa dirty," "We brush our teeth after we eat so that they will be clean and pretty."

In teaching children to be considerate with one another and polite to adults, it's preferable not to use the negative approach of my mother, who called us bad when we were rude or selfish or mean and frequently told us that nobody would like us if we kept on being this way. She was so convincing that we all grew up assuming that we had unattractive as well as evil personalities.

As a parent you can turn such concerns into positive approaches. When a two-year-old impulsively—and naturally enough—slaps the new baby, you can promptly stay his hand and then guide it into a stroking movement, saying, "Stroke the baby. He loves you. He likes to have you do that." If you think that that is teaching only insincerity, you are being too pessimistic. Any child feels love for a new baby, even if it is being obscured by much jealousy. And adult kindliness is made up of a combination of love and sublimated antagonism of one sort or another.

You can help a child of three or more to find the enjoyment of cooperative play (it *is* more fun than solitary play) and of sharing. If he has been involved in a fight, rather than condemn him automatically, on the assumption that he must have a share in the guilt, you first can sympathize with whatever feelings of outrage he has. Then, having detected or at least suspected what his part in the provocation has been, you can explain how this angered the other child or hurt his feelings, and how a similar situation might be avoided or even turned into a happy outcome another time.

In misunderstandings and quarrels involving both the children and the parents or other adults, I'm convinced that grown-ups don't need to fear losing face when they admit that they have been too hasty or made a mistake or got angry. They will have just as much moral authority afterward.

More important, they will be teaching their children by example, which is much more convincing than a lecture. Their children will learn that everyone is human, that misunderstandings and quarrels have two or more sides, that right or wrong is not the real issue, that no one should be embarrassed about losing face, that the grown-up thing is to try to understand, that honest discussion is the way to reach reconciliation.

These particular words are too pompous to be meaningful to children, but children get the message clearly from their parents' example.

I don't want to give you the idea that it is desirable or possible to keep children from developing a conscience and a sense of guilt. (The two overlap to a large extent.) A society cannot function unless a majority of its citizens have a degree of both. Furthermore, the people who seek the most education and become the professionals and executives have to have more than an average amount of both.

All that I am talking about is the desirability of avoiding an excessively harsh conscience, an oppressive degree of guilt, which does not make such individuals more valuable to society. On the contrary, it makes them difficult people to live and work with. This is because they try to ignore the human realities in others and themselves and judge everything in arbitrary, moralistic terms.

It is very easy, in view of the way many of us were brought up, to slip into moralistic disapproval as the main way to control children. But that is actually an *uncomfortable,* inefficient, strained way to do it.

▷ CREATIVE VERSUS SINGLE-PURPOSE PLAYTHINGS

I always bought too many presents and too expensive presents for my children and grandchildren when they were young. It's a common American mistake. But at least I had learned, from being connected with nursery schools, to concentrate mostly on creative playthings rather than on elaborate, single-purpose toys.

Children love most of all to invent their own ways to play with things, ways that express their special interests and drives and problems at that particular stage of development. These ways of playing may or may not have any relationship with what the manufacturer of that toy had in mind. To take simple examples from infancy: a baby will use a doll to chew on or to bang on the side of the crib. I remember watching a misguided child-care assistant trying to teach a twelve-month-old to set a boat upright in a tub when the child only wanted to slap the water with it.

A five-year-old loses interest in winding up the locomotive of a tin train and letting it run around and around on a track, which leaves nothing more for him to do. Instead he may pry off the roof of a passenger car and use it to transport small objects from one side of his room to the other, never mind the tracks and the locomotive.

We bought for our first son, at the age of three, a trunkful of solid wood blocks of various sizes and shapes. They were fairly expensive as playthings go, but he used them often till he was twelve or so, to build towers, skyscrapers, houses, barns, garages, forts, roadways, bridges, mazes, prisons, whatever his fantasies and concerns dictated. Then his younger brother came along and used them for another dozen years. (He's an architect now.)

A set of beads will be used for what it was intended for because it offers the child an infinite variety of colors and patterns to experiment with—to wear or to give as gifts. Similarly a large box of crayons and a ream of paper have endless possibilities for depicting objects, scenes, and happenings that seem to be stirring the child's feelings at the time—whether it's pussycats and peaceful country houses with smoke coming out of the chimneys or fierce dinosaurs and planes dropping bombs.

Speaking of paper reminds me of packages of typewriter-sized sheets of many colors (construction paper, it's called) which small and middle-sized children delight to cut out and paste together— in chains for a Christmas tree or superimposed to make flowers and other objects and scenes. It's another way of making pictures.

The prime example of playthings with which a child can express an endless variety of feelings is dolls, dolls' clothing, dolls' furniture. The girl of three to six, whose strongest drive is to grow up to have all the possessions and activities of her mother, will happily play out these fantasies with her dolls, for hours and days on end. She will care for a baby doll, in every detail exactly as her mother cares for the real baby, sometimes soothing and cherishing, sometimes reproving. Boys will do the same things, if they are not teased, especially if their fathers help in child care. This is the principal way in which children learn to be parents, both in skill and in feelings, and it should be encouraged. Play with child-sized household furniture—stove, refrigerator, vacuum, iron and ironing board —has the same values; cartons can replace refrigerators and stoves.

It isn't just positive feelings that children exercise in doll and household play. Fears, sorrows, resentments, jealousies, and hatreds get expressed and gradually understood and digested, in valuable ways. A boy who has been frightened and felt ashamed during an inoculation has an urge to repeat the scene until he has mastered his fear, which he does by pretending again and again to inoculate a doll, telling the doll that it will hurt a little but not for long. A girl who has resented her mother's punishment may similarly punish her doll, explaining carefully the reason for it, overcoming her sense of outrage by playing out her mother's role and learning, in the process, how she will deal with similar situations with her future children.

I don't want to give the impression that the principal value in play is psychotherapy. But I do mean that the main drive in children's play is to express feelings of many kinds and that this is one of the most important reasons why some playthings continue to fascinate and others soon lose any interest.

There are playthings so tried and true that you can't go wrong— tricycles and bicycles being the most desirable. They are used constantly throughout childhood, sometimes in imaginary play as taxicabs, police cars, Indians' horses, or racing cars, the rest of the time just as transportation. A jungle gym gets lots of play from small children. A tall, sturdily built swing and a sandbox appeal to all ages, as I saw in my own backyard in childhood. (These were among the strategies used by my controlling mother to keep her own children and their friends in view.) Athletic equipment—basketball and basket, football, baseball, bat and mitt—will surely be appreciated by school-aged children, as will sled, skis and ski boots in snowy country.

Carpenter's tools will be used enthusiastically by children as young as four if there is a tactful parent willing to supervise. Don't buy children's tool kits, which consist of saws that won't saw, hammers too light to hammer, screwdrivers that fall apart. Buy adult tools of smallish size, starting with a saw, hammer, and nails thick enough not to bend easily. Get a long board six inches wide and another board two inches wide. Later add pliers, gimlet, and square; later still, hand drill, screws, screwdriver; then plane and sandpaper. But most basic from the start is a workbench with a steel or wooden vise to hold the wood while it is sawed or nailed or drilled. It should be sturdy and heavy. It can be assembled from a kit, to decrease the expense.

Construction kits, ones consisting of wooden pegs and wooden wheels, others consisting of plastic blocks that lock together (for young and middle-aged children), and sets consisting of steel girders and plates, brass wheels and pulleys (for older children) tend to get used a lot because there is no end to the structures that the child's imagination can conceive of.

I'm opposed to giving children war toys, which range from simple pistols to elaborate tanks and spaceships that spew death rays. They are certainly popular with boys, who will play with them enthusiastically and endlessly. But we have scientific evidence that they teach children to accept brutality as a natural way of life and to become, by small degrees, more violent in their behavior. It's not that a child raised in a sensitive family will turn into a criminal, but everyone will be moved in the direction of insensitivity and brutality.

Now I'd like to give some examples of single-purpose toys that evoke no feelings, can't be used flexibly or creatively, and soon poop out. Just this week, on a toy counter in an airport, I saw a tall ladder, up and down which a tin fireman climbed, powered by electricity. Very ingenious. But there is nothing for a child to do but to turn the electric switch on or off, nothing that stimulates his skill or creativity.

Other elaborate, expensive playthings that I've seen soon lose their appeal are chemistry sets (there are five or ten *prescribed* experiments but after that there is no experimenting that children themselves can do; mixing chemicals in some other ways doesn't produce anything) and electronic kits (by following instructions carefully a bright, motivated teenager can assemble a system or two that works, but that's all). I've seen elaborate, expensive games of chance or skill, some of them jazzed up with electrical mechanisms and lights, that were soon relegated to the shelf in the child's closet because they had only one function. On the other hand such games may be challenging to an older child who is highly competitive, especially if he can persuade his parents to play often. There are other competitive games whose equipment is quite simple and which are not expensive, such as Parcheesi and Monopoly, which have proved their popularity with competitive children for generations. Again, parents can expect to be begged and badgered to play.

There are two considerations that are almost as important as flexibility and creativity in playthings. The first is not to buy toys that are too old for the child; they will only frustrate her or him or lead to misuse and abuse. The other is for the adults to try to avoid controlling the play, which will soon destroy the child's pleasure and interest. Both of these mistakes were illustrated by my own mishandling of miniature toy trains with my sons. I craved trains as a boy but was never given any. I had to make the most of occasionally joining in train play with my friend Mansfield. So I could hardly wait—in fact didn't wait—for my first son to be old enough. When he was four I bought him a set of HO gauge trains that would have been more suitable, in their small size and complicatedness, for a fourteen-year-old. He couldn't fit the wheels on the track or couple the cars together. So he pushed one car across the carpet. "No! No!" I cried, "you have to put the wheels on the track," and I tried again and again to show him. Soon his silent resentment at being bossed and his frustration with his lack of skill made him leave the trains for me to play with. A couple of years later he was ready to try again, with a special interest in planning the track layout. My ideas were much more complicated and interesting—to me—than his, and I was soon dominating the planning. Before long he lost interest—for good this time. Ten years later I repeated my folly with my second son. Twenty-five years after that, on the occasion of my second wedding, my bride gave me an even smaller, N gauge passenger car set, I gave her a freight train set, and I worked happily on the track layout for many months. But then it bothered me when my stepdaughter's teenaged friends misused it —by racing the two trains so fast that they went off the tracks on the curves, amid shrieks of laughter. But this time I had the right to control because the trains belonged to me and not to them. (My wife doesn't play.)

When you are in a toy department or a toy store, you have to keep in mind that it is parents (and other adults) who buy most of the toys that children receive and that the manufacturers are thinking of what will appeal to adults more than what will satisfy children. This will help to keep you on guard against buying the elaborate, single-purpose toys that seem impressive at first glance.

You can also remember that children seem to be just as susceptible to fads, clever packaging, and salesmanship as adults. So you can use your good judgment as to whether a plaything that a child craves will have a lasting appeal. A few years ago all young girls felt that they must have a Cabbage Patch doll, perhaps because it has some mysterious basic appeal but, even more, because it was the rage. I read of a father who took a plane to England when he couldn't get the doll in the United States. But at least it did have the lasting appeal that most dolls do. On the other hand, I've had a grudge against the manufacturers and merchandisers who popularized the "banana bike," with its long seat. Its small wheels and low gear make it slow and tiresome to ride, the very opposite of what an experienced racing or touring bicyclist would ever want. But it has sold in the millions because it set a new style for young riders. I would have refused to buy it for my child because it's an inferior design that takes advantage of children's ignorance.

▷ CHILDREN'S THOUGHTS ON THEIR PARENTS

Recently I visited a small private school in New York City's Greenwich Village with the idea of asking children in the lower grades what advice to parents they'd like me to incorporate in the forthcoming revision of *Baby and Child Care*. I didn't get what I was after but I was reminded of some basic truths that are more important.

The first class was made up of children from five to seven years of age. It soon was apparent that I wasn't any good as a discussion leader of a group that age. To each straightforward question I asked, one of the quieter children would start to give an answer. But this reply would immediately be drowned out by several boys who gave fantastic, hilarious responses in loud voices. I asked, "How much allowance should a parent give a child?" The boys' answers were, "A hundred dollars!" "Make that two hundred!" "A million dollars a day!"

The teacher tried to calm them but it was no use. I was reminded of an earlier failure of mine thirty-five years ago, when one of my sons, then eight years old, joined a Cub Scout troop. The whole troop met monthly at a church under the leadership of experienced scoutmasters. But weekly meetings of each den were assigned to parents, each of whom played host and leader for a three-week period to a den of eight boys for some kind of project.

I expected no difficulty, believing that I knew quite a lot about children in general and about young boys and their interests in particular. I bought solid wood model-plane kits of a very simple design: fuselage, wing, stabilizer, and rudder. I also bought sandpaper, bottles of blue paint, and tubes of quick-drying cement.

When the group assembled I sat them down in my son's room, passed out the kits, and read in a loud, clear voice the first two steps in the directions: Sand all the wood parts to a smooth finish. Then fit the wing experimentally to the fuselage to determine which is leading edge and which is trailing edge. But by the time I had finished these few sentences I discovered that I had lost control completely. Seven of the eight had grabbed their tubes of cement and, without pausing to make holes with a pin, squeezed them until they burst, daubed cement onto whichever side of the wings came up first, and slapped them onto the fuselages. The one boy who had paid attention was my son.

The only three things I learned from the whole experience were how good a workman my son was, what skill is required to control a group of children—even eight children, and how poor I was as a group leader. I functioned a little better in the next two sessions, but not well enough to be proud of myself.

After that fiasco thirty-five years ago I watched schoolteachers in action very carefully when I had the opportunity. I realized that in the early grades a teacher (let's say it's a woman) has to have the compelling manner of a hypnotist to hold the attention of a class hour after hour. Her vision has to include every pupil every second. Her voice has an insistence, even if it is quiet, that penetrates every restless head. When a boy starts to cause the slightest distraction, the teacher immediately focuses her gaze on him and directs her voice right at him, as if she were catching him in an invisible net and pinning him down.

I have great admiration for the leadership skill of elementary school teachers. Being a teacher in a medical school, as I was, is much easier because the students are determined to learn the material if they think it's important.

The editor-photographer who accompanied me to the school in Greenwich Village was using a small tape recorder. I was interested that one of the clownish boys suddenly made a quiet aside: "When is that tape recorder going to stop bugging us?" Obviously his sharp mind was working on several levels simultaneously.

I retreated to the next-older class, where the children were aged seven to nine. It was startling to see how much more self-disciplined and calm they were. (I remembered that Ilg and Ames, in their book *The Child from Five to Ten,* had written that there is nothing in childhood as explosive as a six-year-old's birthday party.)

Here the children sat quietly until I recognized one of them and then each offered an answer. Half the answers were serious, responsible, adultlike. The other half were rebellious and sometimes sardonic in flavor. I realized that we were seeing two dramatically opposite sides of childhood: the child who is identifying—at the moment—with the parents, striving to grow up and be more responsible; and the other child who—at the moment, anyway—is feeling oppressed by parents, teachers, brothers, sisters, rules, obligations, penalties. She or he daydreams with glee about kicking over the traces or at least takes satisfaction in leveling perceptive criticisms.

When I mentioned revising *Baby and Child Care,* a boy said in a discouraged tone about his parents, "They read the book but they don't do what it says."

When I asked for suggestions a girl said gently, "They could be more patient." I requested a show of hands, and half agreed with the criticism.

"I wish they'd listen more," a girl volunteered, and all but a few sided with her.

Another girl burst out with great fervor, "When your baby sister starts running around the house and taking out your games, you shouldn't be responsible for putting them back." There was universal, vigorous agreement with this combined reproach against parents and younger brothers and sisters.

A boy complained of a brother who showed no respect for the speaker's possessions, and I asked if it was a younger brother. *"Of course!"* he exclaimed, and sympathetic, grim laughter ran through the class.

The strongest response of the day came to the question of whether children who have younger brothers and sisters are really fortunate, despite well-known annoyances. *"No!"* they shouted in a sustained, unanimous roar.

There were a few complaints of bossing and bullying by older brothers and sisters, but these were mild by comparison. Though I was familiar with the resentment against brothers and sisters from previous discussions with children, I was startled at how vehement it was when it focused on younger ones.

I asked whether they thought children should be allowed to set their own bedtime. Some of them relished the idea of staying up as late as they wanted, as would be expected, but I was surprised how many were content to let their parents protect them from fatigue. One girl suggested that they might not find staying up was so great if they had an actual chance to do it. A majority came around to a compromise of wanting to stay up late on Saturdays.

I told them that a meeting of the Children's Liberation Movement had come out for the right of children to leave home if angry, and I asked if they agreed. This was greeted with a unanimous, resounding "No!"

A gleeful boy told a long, complicated story of larceny: how he got his mother to give him money for some plausible reason and then extracted the same amount from his father without admitting that he'd already touched his mother. He eventually was detected. But he showed no remorse in telling the story. His classmates seemed amused rather than shocked, although no vote was taken.

In a thoughtful mood, the class was unanimous that parents should not hit their children. One child added that if you're crying and your parent tells you to stop and then hits you when you don't stop, it only makes you cry more.

When I was envisioning making the school visit, I had thought the children would welcome an opportunity to criticize parents to a stranger in this indirect, relatively anonymous way; I had assumed the votes would go overwhelmingly against domination by parents and in favor of freedom, if not anarchy.

So I was impressed by the reasonable tone of the criticisms and by the limits to their freedom the children were willing to accept.

I think it's worth emphasizing again, though I've written about it before, that children as they grow up not only are feeling and acting, and sometimes misbehaving, like children. At the very same time they are silently identifying with their parents. They are learning how to be adults and parents. They are watching the seemingly exciting things that adults do: driving cars, getting money at the bank, going to parties. But they also are aware of the stern things that parents do: scolding children for making messes and breaking things, for not wearing rubbers or mittens, for quarreling so noisily that they give their mothers headaches. You can see how clearly this kind of identification is registering when you hear children warning their dolls, scolding them, punishing them.

Less well known but equally vital is the way parents identify with their children. That's why parents speak baby talk to their infants —separating out a word or two at a time for emphasis and clarity. That's why they pick simple playthings that they sense will appeal in early stages of development. That's why they move closer when they anticipate that their small child may move into a dangerous spot.

You may think that these parental actions are so obvious and universal that they don't need mentioning. But observations have shown that some parents are so out of touch with their babies' situation and feelings that they hold a bottle at a level so that no milk is in the nipple, hug babies tight when they are struggling to get free, joggle them and jabber at them when they are drooping or crying with sleepiness.

Having had five younger brothers and sisters, I remember clearly the strange facial expression that my mother put on when she was spoonfeeding the current baby, with whom she identified. (She *loved* babies.) As she advanced the loaded spoon toward the baby she always opened her mouth and protruded her lower lip as if *she* were going to accept the cereal and try to keep it from spilling down her chin.

Good parents are constantly anticipating and sympathizing with their children's delights and anxieties. They sense that they will marvel at steam shovels and elephants. They tell or read them stories. They explain eggbeaters and strange-looking people and thunderstorms. They reassure them that pains and bruises will go away and that nightmares are only dreams.

This sensitive parental identification with children—or the lack of it—is what makes all the difference between children who turn out dull or bright, stodgy or imaginative, shy or sociable. The parents' ability to identify is as crucial for children's development as children's ability to identify with parents.

CHAPTER EIGHT

Difficult Relationships

▷ WHEN ONE CHILD IS
  PARTICULARLY IRRITATING

▷ DIFFICULT NEIGHBORS

▷ GETTING ALONG WITH YOUR
  CHILD'S DOCTOR

▷ JUDGING YOUR CHILD'S TEACHER

▷ WHEN ONE CHILD IS PARTICULARLY IRRITATING

"I don't know what to do about my husband," the woman began her letter. "Jack is a wonderful father. He'd do anything for our two boys. I'm sure of that. What worries me is he spends a lot of time with Kevin but he kind of avoids Andrew. He's not cold or unkind, exactly—it's hard to describe. He just doesn't seem to *love* Andrew as much, and I don't understand it. Andrew feels hurt, I know, and he and his father haven't been getting along lately."

Many parents—mothers as well as fathers—write to me about

the same problem: one of their children appeals to them more than another. They assume this means they love one child less. But it's not that simple. To be sure, they probably respond differently to different qualities in their children. One parent, for example, may particularly appreciate athletic ability; another may appreciate high intelligence. Some parents value outgoingness; others will be drawn to a sensitive, thoughtful child. Similarly, one parent may be irritated by procrastination, another by hyperactivity.

But all good parents love their children equally in the sense that they are equally devoted to each of them. They buy them nice clothes and toys, educate them as well as they possibly can, try to satisfy their emotional needs and stand by them if they get into trouble. This deep devotion is what makes children feel that they belong. It is the most valuable aspect of love by far.

To look at the same issue from another angle, we may deeply love our best friend or spouse and yet be intermittently antagonized by some characteristic or habit that wouldn't necessarily bother someone else.

We are all human, and whether we show it or not, we are usually disappointed if a child lacks a quality we value highly. For some parents, however, the problem is more painful: they have one child who irritates them, not just occasionally, but much of the time and perhaps for no reason that seems sufficient.

The most common cause of this kind of incompatibility is antagonistic feelings left over from the parent's own childhood, feelings that were originally directed toward a sister, brother, mother, or father. I'm thinking, for example, of a mother of a five-year-old boy. As a child, she had intensely resented her older brother because he was something of a bully, grabbing away her toys and spoiling her quiet games. To her, he also seemed the favored child, the one who received the most attention and privileges. As an adult, this woman transferred these negative feelings to her son, who somehow reminded her of this brother.

Another frequent cause of incompatibility is that certain qualities about the child remind the parent of traits he dislikes in himself or traits that he was criticized for or made to feel embarrassed about as a child. A father I know was frequently picked on by other boys when he was a child because he was timid. Because of these humiliating experiences he is now quite intolerant of his son, who, as it happens, is gentle and unassertive. Parents may or may not realize that problems caused by faults they had as children—procrastination, meanness, oversensitiveness—make them intensely critical of these same faults in their child.

If it is your eldest who gets on your nerves (as is often the case), it may be because, like most parents, you are more intensely involved with your firstborn. You want that child to have all your good qualities and none of the bad. By the time your other children come along, you are probably relaxed enough to view them as separate individuals who can be allowed to go their own way.

Parents who are honest with themselves simply take these differences in their responses to their children for granted. But some parents can't help feeling guilty.

Children can always sense guilt. Their usual response is to punish the guilty parent, for example, by being uncooperative or impolite or demanding or passive. This further antagonizes the parent, who then feels even guiltier. It's a vicious circle that parents can usually break only by getting beyond the guilt and taking constructive steps to improve matters.

The first step is to be firm with a child who is badgering you with excessive demands ("Why can't I have a doll as big as Suzie's?") or criticisms ("This food is crummy.") or outright rudeness ("You're a mean mother!"). If you secretly feel you deserve to be punished, you may try to put up with this behavior, but sooner or later you'll explode. A much better (though more difficult) response is to take control, not angrily but briskly and matter-of-factly. Just say something like, "If you don't want to play with your doll, pick one of your other toys," or, "Please don't be rude. It makes me unhappy." If the child keeps bugging you, say, "I don't feel like arguing anymore," and don't.

If a little girl complains to her mother, "You like Danny better than me," the mother can respond, not defensively or argumentatively but lovingly, with smiles and hugs. "I can see why you think that," she might say. "It's hard to stay angry at Danny, because he's so funny. I love his sense of humor. And I love you—for many reasons. I love you because you work hard and do well at school. I love you because you like to help other people, and sick animals. When you grow up I know you'll come to visit me, no matter how far away you live." This mother is not criticizing her son in order to console her daughter; she is shifting the discussion away from her son and onto her daughter's virtues.

If mother and daughter truly don't get along, honesty is equally important and may clear the air. "I do get cross with you often," the mother might say, "and I feel bad about that. I know you get angry with me too. Maybe it's because we're so much alike; we know each other's faults. The next time I make you mad, please tell me. Then we can talk about how you feel." It will impress the girl to hear that her mother accepts her anger, wants to get along better, and really loves her.

A second step is for the parent from time to time to deliberately compliment the child for a good quality or a job done well. The danger of simply avoiding the child is that your relationship may never change and possibly will get worse. The husband of the woman who wrote to me, for example, should let his son know that despite their differences, he is loved. This will please the boy and make him more agreeable for a while. That in turn makes it easier for the father to praise him again or to spend time with him. Their activities need to be chosen carefully, however, so that they don't backfire. If a father is unhappy because his son is clumsy and unathletic, the worst thing they can do is shoot baskets together.

The child may never complain, but inside he'll feel insecure. His way of coping—by being grumpy or uncooperative, aggressive or whining—can make the situation worse. Parents must act to stop this sort of chain reaction of negative feelings. If they are willing to be openly loving, they'll find their child is willing too.

If a relationship remains bad, psychiatry should offer help to the parent and perhaps to the child.

▷ DIFFICULT NEIGHBORS

A majority of neighbors—adults and children—are a pleasure to have near. But in most localities there are a few stinkers who may make life difficult for your children and you and who are a problem to deal with.

I'll first mention the disagreeable adults who are suspiciously on the lookout for trespassers and will pounce like spiders if a child puts one foot on their grass. The tougher kids in the neighborhood are not upset by crabby neighbors—they enjoy teasing them by running across their lawn or dropping litter there. It's the sensitive young child who is worried by the exaggerated stories he hears about the ferocity of the cranky couple; he may have had bad dreams about them and may be afraid to go down their street.

The parents can help in such cases by pooh-poohing the wild

stories, explaining to their child that there are lots of cranky people in the world who are always ready to get mad, and that all that is necessary is for the child not to provoke them.

Children take their cues about how to view strange behavior and strange people from their parents. If the parents are outraged or alarmed, children will be even more perturbed. If the parents take eccentrics for granted, the children will learn to do so too. I can remember vividly how my mother, who feared very few men or beasts, would tense up when passing a drunk on the street, and I assumed throughout childhood that all drunks were dangerous fiends.

A most troublesome neighbor child is the bully who delights in picking on smaller children, teasing them, hurting them, or frightening them with threats. The bully is usually a boy. There is no simple solution here. If parents take the attitude that he is a cruel monster, their children may become increasingly fearful of him and by showing this in their manner when meeting him, provoke his sadism.

As a child I was scared of all bullies and dogs. In retrospect I can see that this stuck out all over me and must have suggested at least a little teasing to every mean child I passed on the street. I remember at the age of eight going downtown in New Haven to a Saturday-morning gymnasium class and spying a group of tough guys approaching on the other side of the street. I hurried forward and tried to look everywhere except at them. But they spotted my timorousness and swarmed across the street to accost me. One said truculently, "Oh, so you want to fight, do you?" and started to take off his coat. While his arms were still entangled, I turned and ran—faster than I'd ever run before or have run since, much too fast for anyone to catch me—and didn't stop or look back for half a mile.

If parents rush out to scold a child who has been bullying their children or telephone his parents, this convinces the victims that they can't protect themselves but can be saved only if their parents are present. So in general, I think, it is better for parents to take the philosophical attitude that their children must fight their own battles. But if one of their children is being persistently abused by a larger child, they may decide that they will have to speak to the bully or call his parents, preferably when their own child is not aware of this interference.

To keep your children from growing up afraid of other children,

I feel it's important to get them used to playing regularly with other children from the age when they first can walk. At that age their feelings aren't so easily hurt and they aren't likely to acquire fear of other children. If they can learn a matter-of-fact attitude toward the occasional blows and snatchings of their contemporaries, it will form a partial protection against bullies, because bullies particularly love to go after frightened children.

Next comes the neighbor child who, despite having been scolded often, persistently tries to involve other children of the same age or of younger age in sex play. I'm not thinking primarily of three-, four-, or five-year-olds, who easily and naturally fall into sex play with others their age by playing doctor or by looking or by touching. Most children this age can be inhibited easily by the request of a parent, at least temporarily.

The child I'm thinking about is usually a boy seven to twelve years of age who has a reputation for being somewhat mean, disobedient, and generally a troublemaker. Often he is a child who is somewhat neglected by his parents and is always hanging around other children's homes, usually the homes of younger children, because he's not very popular with youngsters his own age; this is not an attractive child or a desirable playmate. Sex play initiated by an older child can be more disturbing to a young child because it is harder for the younger one to resist or understand.

There are two aspects to coping with such a child. The first is the attitude you should take when your own child indicates to you that sex play has been proposed or initiated. I would say to my child that I don't think sex play is a good idea in childhood; sex is for grown-ups. I would explain that I don't want him (let's say it's a boy) to do it, and he can tell that to the other child. (Other parents may have different ideas.) From my point of view, it's not necessary or wise to make your children feel guilty about sex or to give them the impression that they have been harmed or corrupted by molestation from another child. Better to keep it casual.

What can you do about the child who initiated the sex play? I think it's appropriate, especially if he persists in further attempts, to tell him matter-of-factly the next time you see him that you don't want him to play that way with your child. If this doesn't have any effect, you can ask your children not to play with him at all or you can consider speaking to his parents.

The commonest problem with approaching another child's parents—whether about sex play or bullying or walking off with your children's playthings—is that in a family in which these things often happen, the parents frequently are lacking in responsibility and may simply become angry at anyone who criticizes their child.

If it's your children who are being accused of picking on other children or leading them into sex play or stealing, it's wise, I think, to hear out the complaints in a courteous manner, even if your first reaction is that a mistake has been made. This is by far the best way to calm the indignation of the complaining neighbor. "A soft answer turneth away wrath." More important, it's the quickest way to rehabilitate the reputation of your child and your family in the neighborhood generally, just as getting angry and refusing to listen sets the neighbors more indignantly against you. Your cooperative, concerned manner reassures the neighbors that you will try to prevent any repetition of the behavior.

Suppose the problem is that you have just moved into the neighborhood and the local children are excluding your child from their play. This is a common occurrence, children being the clannish creatures they are, especially in the six-to-twelve-year-old period.

You can buy a little popularity for your child (let's assume it's a girl) for a while by giving the local children an especially good time. You can serve fruit juice or fruit and crackers or cookies in mid-morning and mid-afternoon. You can invite children to meals, preferably one child at a time—two is company, three or more is a crowd that may discriminate subtly against your child—and serve such invariably popular food as hot dogs or hamburgers. You can take a neighbor child along on picnics, excursions to zoos, museums, sporting events. (These suggestions work especially well for parents who live in apartments and don't have backyards where other children can gather.)

If your child is really unattractive, you can't buy her much permanent acceptance; if she is unusually charming, you won't need to try. But what I'm suggesting is that treats will induce clannish children to let down the barriers more quickly, so that the newcomer will have a chance to show her good qualities.

Having a backyard is an advantage. If you have young children, you should be able to keep them and neighbor youngsters under observation most of the time by making your yard a popular gathering place. This will help you to control various sorts of difficult behavior in other children and in your own.

My mother, who was a great controller, used this method with success. There was a large sandbox, which got a fresh load of white sand each spring. There was a swing of unusual design. The seat was about four feet wide and was suspended by four vertical ropes, making room for three swingers to sit side by side. Six could swing standing up, three facing three. There was a good-sized seesaw and an apparatus I've never seen elsewhere—a broad jouncing board eight or ten feet long supported securely by sawhorses attached at each end. A trampoline would serve the purpose even better.

For a few years we even had a merry-go-round of a simple design. It looked like a seesaw, but instead of tipping up and down, it rotated horizontally. There also happened to be three cherry trees in the yard, which were ideal for climbing. Our yard was always full of children, including the younger Spocks. We didn't have a tree house but a tree house is always popular, either one that's actually in a tree or one simply built on stilts.

How much can you as parent boss the other children of the neighborhood? I'd say as much as is necessary when the children are on your premises. However, just as in the case of managing your own children, I think it's important to try to avoid turning into a scold with neighbor children. Aim to be a friendly leader, yet firm. You can keep track of the play situation unobtrusively.

If matters are getting out of hand—and I don't mean every little quarrel or blow—you don't need to rush out with angry reproaches that make one child feel like a villain and the other a martyr. Just drift out as if you happened to want a breath of fresh air. This usually stops the hostilities promptly and reminds the more troublesome children that you always are close by.

Of course, there will be occasions when you have to explain to young children how to share and how to reason with one another instead of grabbing or hitting. You also may have to go further once in a while and be very firm with a difficult child. But even here it's more effective in the long run not to seem to be an enemy, since the child's mean behavior probably is related to feeling unloved already. Put your arm affectionately around the child while you are making your point. Invite the difficult child to a meal or on an excursion.

▷ GETTING ALONG WITH YOUR CHILD'S DOCTOR

You probably don't need to be reminded that doctors are as human as anyone else—as human as parents—and that no two are exactly the same. So it's no wonder that sometimes parents have to work at finding a doctor who is right for them—and for their child. What you should remember is that the relationship between parents, children, and the family doctor or pediatrician is a close and important one. Whether that relationship is satisfying or frustrating is partly up to you.

The first and perhaps most crucial step in getting what you want is to take care in making your original selection. Some like an advisor who is unusually specific and detailed, others want one who seems casual, easy-going. Some parents like an older, well-established type and others feel more comfortable with someone close to their own age. Some respond best to a male doctor, others to a woman. When making inquiries—of friends or of physicians in other specialties such as obstetrics whom you may know—express your preferences.

The next step is to make an appointment with one or more doctors for an exploratory visit and interview. That first visit is your opportunity to discover a bit of what the doctor is like and whether you suit each other.

If I were a parent expecting my first child, I would confess to the physician that I was an anxious type (even if that wasn't true) and that I imagined I would raise lots of questions, perhaps silly questions, in the early weeks of my baby's life. Then I would watch his reaction. Does he tighten up at the prospect of a hundred trivial, time-wasting questions? Or does he laugh reassuringly and say that he expected a barrage of questions at first? I want to make a point of "silly questions" because they are an uncomfortable issue for many parents in the first two or three months of the first baby's life. It's no exaggeration to say that half the questions you'll ever want to raise will come up in that period—and you are entitled to the answers. If you've been persuaded that this will make you a nuisance, you'll spend half your time in a stew, needing information or reassurance but afraid of irritating the doctor. It shouldn't be that way.

My advice, then, is to sound out a prospective doctor on this subject. If he shows traces of impatience, drop him before you get started. If you have already made a commitment, then you should try to work things out. Summon the courage to say that you have the impression that the number of questions you raise bothers him. If he's any good, he'll apologize and encourage you to ask away. If, on the other hand, he implies that you *do* have too many questions, I'd leave him and find another doctor.

The parent, of course, is not the only person whom the doctor should please. The real patient is the child, and the doctor should please her too—as well as a syringe-wielding person ever can. Some physicians take the trouble to make friends with the child and speak to her directly when that's appropriate. If the child is frightened and starts crying, the doctor shouldn't be brusque; he should allow time for the parent to hold and soothe the child. (Of course, I know that this "parent" will generally be the mother, but I would like to encourage fathers to take equal responsibility for their children's care.) If your doctor ignores your child or usually addresses you as if she weren't even there, you can include the child in the conversation yourself. If the doctor doesn't respond to these hints, you should probably look for someone whose priorities are closer to your own.

Another source of parents' frustration is the telephone. Most pediatricians set aside an hour, often the first thing in the morning, and ask parents to try to call then, unless there is an emergency or a new development in an illness. But it can be very irritating for a parent to get busy signals for a full hour.

You may find yourself less annoyed with the doctor if you realize that this telephone jam is often caused by parents who misunderstand the purpose of telephone consultation. I remember in the early years of my practice a mother's waking me at seven o'clock on a Sunday morning. "I've got a list of problems," she announced, "that I've been wanting to discuss with you." If I'd been more experienced, I'd have explained to her cheerfully that an office visit was more appropriate for a long conversation. The telephone should be used mainly to obtain brief answers to anxious questions in the baby's first month or two, to report new illnesses (and see whether an office visit is advisable), or to report progress in an illness that has already been discussed.

Some parents complain that their office visits seem rushed. If a mother has brought a list of questions, she may find herself only halfway through when the doctor stands up, as if dismissing her. Or he may respond to questions in a soothing, paternalistic way without really taking her concerns seriously. Your doctor may be unaware of the impression he gives. I had an extremely educational experience early in my practice when an outspoken mother abruptly asked me, "Just how long are my office visits meant to be, anyway?" Recovering from my surprise, I said, "They are meant to be half an hour." She replied, "Well, I'm glad to know that, because you always make me feel I'm being rushed."

Now I was even more surprised. I had always thought of myself as leisurely, but I realized what that mother was picking up. I was constantly frustrated at that time because I wasn't yet supporting my family. It was 1933, the bottom of the Depression, and when I started out as a pediatrician in New York, I had very few patients. I was also pioneering in trying to find the connection between psychoanalytic concepts and the everyday problems that mothers were asking advice about, such as thumb sucking and resistance to weaning. It was tough going because no one had previously studied or written on these particular matters. (A standard answer up to then had been, "Thumb sucking is a bad habit, so stop it with bitter tasting medicine on the thumb or aluminum mittens or tying the babies wrists to the sides of the crib.") I felt these pressures constantly and without even knowing it, was transmitting them to my patients. From then on I tried hard to cultivate a relaxed, attentive manner, the most valuable and appreciated trait any physician can have.

Most doctors are under various pressures. If yours makes you feel rushed, your first recourse is to speak to him frankly. Frankness doesn't have to mean angry accusations, which tend to make people—including doctors—defensive. It may be more tactful for a parent to say, "Part of the trouble may be my oversensitivity. But I feel we have this or that problem." The parent's readiness to take part of the responsibility for misunderstandings invites the doctor to be equally humble and generous.

If you tell your doctor frankly what you need, you may be reforming him for the benefit of his other patients—and himself. But if he can't or won't change, the power is still in your hands. It is a parent's privilege to change doctors, and it's really very simple to do: just don't go back. You needn't call and explain to justify your position. Get recommendations from friends or from your local hospital, and try somebody new. It's as easy as that, unless you live in a one-doctor town.

▷ JUDGING YOUR CHILD'S TEACHER

I'd say that the most important criterion—by far—is whether your child likes her or him.

But, you may say, might not a child like best a person who is not an effective teacher but who seeks popularity by being pleasant and making lessons too easy? That's a logical-sounding fear, but it is not correct at all according to my experience. In fact, children are quite critical of an undemanding teacher. I've heard them say, "Miss Jenkins is nice but she doesn't teach you anything."

Children learn best by identifying with an adult who likes them and whom they like and admire. In the many parts of the world in which there are no schools at all, children learn hunting or fishing or agriculture or weaving or baby care or cooking by identifying enthusiastically with the parent of the same sex, whom they admire and love and want to grow up to be like. At the other end of the educational scale we can see in a training hospital that the young residents are learning to be physicians by eagerly patterning themselves after the older staff doctors whom they admire and who respect them. (No students of any age want to pattern themselves after a teacher who doesn't like them.) When children like a teacher it means that the teacher loves them and tries to understand their individual problems. This is a major factor in successful teaching.

It's a mistake in general to think of the subjects children study in school as being difficult to learn and as therefore requiring unusual technical skill on the part of teachers and hard work on the part of pupils. Subject matter at each grade level is relatively easy for a majority of pupils to learn without great effort *provided* they don't get scared or blocked at certain points. They get blocked because they are scared of the teacher or scared that they don't and can't understand. So the friendliness of the teacher and the patience of the teacher in understanding where the block occurs and in helping a child over it are crucial elements in any teacher's capability.

Another reason why some children can't learn, of course, is that their learning capabilities are not up to the material presented in that class, either because their intelligence is below average or because the teacher's expectations are not realistic. I was in a small, informal class of six at the age of eight where the teacher, untrained, pushed me in a hurry to long division. It seemed so overwhelmingly complicated at that age that I wept every day. The trouble there was that few children of that age are capable of long division.

"Learning capabilities" doesn't mean just intelligence. Ten percent of boys who have good intelligence still are slow in being able to remember the shape and position of letters: they confuse *d* and *b;* they confuse *god* and *dog.* This makes them, first of all, slow to learn to read, but much more damaging is their loss of self-confidence, their feeling of panic that they won't ever be able to learn to read. Other children are slow in catching on to certain mathematical concepts. (Girls are more apt to have this difficulty.) Such learning disabilities can be suspected by a well-trained teacher, diagnosed by tests, and treated by special methods.

To get back to judging teachers: a second sign of a good teacher, whether at the nursery school level or the high school level, is whether she or he spends all of the time talking at the whole class or is able to spot the individual who is stuck and help that student to get unstuck.

One kind of poor teacher threatens slow students that she will give them low grades or not promote them. This is more likely to paralyze backward pupils than to stimulate them. The teacher's job is to make the work understandable enough, interesting enough, challenging enough so that the pupils can't help but get involved. This means designing projects, exercises, angles, trips that will make the subject matter seem real and exciting. It means giving serious students who are extra bright assignments that are extra challenging and giving slow students less difficult assignments so that they won't become discouraged but will get a sense of achievement every day. Of course classes have to be small to make this possible. A teacher who uses physical punishment or sends a student to the principal for punishment has failed and has given up, in my estimation. I don't care what the laws of the state or the rules of the board of education say.

A good teacher encourages initiative, responsibility, and creativity. These qualities are essential to all students if they are to be ready to take on jobs in adulthood that are better than humdrum or bottom-of-the-ladder. These qualities can't be taught by books or by the preaching of the teacher—or of the parent. Children develop them by being given opportunities—every day—to carry them out in practice. The wise teacher gives her pupils daily opportunities to take the initiative, to make their own plans for some of their work, to try to solve certain problems by themselves—even if they make mistakes. She encourages them to be creative and original in their writing, in their art work, and in their dramatics. And after letting pupils plan some of their own projects, she lets them carry these out—with minimal supervision. You can only teach a child to *take* responsibility if you *give* responsibility.

How will you know whether a teacher is helping individuals and is encouraging initiative, creativity, and responsibility? You may get hints and clues from what your child tells you about school. But best of all is to visit. Not for a half hour but for at least half a day.

What if your child complains of a frightening teacher or one who can't seem to make the work understandable? First of all you need to know that it is usually the sensitive, overly conscientious pupils, at the start of first grade or second grade in the fall, who are most apt to be overawed or scared by a teacher. They show this not only in their complaints but in not being able to eat breakfast or in vomiting on the way to school. This fear of not being able to satisfy the teacher at six or seven years is an aspect of the shift from being totally a child of the parents, in the first five or six years of life, to beginning to be a person of the outside world where one has to cooperate, take responsibility, and be increasingly independent.

I think it's helpful to listen sympathetically when a child complains of a teacher but not jump to the conclusion that the teacher is mean or incompetent. You can say, "I can see how that would upset you, to have the teacher correct you in front of the class." Next you can offer to visit the classroom, to see what it's like. Just going there may tip the teacher off that there is some problem and make her more considerate of the child's feelings.

Next you could make an appointment for a conference, not to complain but to ask how the child is doing. Then you can refer to the problem, not in terms of blaming the teacher but of explaining the child's excessive sensitivity: "He worries whether he can do well enough," or, "When he can't understand something right away he gets panicky and gives up."

The overawed child usually gets a thickened skin in a few weeks and learns that the teacher's severity is not as dangerous as it seemed. If this does not happen and the child remains tense and unhappy, the parents can approach the principal for help. In this case it is just as important that the parents not put the blame mainly on the teacher, which usually only forces the principal to defend the teacher. They can put it instead on the child's sensitivity or slowness. A principal can read between the lines and may, herself or himself, suggest that the child be transferred to another teacher.

If this doesn't happen and if the child lives within a reasonable distance of another school, public or private, transfer may be considered. This solution usually has the disadvantage of making the child attend a different school from the other children of the neighborhood. Children of school age want very much to be "regular."

This discussion of placement brings up two other issues. Parents with high standards and ambition for their children sometimes try to persuade a school to put their child in a higher grade or class than the school people feel is wise. This often proves a mistake because the child placed too high may be unable to keep up and then feels disgraced by being demoted.

Parents of an unusually bright child sometimes assume that he is bound to be bored in a class of average children. This isn't necessarily true at all. If the class is not large and the teacher is well trained and imaginative, she should be able to enrich the bright child's assignments, for example with extra reading in the classroom, in the school library, or in the town library. This is the same principle used in the much praised one-room school, where there would be four or more grades in the same room and the teacher would assign different work for each child.

CHAPTER NINE

Several Behavior Problems

▷ BAD LANGUAGE

▷ STEALING, LYING, AND CHEATING

▷ WHINING

▷ ANXIETY ABOUT STARTING
SCHOOL

▷ BAD LANGUAGE

It's a bit embarrassing for me to discuss what parents should do about "bad language"—which in the past was always assumed to be undesirable—at the very time when many parents purposefully, even proudly, have taken to using excretory and sex-related words in their ordinary conversation. Many of the people who make a point of using four-letter words consider this just one aspect of their general conviction that it is always better to be natural and honest. And when people such as myself act uncomfortable about

216

such language, they see it as a kind of stuffiness that is a holdover from the past.

But standards of behavior weren't invented in the dim past by killjoy religious leaders or police chiefs and then imposed arbitrarily on unwilling people. They have been expressions of basic human ideals or of the particular society at a particular time.

One of these human desires is for beauty. This is what makes us create or respond to attractive clothes, to adornments, to well-designed buildings and—with respect to language—to the inspiring sounds of poetry and song and eloquent speech. In this sense the desire to use beautiful language is much more basic than the impulse to use words to shock or to insult, which expresses revolt against the conventions.

Another human need is for laws and social conventions that control the aggression of others and of ourselves and that assure us of pleasant relations with people. Though they hem us in, they protect us and give us comfort.

Since most of us were brought up in families in which, to one degree or another, we loved our parents, respected their authority, and patterned ourselves after them in behavior and ideals, we tend, other things being equal, to respect their traditions and standards.

These influences—the love of beauty, the acceptance of rules, the respect for family traditions—are positive forces that make us *want* to behave with correctness and style. It's when we feel that they are too artificial or rigid that there builds up an impulse to defy them. Eventually, though, the drive toward formality and standards reasserts itself.

So my own opinion is that despite the current trend toward crudity in language, there will be a swing back—whether it takes twenty years or a hundred. Parents who want to keep their children's language fairly proper can use my prediction as support. If I'm wrong, their children will be swept along in the new style sooner or later anyway.

So-called dirty words of the fecal sort first crop up at about four years of age, when many children become deliberately cocky. They are developing a primitive sense of humor. They enjoy playing with words. The words are literally dirty, in the sense that they are apt to be concerned with bowel functions.

A four-year-old's dirty jokes are not very dirty and not very funny. A good example is the jolly insult, "You're a big BM." The children laugh uproariously. Then another child says, "You're a stinky BM." More hilarity. Like poor adult storytellers, they try to get more laughs out of essentially the same joke: "You're a stinky pee-pee," "You're a stinky poo-poo." (A perceptive observer once said that the passing of gas by rectum was the first joke. Four-year-olds confirm this with enthusiasm.)

Sex is less likely to be a subject for crude joking during the four- and five-year-old period, because sex has not yet been as strongly repressed as soiling and playing with BMs. Sex is still a matter of open, serious preoccupation, and children are grappling with the meaning of genital differences, wanting to marry the parent of the opposite sex, wanting to have babies.

But then several factors cause a gradual repression of sexual interests at six or seven years and beyond, as discussed in Chapter Ten. As sexual interests become more forbidden in the six-to-twelve-year-old period, the urge to joke about sex or to use it for shocking effect becomes greater. At this age too, children are turning away from their parents as models and are trying to be just like their contemporaries in behavior of all kinds—unappetizing table manners, slovenly personal appearance, ungrammatical language and dirty words. They may or may not know the meaning of the words, but they do know they are naughty.

In adolescence there is a further accentuation of the need to be like one's friends and to prove one's independence from parents. (It may not be so much that the parents are holding on as that the child is afraid to let go.) To shout or mutter forbidden language seems like a glorious way to defy.

(In the case of adult dirty jokes, the fun comes from daring to use words or bring up topics of conversation that are conventionally forbidden. But if there is humor in the idea—and an unexpected punch line—the sin is sugar-coated with the humor, and the listeners all laugh. In this way they join the teller in his or her sinfulness and forfeit the right to disapprove.)

As to how parents might respond, I have two general principles. First, I believe that in the home parents are entitled to expect, within reason, the kind of behavior from their children that they consider right—and language is within reason. Second, I've always been convinced (though many parents will be skeptical) that parents can secure the kind of behavior they want *if* they really want it. (You can see plenty of parents who keep yammering at their children, or even hitting at them, out of irritability, without making any effort really to control their behavior.)

If you say to children that you wish they wouldn't use again an offensive word they've just said, but your facial expression shows you're actually amused by this precocious worldliness, children will pay more attention to your face than to your words. If you pretend to hit the ceiling in horror, you add extra inducement, because it's fun for children to find that they can levitate an adult that high. But if you feel sincere disapproval or irritation, I think it is quite all right to show this. However, I wouldn't act as if the child was basically evil to have used such language. After all, the child originally learned the words from someone who probably wasn't vicious, perhaps even from a parent, and the child was only experimenting with being grown-up in this way. All that is necessary is to ask the child in a reasonable, sincere tone not to use such words. It's the words you disapprove of, not the child's character.

I think the easiest way to handle what the parents may feel is a moral or ethical point, but too subtle to explain to a young child, is to say something like, "Most people don't like to hear impolite words like that, and I don't either."

When I say that the ethical issue may be difficult to explain to a young child, I'm thinking, for instance, of the four-letter words for intercourse and bowel movement. Very few parents today want to give their children the idea that either intercourse or a bowel movement is bad or disgusting. Then why is crude language about these activities offensive to so many people? The main reason, I think, is that the vulgar words traditionally have been used in a hostile spirit, when one person cursed or disparaged another. Usually there is no actual connection with genital or intestinal function. And even when genital function is referred to, as in a dirty story, it is typically an act of intercourse that is loveless, exploitative, perhaps brutal. Curses invoking God or Jesus also are not only antireligious but hostile.

If an older child questions your disapproval of crude words, you can get into an explanation such as I've just given. For the young child I think that general phrases such as "not polite" or "people don't like to hear them" or "they hurt people's feelings" are satisfactory enough. Children get the idea all right.

But if you yourself don't think crude language is bad and if you use it when you're upset or hurt, you don't have to make it a moral issue with your children. Certainly the use of off-color words in itself will not corrupt a child's character. Children's characters are formed by their parents' characters.

So another approach is for the parents to appear quite relaxed. They can smile wickedly to show that they have their naughty side too, while counting on their lack of shock to help the child lose interest in the *persistent* use of bad language. The trouble here is that the child may very well feel free to use these words in other people's homes and may thereby get a bad reputation in the neighborhood. Some parents may even forbid their children to play with the cusser. I wouldn't risk this myself.

▷ STEALING, LYING, AND CHEATING

Outright stealing is only an occasional problem with children. Arguments between them over property and sharing are incessant.

In some simple societies, most property is held in common by the extended family or by the community; there, stealing is not often a problem of the individual. If a neighboring tribe makes a raid to steal cattle or other property, however, it's a community problem. So the same impulses are present but are expressed through the group.

We live in a country where individual property rights are taken very seriously. We go to work not as part of a cooperative effort to serve the community, as in some societies, but to acquire money for ourselves and for our immediate families. Almost all the things in the home, except perhaps the furnishings, are considered the possession of one family member or another.

As soon as a small child begins to be aware of such things— between one and three years of age—he learns that he must not play with fragile objects because they belong to his parents. If he picks up a toy belonging to his older sister, she grabs it from him and yells, "That's mine!"

He acquires the idea of individual property not only because its importance is frequently drilled into him but also because it fits in with his growing sense of self and assertion of self. Early in his second year he becomes conscious of the fact that this body is *his*. He like games of pointing to *his* nose, *his* eyes, *his* ears, *his* toes, when his mother names these parts. He wants to hold his own spoon. And he resists bowel training at times because the bowel movement is *his*. Even when he cannot form sentences, he says, "Mine!" with great determination if another child tries to pick up a plaything of his.

The awareness of his own property rights develops faster than the recognition of the rights of others; at one and two years of age he can't resist picking up another child's appealing plaything—and may even try to take it home—whereas he wouldn't let that child take anything of his.

Some conscientious, public-spirited parents have tried hard to teach their children to share during the one-to-three-year-old period. My own inclination is to suggest that you wait until sharing comes more naturally. I don't mean that you can't suggest sharing occasionally between the ages of two and three, and I'd keep encouraging it if the child takes to the idea. But most children under three have too great a need to hang on to their own things and too little enjoyment of sharing to be able to yield—even for a few minutes. In fact, I have the impression that when parents make too insistent demands for sharing, it only makes a child more "selfish." He feels that not only other children but his parents too are trying to deprive him of his possessions.

When a child of one or two tries to appropriate and take home another's toy, it's obviously not stealing. I only bring up this point to suggest to parents that they not try to make a small child feel even mildly guilty about it, not overimpress him with the sacredness of private property. You can just say, "Henry wants it, so we have to leave it."

When a small child tries to use a possession of another, and the other objects, I think it's preferable to let them tug it out between themselves for a while. It's good for children to learn to stand up for their own rights. Usually the one who is the owner has stronger feelings of possessiveness and therefore a stronger tug. But if the owner is being consistently victimized or physically abused, a parent may have to intervene. This can be done quite casually by stepping between the battlers and prying the toy loose; there is no need to become accusatory or moralistic.

As children approach the age of three, most of them begin to develop enough affection for other children and enough enjoyment of the special delights of cooperative play that they can start to share. But the encouragement of parents will make a big difference. You can say, "First Charlie rides in the cart and Peter pulls it. Then Peter climbs in and Charlie pulls it." "First Mary throws the ball to Peter and then Peter throws it to Mary." Or, "Mary rides on the seat of the tricycle and Sally stands on the back. Then they change."

Such sharing is new and exciting at about the age of three; the child's beginning social outgoingness makes him able to enjoy it. With a little encouragement the child doesn't have to feel that sharing means a deprivation of possessions; it is a new and more grown-up way of enjoying them.

In the age period between six and twelve there is an intensification of the sense of possessiveness. Children want their own rooms. They have the drive—at least at times—to organize their possessions and to guard them. Many of them want to make collections —of stamps, rocks, trading cards, and even junk. They think up schemes to make money.

From my own observations, the age at which surreptitious stealing first becomes a fairly common problem is at about seven. A child may be discovered to have removed a fellow pupil's trading cards from his locker. Or he takes and hides a teacher's desk ornament. Or he sneaks money from his mother's purse. Or he lifts a jackknife or a toy pistol from the counter of a neighborhood store.

This sort of stealing is the kind that's done in a solitary, secretive way by a child who has been brought up in a reasonably strict family in which stealing is totally unacceptable. (This is quite different from the stealing, for example, done by a gang of boys whose parents don't strongly disapprove.) The child psychiatrist who works for a while with such a child may find any one of a variety of special factors, such as a sense of deprivation, an envy of a brother or sister, or other resentments and anxieties, that may help explain his stealing. But when I was a part-time school physician, consulted by the teachers about all kinds of problems, I was impressed with a couple of elements that were commonly present. Most of the children were about seven years old, and none of them were what the teacher would consider really popular.

I think of the six-and-seven-year-old period as one in which the child, for complex, unconscious reasons, is turning away from his very intense early-childhood attachment to his parents—admiration and imitation of the parent of the same sex, romantic love of the parent of the opposite sex, deep dependence on both for his security. He is now seeking a more grown-up, independent position for himself. He wants to model himself after his peers, not his parents. He craves close friendships with others of his own sex and age.

One of the factors that helps him make the transition from parents' little child to young man (or woman) of the world—at about seven—is ease in making friends. His new, close ties with them help compensate him for the loss of closeness to his parents.

I think that the child of six, seven, or eight who doesn't have the knack of making friends easily may unconsciously get caught in no-man's-land. He has moved away, somewhat, from his parents but has not yet formed equally warm relationships with others. The deficit of love makes him hungrier for possessions instead.

The things children steal in this age period give support to this concept. The teacher may have told her class that the ornament that disappeared meant a great deal to her because it was given to her by a dear friend. Trading cards are a means of coming closer to classmates and a basis for being admired and envied. Sometimes a child who steals money uses it to buy candy, which he then distributes among the children with whom he craves popularity. Or he may pass out the dimes and nickels directly.

In my experience there is another peak in the frequency of stealing at about thirteen, when children are going through other changes—in body, in feelings, in friendship—that cause anxiety. At that age some thefts are still motivated by loneliness; in other cases, the child is trying to keep up with or impress her group. A girl or group of girls may shoplift cosmetics. A boy may steal from stores too or even commit a minor burglary with a group of his friends.

When a child is found to have stolen something, it isn't necessary or wise for the parents to condemn him harshly or act as if they will never be able to love him again. And it's wiser not to ask, "Henry, did you steal this?" That only pushes the child into implausible lies that lead nowhere. A first step, which shows him clearly that the parents can't allow stealing, is for them to plan prompt restitution. Either the child alone or child and parent should go—right away, if possible, otherwise the next morning—to the child, the teacher, or the store from which the object was taken. If the parent has to be spokesman because the child is too embarrassed, he only has to say that the child is sorry and won't do it again.

As for discussing with the child what has happened and why, the parents may explain along lines such as the following: They know that the child is not a bad person. They know that the child didn't steal to be bad. Everyone occasionally wants something that belongs to another person, but we can't take it because that wouldn't be fair. When a person takes an object that doesn't belong to him, it is usually because he's unhappy about something—though he may not be able to say what it is. If he knows something he is unhappy about, his parents would like to know and try to help him.

Certainly the parents shouldn't allow the wool to be pulled over their eyes if the child tries to explain—and usually his guilt shows clearly—that he *found* the pack of cards or brand-new knife or money.

Children who steal once in the early school years usually are chastened by being detected and having to make restitution and by learning that their parents won't let them get away with it. Most of them never repeat such thefts.

Those who persist in stealing can be assumed to have more serious problems—perhaps in their social relationships with other children or in their more basic relations with their parents. Then it would be wise to consult a child guidance clinic or a family social agency in order to prevent increasing alarm and disapproval on the parents' part and a progressive hardening of the heart in the child.

If a three-year-old says there is a giraffe in her bedroom, she isn't lying, she's pretending. When a seven-year-old says she didn't eat ice cream before dinner, but there's an empty ice-cream carton in the garbage pail and chocolate stains on her blouse, that is lying, because she is trying to deceive and is old enough to know it.

Children who have been brought up lovingly and responsibly most often lie because they have done something that they fear will bring down severe parental disapproval or punishment. Yet in most cases these kids haven't done anything worse than the average child does, so the question then becomes, why do they feel so guilty? The answer may lie in the degree of communication between parent and child.

In many cases the parents of children who lie have unusually high standards of behavior or school performance. High standards are not harmful in themselves. They can be transmitted successfully and easily if the parents are close to their children. The difficulty comes when the standards are high and the parents seem distant and awesome.

I don't mean that the first time a child tells a small lie to save his skin the parents have to worry about their discipline. They only have to say, in a friendly but serious manner, "I want you to tell me the truth and I will always tell you the truth. Then we can always believe each other." But if the child continues to lie, then it's up to the parents to ask themselves why their child feels she must be deceitful. Children are not liars by nature; if a child lies often, it means she is under pressure of some kind. If she's doing badly at school and lying to cover up about it, it isn't because she doesn't care. Her lying shows that she does care. So the parents need to look further. Is the work too advanced? Are the parents setting standards so high she can't meet them but is afraid to say so? The child's teachers or guidance counselor may be able to help parents figure out what the real problem is.

In the meantime parents shouldn't let the child think she is fooling them. But it's also not wise to confront her angrily or demand to know why she lied. Instead, to create an atmosphere of mutual understanding, a mother might say gently, "You don't have to lie to me. Please tell me what the trouble is. I'm sure we can help you work it out." The child may need adult help to realize what's troubling her. Even if she does know, she may not be able to tell her parents immediately. But if they show understanding and sympathy, they'll probably win her trust. If, however, chronic lying continues, a counselor could be consulted.

No matter how unimportant the game, children hate to lose. So sometimes they try to cheat at such games as Monopoly or checkers. And the parents are often surprised to discover that it may be their example that is encouraging their child to cheat.

Human beings are naturally competitive, but in the United States competitiveness is encouraged to a harmful degree, I believe. If a parent takes Little League too seriously and is visibly upset when the child's team loses, many children will take the next logical step and assume that it's better to cheat than lose the game. If parents are overemphasizing grades and constantly comparing one child's performance with another's, they may soon find the child copying from another student's test paper or even forging their signatures on a report card.

When a child cheats at games, it's usually enough if the parents point out that what she has done is unfair. If she cheats again, the parents can explain again. Then, even if the child remains overly competitive, she learns that she will usually be detected if she cheats, which in itself is a partial deterrent. Cheating under the age of six is less significant than after.

Cheating in school is a more complicated problem. If a child needs help with schoolwork she should get it, from her teacher or a tutor (the tutor may be a parent, but only if the parent is patient enough). She should not be left to flounder and then feel she must cheat to cover up her inadequacy.

In any case, when a child steals, lies, or cheats, it's wise for the parents not only to give clear ethical guidance but also to try to find out what started the behavior to begin with and deal directly with that.

▷ WHINING

There are various causes when children whine. Chronic physical disease can produce whining. So can acute unhappiness, as in the case of many children during the first year after their parents' divorce. But in this chapter I'll discuss only the habitual whining of the child who is physically well and has no serious reason to be miserable.

In one sense such whining is not a serious disturbance and doesn't lead to worse problems. But it's a pain in the neck to other members of the family and to their friends. (It happens to bother me tremendously.)

It's in the preschool and early school years that you hear whining oftenest. The words that go with the music are varied. "There's nothing to do," the child keeps complaining on a rainy day. Or, "Why *can't* I stay up for this program?" when the parent already has said no several times. "Why can't we make more popcorn?" "Why can't I have Sarah over to play?" "Why won't you read me one more story?"

I'm not talking about a single request but the same request repeated again and again in a complaining tone, despite an equal number of refusals by the parent. Most of the requests are quite natural, in the sense that they are for things or activities that all children enjoy. What is special about whiners is that they won't take no for an answer and that they appear to need the requested privilege or possession so desperately.

And I've noticed two other significant things about whining. Many whiners whine at only one parent, not both. (There are exceptions.) So whining often expresses not simply a habit or a mood in a child but also an attitude toward one parent or a slightly disturbed relationship with that parent.

Often, too, a parent who has two or more children will tolerate whining in only one. I remember once going sailing all day with a family in which the mother was a no-nonsense person with her three other children—they were polite, cooperative, independent, cheerful individuals—but the five-year-old girl bugged her mother all day, complaining of boredom, of hunger, of thirst, of being cold, when she herself could easily have found remedies for any or all of these small needs. The mother would ignore her for a while. Then she'd suggest that the girl get what she wanted. But she'd say it in an indecisive or apologetic tone, as if she felt guilty that she was not acting for the child. She'd never get masterful, even after an hour of steady whining that made me long to send the child to the cabin.

What is it that makes parents tolerate whining and bugging from one child but not from another? In many cases it appears that they feel guilty and submissive. Unconsciously, at least, they feel that the child has the right to keep making excessive demands, that they are guilty of something—of stinginess, perhaps, in not giving the child what she wants, or of not loving her enough, or of not knowing what a child is entitled to. At the same time it's apparent that such parents don't give in freely, as if eager to please the child; they do so grudgingly, as if feeling that they must.

There are various possible reasons for us parents to feel unconsciously guilty toward one child. We might not have been fully ready for the pregnancy, might have resented the unborn child.

Or the child may remind us of a sister or brother or parent who made life miserable for us during our childhood and aroused a great deal of both hostility and guilt in us, emotions that now determine our behavior.

It is also possible that we've got off on the wrong foot with a child who was, for instance, a fretful or very demanding baby.

Extremely conscientious parents who were brought up with a lot of criticism from *their* parents, and who as a result are easily made to feel inadequate, often begin child care with at least a mild sense of guilt about their lack of knowledge on the subject and with a fear that they'll do the wrong things.

Therefore it's often some kind of submissiveness or guiltiness that makes parents give in to unreasonable demands in the first place. But if the demands become more frequent and more insistent, the parents are increasingly inclined to resist—or at least to procrastinate or to argue back. If they could resist promptly, firmly, matter-of-factly, that would end the argument, because children always know when the parents really mean no. But the parents of whiners usually can't be that definite. They pretend not to hear the request at first, or their irritable tone of voice betrays their expectation of being defeated again. Children are experts in picking up these clues to uncertainty—and in acting on them.

After a while it's apparent that what has developed is a power struggle in which the child is using whining mainly to make the parent give in and the parent is trying to resist without feeling too guilty about it. The fact that it's really a battle of wills is shown by the way a child often keeps whining for something that she could easily get for herself or for something that she really doesn't want at all. She simply wants to make the parent—against the parent's will—read a story for the third time, run an errand, cook something, find something, buy something. And often the parent could easily grant the request but sensing that the child is playing a game of wills, instinctively resists giving in—but not sharply enough to end the conflict.

There are at least two good reasons why children want to exert some power or control over parents, aside from wanting the object or privilege they are asking for. The first is that most parents are regularly using parental power over their children in one form or another and there's a natural desire in children to turn the tables. The second is that parents who can't be definite and who have to put up with begging and bugging can't help but feel irritable and antagonistic toward their children, and this arouses an answering antagonism in the children.

What can you do if you have the problem of habitual whining? There are definite, practical steps you can take. But first you have to decide whether it is some attitude on your part that feeds the whining. You may be using some expression of evasiveness or hesitation or submissiveness or guilt, mixed with the inevitable irritability that comes from being a victim.

This is the most difficult step, because parents are usually quite unaware, quite unconscious, of any submissiveness. (They are apt to be much more aware of their impatience.) If you can't see any submission in your behavior, it may be well to consult a social worker in a family social agency who will help you analyze the cause of the whining and other factors in the family situation.

Though I've half-jokingly confessed my own irritation with whining in children, partly to show my sympathy with other par-

ents, I don't mean that a cranky or angry attitude is the right one—
far from it. For that reveals to the child that you have often been
frustrated by failure to hold your own before and you expect to be
frustrated again.

When parents have self-confidence about managing their children and are doing it effectively, they usually can show a *friendly
manner,* combined with clearness and firmness. The child is kept in
a cooperative mood by the friendliness, and the parent's definite-
ness gives the child the explicit guidance that's necessary for cooperative action.

Now for some illustrative examples.

If your child asks to be read or told just one more story when
you feel bored and tired with what you've done already, say cheerfully but definitely, "I'm tired now and I want to read my own book.
You can look at your picture books." After all, you have control of
this situation; if you act sure of your right, you child will soon
realize the futility of begging.

If your child whines that there is nothing to do, it's smarter not
to be drawn into suggesting a variety of possible activities, which
the child, when in this mood, will scornfully shoot down one by
one. And it's smarter not to explode with an indignant tirade about
spoiled children (which was my impulse as parent and grandparent), this being only a confession of frustration. You can toss the
responsibility back to the child, without getting bogged down in
futile argument, by saying, "Well, *I've* got lots of work to do, and
then I have a dozen pleasant things to do afterward, if there's time."
In other words, "Follow my example; find things to do for yourself.
Don't expect me to amuse you or argue with you."

If I were being regularly tortured by a whining child, I'd make as
many rules as necessary to cover all the usual pleas and then stick
to them with great determination. Bedtime is *always* to be a certain
hour, no matter what the plea. (And you should supervise this
rigidly until the child accepts it.) Only certain television programs
may be viewed. Friends may be invited to meals or to spend the
night only on a certain schedule. No special food, drink, or toy will
be bought for the child during ordinary market shopping.

At the end, I want to be sure that I am not misunderstood. I am
not saying that babies should not be picked up or that children
shouldn't be read to or have things bought for them in stores. I'm
writing here about the special problem of the chronic, continual
whiners who make themselves and their parents miserable. It is a

pattern of excessive demandingness and power playing. The pattern takes weeks and months to become fully established and quite a while to overcome.

Babies need to be picked up and held and carried when they are tired or sick or are just looking for some company and loving. In fact, careful observations have shown that babies not only need attention but also need to feel confident that they can *make* their parent give them the attention. When parents are inattentive because they are unloving or depressed, their babies become depressed too.

Children after infancy also need attention and the confidence that they can get attention. They need hugging and being read to. They need the clothes and playthings that are appropriate for the family's finances. It's right for them to be able to ask occasionally for a food that they particularly love and to be taken on some excursion that is particularly exciting.

So do give freely what your children ask for, as long as it is what you feel is their due and is what you want to give. But learn to protect yourself when the demands become incessant and petulant and when they leave you frustrated.

▷ ANXIETY ABOUT STARTING SCHOOL

The introduction of small children to school in September may create inner tensions, especially in those who've never gone to any kind of school before.

For children of three or four starting at a nursery school, a Montessori school, or a day-care center, the underlying stress comes from fear of being separated from their parents. This anxiety is quite prevalent at about two years of age, when it causes many bedtime problems. After that it tapers off. It causes school difficulties in only a small percentage of three- and four-year-olds. Such anxiety also may exist, though less frequently still, in those entering kindergarten and first grade.

The children who develop anxiety may be eager enough to go to school when they start out from home. But once they get to the school, the unfamiliarity of the scene, the teacher, and the other children may make them shrink back against their parent's legs rather than participate. And whether they have become involved in play or not, when the parent starts to say good-by they may cling tightly. If the parent tries to pull away, such children sometimes put on quite a scene.

Underneath the separation anxiety there may quickly develop another factor altogether—the impulse to use their anxiety as a means of controlling their parents. Children are being more or less continually controlled by their parents, of course, and this fosters the impulse in them to control. You can see this in the bossiness with which they talk to their dolls.

If they are frightened about separation and if they see that their parents feel intensely sympathetic, they sense they can use that sympathy to keep their parents from leaving them. As the weeks go by, sometimes an outsider can see that the anxiety is no longer a big factor but that the drive to control has become very strong indeed. The parents are less likely to recognize the child's controlling behavior because they are so sympathetic to the anxiety.

It's sensible for parents to consult the teacher ahead of time about the prevention of separation anxiety. The teacher probably has had considerable experience. It is even more important to work closely with the teacher if difficulty does develop, because the teacher can help the parent judge whether the child's desire to control is becoming a factor.

In order to minimize the chance of anxiety, some schools suggest that the child and parent visit school together once, twice, or more before the child is left there alone. Kindergartens and first grades in some localities ask children and parents to visit the classroom in late spring, while the previous class is still in session, so that children entering the following fall can get a clear and reassuring picture of what actually goes on.

If a child does begin to cling or cry when the parent starts to leave, in most cases the parent should take the cue from the teacher about whether to stay a while longer to see if the child will get so involved in play that she or he will not want to leave when the parent does or to walk away—after saying good-by—with as much calmness and assurance as the parent can muster.

The point here is that if the parent is so sympathetic as to show almost as much anxiety as the child does, this is a signal to the child that she or he is right to dread the separation. But if the parent acts quite sure that there is nothing to be afraid of, this reassures the child in the most convincing way. It won't work for the parent, in embarrassment, to get angry or agitated with the child; this has an upsetting rather than a reassuring effect.

It is a mistake for a parent to wait until the child is absorbed in play and then quietly disappear. An anxious child concludes from this experience that the parent can't be trusted. It is better for the parent to say good-by clearly, either at the door on arrival or after staying for a while.

If the mother has taken the child to school and the child has refused to let her leave, it's sensible to let the father try the escorting the next day. Since the majority of young children are more closely tied to their mothers, it's plausible that separation from her seems more threatening to them. I've been involved in separation problems in which it turned out that a child who clung to the mother was quite willing to separate from the father at school.

Usually after children have attended for several days they become so delighted with the joys of school that the fear of separation is erased. Then the child's parent, or the parent whose turn it is in the car pool, usually can manage the separation.

Occasionally a young child, most commonly one under four years—let's say it's a girl—takes well to school for several days and then, when hurt accidentally or on purpose, cries and wants her parent to comfort her. If the crying goes on for a long time, meaning not that the injury was so bad but that the child realizes how desperately she wants her parent, she may balk the next day about leaving home at all. I think the wisest course is for the parents to act as if *everybody* who starts school keeps going, no question about it, and to take the child by the hand breezily or pick her up. I wouldn't use force, however.

In general, it's the children who have been very close to highly conscientious, protective parents and who've had only limited experience with other adults and children who are apt to have separation anxieties. Naturally too, it's more often first children, because they're usually closer to their parents and haven't had other children at home to play with.

The most fundamental way to prevent separation anxiety at three or at five years is to get a child used to outsiders from infancy—grown-up outsiders and little outsiders, acquaintances and care givers. This familiarization is twice as important for a first child as for subsequent children.

From the age of three months it's good for babies to see visitors regularly in the home, to go to market, and to visit family friends. I like the way young parents now carry babies on their backs or chests when hiking, going to dinner at a friend's house, or wherever else they go.

As soon as children can walk they should be outdoors where other young children play part of every day, so that they can get used to the shouting, the grabbing, and the rough-and-tumble. They should be rescued only if they are being persecuted persistently by a mean child, but this happens rarely. Of course, a parent has to be in attendance until a child learns to stay out of the street.

If there is no public park, playground, neighborhood gathering place, or hospitable neighbor's backyard and you live in a private house, you can equip your own yard with swing, seesaw, and sandbox. That will make it a magnet for neighborhood children.

Independence in children is fostered partly by their getting used to other adults and children, partly by their being encouraged to follow their own pursuits, and partly by the parents' not being overprotective.

I remember a staff conference in a well-baby clinic that involved a two-year-old who screamed with terror from the time she got in sight of the clinic and who fought so violently against it that the examination was really worthless. The mother was an anxious recluse who clung to the child as much as the child clung to her. This is an extreme case. But it is natural for a few highly conscientious parents to be on the overprotective side, tending to worry about the risk to their children from diseases, accidents, getting lost, and being picked on by mean bullies. Children are acutely sensitive, especially when they are young, to the anxieties of their parents.

Of course, there are other parents at the opposite end of the scale who are so careless that their small children easily get hold of poisons, play in the street, and are allowed to stand on the seats of automobiles. So you have to strike what's called a happy medium (really a slightly worrisome medium) that means you have to take some risks—but not crazy ones.

By first and second grade there is another kind of anxiety in some children that causes problems at the beginning of school in September. I became aware of this problem when I was physician for an hour each morning at a private school for girls. Every fall there would be one or two girls, most commonly in second grade, who vomited on the way to school or—even more embarrassing— on arrival there. A commoner and milder form of this tension makes children unable to eat breakfast on school days.

These disturbances occur in children who are unusually conscientious. I think they are caused by a child's awe of the new teacher and the class—in other words, the fear of not measuring up to the expectations of outsiders. The difficulties may last for a few days or for weeks, depending partly on how they are handled.

My interpretation is that children of six, seven, and eight are making a crucial inner transition from being homebodies closely attached to their parents (even though they may have been to nursery school and kindergarten) to being semi-independent beings who are shifting their focus to the outside world, particularly the world of their contemporaries. This is the age when they stop aping their parents and want instead to look like, speak like, act like, their classmates. They stop playing house and get interested in the three Rs and science.

So fitting into the school scene—suiting the new teacher and the other pupils—may become such a serious challenge for those brought up with high standards that their stomachs are tied in knots.

There are several positive approaches to the problem. The first is to let the child who is temporarily robbed of appetite go to school without any breakfast at all. Pressure by the parents to "eat something so you won't go to school on an empty stomach" (as if an empty stomach might cause collapse) only puts the child between *two* grindstones. The parent can also confess that she or he has always been nervous about starting in a new school or job, not only as a child but as an adult too. This is apt to come as a surprise and as a comfort.

Another approach is for the parent to speak to the teacher about this evidence of tension so that the teacher can look for opportunities to be friendly, personal, approving—to counteract the authoritarian, judgmental image of the teacher that so many children have.

The good thing about the school problems I've been describing is that though they may be troublesome, they don't indicate any deep disturbance and they usually are soon over.

CHAPTER TEN

Influencing Personality and Attitudes

▷ CURIOSITY, IMAGINATION, AND CREATIVITY

Curiosity, imagination, and creativity in children make a powerful three-part force that constantly pulls them upward to new
levels of maturity. This will show up in their schoolwork, in their
future jobs, and in their lives generally.

In infancy, curiosity comes first. It is eager and inexhaustible. It
can be seen in the fixed gaze that two-, three-, and four-month-old
babies direct at an object, say a toy or mobile hung above the crib.
It is shown in the stirring of the baby's still-inexpert arms as she
feels the impulse to reach out and touch the object, though she has
nowhere near the skill needed to accomplish this yet.

From the middle of the first year, curiosity extends from eye to
hand. Objects are turned over and over, banged experimentally
against the furniture, brought to the mouth for tasting. The constant tasting reminds us that most other animals have to do all their
exploring with nose and mouth. How frustrating this seems to us!

In the second year, as crawling and walking make it possible,
curiosity drives children to endless explorations of places like cupboards, drawers, and closets. They test bodily skills by climbing up
stairs and onto furniture, by pushing and pulling everything that's
not nailed down, by experimenting with containers as they set out
to find if small containers will fit into large ones and if large ones
will fit into small ones. The answer to the latter seems obvious to
adults, but the child has to try it again and again.

We harassed parents call this all-day exploration "getting into
everything," and our impatient tone implies that this is a nuisance.
But we can see that all this is very, very serious business to the
child. She is striving to master her world and to grow up. The fact
that each baby goes through the same stages of exploration—pushing objects for months before thinking of pulling, climbing stairs
long before trying to descend, emptying drawers and then filling
them—shows that there is an orderly and elaborate pattern of instincts unfolding, a pattern that has developed over millions of
years in the evolution of our species and that has proved efficient
in finally producing maturity in the individual.

Of course, curiosity for the purpose of useful learning continues
to drive the child all through childhood—and through adulthood
too, though it gets less feverish with age. There is curiosity about
one's body, about animals and bugs, about the origin of babies,

about death, the meaning of rain and thunder, the workings of machines, the mysteries of the three Rs. In adolescence and youth there's a new and more intense wave of curiosity about sex, romance, one's emotions, and the workings of one's body.

Some parents have no idea of the importance and value of curiosity. When their one-year-old looks at magazines and then deliberately tears them, or pushes a chair around, they shout or slap. When their three-year-old asks "too many questions," they demand silence. They do not realize that if you consistently stop exploration and questioning, if you fail to provide things to play with (and they can be very simple things, such as pots and stirring spoons), this will eventually inhibit not only the child's curiosity but also her intellectual and emotional growth.

This doesn't mean that parents ought not interfere at all in their child's explorations. Old magazines can be substituted for new ones, an empty carton substituted for the chair that the child is pushing around. If your three-year-old has got into the habit of absentmindedly repeating the same question and not listening to the answer (which sometimes means that the child is preoccupied with another, more troubling question, such as the meaning of bodily sex differences, but doesn't quite dare ask), you don't have to go on repeating the same answer. You can cheerfully call attention to what's happening and ask if the child really wants to ask something else.

Imagination grows out of curiosity and experiences and is feverishly active in childhood, especially in the three-to-six-year stage. After receiving an answer to her first question about death, the child of three can be seen mulling over this disturbing information; then she is apt to ask, "Do I have to die?" One of my sons at that age was looking at a picture in a magazine of a head protruding from an iron lung and asked, with some anxiety, what it meant. I tried to be casual in explaining that the man had had polio and couldn't breathe by himself, so the machine did it for him. Suddenly my son put his hand to his chest and cried, "I can't breathe!" His distress lasted only a few seconds, but it showed how quickly and intensely his imagination and his capacity to identify had put him in the other person's situation.

But imagination isn't all morbid. Read a small child a story and she interrupts to ask dozens of eager questions that show her mind is racing ahead of the story and off to one side or another, like a dog on a walk through the woods. She is putting herself into the story, putting her feelings in, and seeing all kinds of angles and possibilities that aren't in the story as it is written. If you get into the habit of making up stories for your child, she may decide to tell stories to you.

Young children love stories about animals even more than stories about children. One reason, I think, is that they can cut loose from all the limitations and rules of their own civilized lives and from the control of their parents. They can dream of running free in the forest, living in a hollow tree, flying with the birds, living with creatures who don't scold or make you wash your hands before supper.

This desire for escape from control and disapproval shows up in the imaginary companions that a few children, usually only children, invent and talk about constantly for months. One of the needs in such a situation is obviously companionship. But it is clear in addition that in most cases the imaginary friend is doing—and getting away with—all the naughty but delightful things the real child is too well disciplined to try. If this seems to be the case, it's a signal to parents to ease up a bit in the expression of disapproval and to joke with the child in a sympathetic spirit about how she too would like to do the things her imaginary friend does.

Then there are the imaginary adventures children enjoy on their own, without an unreal companion. What do you do when a four-year-old child with a rich imagination comes home and spins elaborate stories of adventures that can't be true but are told as if they really are? On the one hand you don't want to squelch the child's imagination or make a federal case out of a good story. On the other hand you don't want her—or at least I didn't want my children—regularly losing track of the difference between fact and fiction or thinking that their parents can't tell the difference. A sensible compromise is to say with friendly admiration, "You are a wonderful storyteller. Someday you can write storybooks for children."

But I've been focusing too much on the unusual kinds of imagination. The commonest and most constructive manifestations are in the all-day, everyday kinds of play that preschool children engage in. They "play house," which means to play family. The pretend-father imitates the daily activities and attitudes of his real father. The pretend-mother is inspired to copy the schedule of her mother, whether it means going out to work or staying at home for a while and then going to market. A boy spends hours constructing part of a town out of blocks and then driving a miniature car or truck in and out of garages and through the streets, perhaps getting involved in a traffic accident. A girl and a boy prepare an elaborate meal in a play kitchen.

As they grow into the school years, children's thoughts and their play shift away from family dramas. They get absorbed in nature and science and technology. They dream of creating inventions and carrying out heroic deeds. In adolescence and youth the dreams shift again—to romance and to great but more realistic achievements.

The main point I want to make is that imagination is not just an amusing and unimportant aspect of childhood. It is a powerful stimulus to the development of maturity. It encourages children to see all the meanings in their daily experiences and to explore new ground. Each new idea is the starting point for further ideas. There is a constant enrichment of life from within, with each step leading to more-enriching experience in the outside world. So imagination broadens life, makes it more exciting, hastens growing up, enables the individual to go further in his field.

Imagination should certainly be fostered. Most basic to this is a loving family. But there are other, more specific things parents can do. One is to be genuinely interested in their children's questions, to give them satisfying answers, to make their children feel that there are no taboos regarding curiosity and learning and dreaming. Another intense stimulus to imagination is reading to children. Reading isn't done nearly as much as it could be and used to be. Nowadays television often takes the place of reading. Programs that widen children's awareness are wonderful, but these are few and far between. Even if there were more good shows, I don't think it is good for children to sit for many hours watching television. Especially with all the brutality. It is too passive an occupation. Parents have to limit the watching so that children have more time to develop their own imagination and to carry it into active play.

Imagination and creativity are close; they overlap. Imagination is where ideas come from. Creativity makes the end product possible.

There are parents, in these fiercely competitive days, who believe that the most valuable contribution a nursery school, Montessori school, or day-care center makes to children is in the specific skills they learn—skills such as buttoning buttons, tying shoelaces, using a pencil, recognizing their numbers and the letters of the alphabet. Learning such skills is fascinating to children and is helpful in their gradual approach to formal schooling, provided they aren't pushed too hard and far but are going at their own pace. But more valuable still, I feel, are the spontaneous dramatic games that children invent themselves—about family situations, illness and health care, trips, animals. These activities help children to learn cooperation, to understand and to digest their daily experiences, to overcome life's inevitable anxieties and frustrations (for example, to outgrow fear of the doctor by playing doctor), to learn how to be parents someday. I believe that more is learned between the ages of three and six about being a parent than at any other time or in any other way, at least until actual parenthood is reached.

Other valuable activities for young children are painting their own pictures, modeling with clay, marching and dancing, making music with a rhythm band. These activities free the feelings, broaden the meaning and the richness of life—in childhood and for the rest of life. But creativity is not limited to the fine arts. In the school years its function is plain in the building of a model plane or a table, in designing and making clothes, in putting out a school paper or yearbook. In these ways children learn to take initiative and to trust themselves.

What I have been leading up to is this: the adults who lead creative lives in their jobs, in their hobbies, or in their interests—the people who write, who design clothes or industrial products, who paint, who sculpt, work at crafts, invent, who compose or play music, who act, dance, write advertisements, who are architects and landscape designers, who produce and direct plays and television programs, who are writers and editors—all these must have been imaginative and creative in childhood too. In fact, you can include scientists and executives and people in many other occupations that are not necessarily thought of as creative, since in order to make a more-than-routine contribution in almost any field you must have the capacity and the eagerness to see beyond your nose and to branch out into new territory.

So it is well for parents whose one-year-olds are "nuisances" to remember that their constant explorations represent hard work toward developing their potentials as adults, and that parents can support their efforts by giving them simple things to play with. reasonable toleration, some time, help, and appreciation.

▷ FOSTERING SOCIABILITY

It's possible for children to grow up to be socially well adjusted without ever having had much chance for friendships with other children, but I wouldn't recommend this as the best way.

I've known quite a few children who had no play experience—except with their accommodating parents—until they were two, three, or four years old. But in their first experiences with children their own age they were frightened, or at least put off, by the way the other children behaved, coming up to them abruptly, not bothering to smile or say anything polite, perhaps grabbing a toy to try it out, often turning noisy and rough in play. Children encountered for the first time can seem as strange and dangerous to inexperienced children as gorillas would to us grown-ups.

I'll always remember a girl of sixteen, an only child, who had been raised on a remote estate in Switzerland and who, instead of going to school, had been taught by tutors. When she and her family moved to New York, they lived in a hotel on busy Madison Avenue, and she began to attend a good but noisy school. Within a few days she was weeping with nervous fatigue. She made an adjustment to the sound and confusion after a while. More slowly she made friends with a couple of the quietest girls in her class.

Parents should begin by recognizing that every child is born with his or her own unique personality, and some children are more ready for sociability than others. One child may be distinctly outgoing, energetic, capable of withstanding social bumps and physical bruises. At the opposite extreme is the cautious, quiet, sensitive individual whose feelings are easily hurt and who responds by pulling back into a shell. As a parent you can't turn one into the other.

Another influence on sociability is birth order: many firstborn children are less sociable than average. (I have special sympathy for them because I am an eldest child myself.) First children model themselves exclusively on their parents because there are no older brothers or sisters to copy. As a result firstborns tend to be more serious-minded, more mature, more self-conscious than second and third children. They try harder and may be less playful, so sociability does not come as easily. This is as or more true for only children.

When a first child, let's say it's a girl, just begins to be around other children, sometime after the age of two or three, she is not prepared for their noisiness, their roughness in play, their tendency to grab. They scare her, make her shrink back. She's used to the politeness and considerateness of her parents and their friends and may feel at least a little suspicious and resentful of other children.

But there are compensations for first children and their parents. Oldest children are more likely to be good students. They are more likely to go into the "helping professions"—teaching, nursing, social work, or medicine. And the people listed in *Who's Who* are disproportionately first children.

A second child, of one, two, or three years is more apt to be left to his own occupations much of the time, but when, being human, he wants company, he toddles over to his mother. He makes the first greeting and has the real gratification of *evoking* a response. When he wants to be read to, he fetches the book and asks. When he wants his sister or brother to play with him, he may suggest it. These initiatives are part of learning how to make friends.

How fast a child without much experience can get over the strangeness of other children and go on to the pleasures of companionship will depend partly on what kind of relationship he has had with his parents. If it has been one of enjoyable give-and-take, he will eventually find the way to establish the same kind of relationship with contemporaries. But if his parents have kept him in the center of the stage or have kowtowed to him, it will take him a longer time to find out how to have fun with others on a democratic, mutual basis.

Generally it's easier for a child to learn friendliness in the earliest years. If he gets the knack at the start, when he is least self-conscious and learns the fun of mutual exchange, then he increases his skill and his self-confidence with each subsequent acquaintance. But if he makes a slow or poor start and feels rebuffed, he comes to anticipate unfriendliness. As he is subsequently thrown into contact with others, he has a chip on his shoulder—or at least a scowl on his face—which provokes the very unfriendliness he fears. Each social failure subtracts from his self-assurance and increases his bristliness.

Learning friendliness does not really mean learning a set of rules from one's parents like, "Be polite to your friends," "Share your toys," "Do what your visitor wants to do, not what you want to do," though parents often do have to give such reminders.

Friendliness is basically a love of other people, an enjoyment of them, and a spontaneous desire to please them. It comes most fundamentally from the fact that we are social beings, ready to love company if things go right in our development.

The development of our sociability has to be given a good head start by our having parents who are delighted with us in infancy, who smile at us, hug us, talk baby talk to us. Then, after the age of one or two, the warmth engendered in us by our parents turns increasingly outward to other people—adults and children.

At one year, you will notice, a baby observes a stranger for quite a few minutes at first. Then if the stranger has shown quiet friendliness—by smiling, not by rushing up to him and talking a blue streak—the child gradually will approach the stranger. He may hold out a toy, not to relinquish, but to serve as a sign of friendship.

At two years a child enjoys playing alongside another child and perhaps doing the same things; this is parallel play, so-called, not cooperative play. By about three years, loving children begin to find the fun of playing together—acting as husband and wife or bus driver and passenger. One pulls the wagon and the other rides, and they take turns. Of course, a parent or teacher has to make suggestions from time to time, but the readiness for cooperative play is in the child.

By the age of six or eight, children are able and prefer to be away from adults for most of their sociable play, so that they can prove to themselves their ability to function independently and in a grown-up way.

But this is also the age when they tend to be clannish and intolerant. In trying to find their own standards they naturally flock with those who have been brought up with similar outlooks and tastes, and they look down critically on those who are not just like them. Because of this intolerance, the child who seems "different" or the child who has never caught the knack of submerging himself easily in a group is apt to find the period between six and twelve rather painful.

Adolescents are not much more tolerant either. Most of them are almost slavish in their conformity to their own group styles and customs and scornful of nonconformers. There is such a need at this age for intense emotional attachments, however—both with those of the same sex and with those of the opposite sex—that the child who is not expertly sociable or who has an unusual personality or unusual tastes tries particularly hard to find, to win, and to hold the friendship of one or two kindred souls.

There are several ways, I think, in which infants and small children can be delayed in the development of their friendliness. They may not get the ideal balance in the various kinds of attention their parents give them, or they may not get a good balance between adult and child companionship.

One example—and a rare one—is when the parents simply aren't very outgoing. They don't hug, they don't smile, they don't talk to the baby. This is not because they aren't devoted to him; they've just been brought up to be reserved and solemn. But a baby needs an *obvious* show of affection, and I don't mean boisterous attention or tickling that makes him hysterical.

Another general type of imbalance that's rather common with a first baby occurs when the parents fuss over him a great deal in one way or another. Then he becomes too self-centered, at the expense of his outgoingness. For instance, the parents may hover in an anxious spirit, worrying constantly that he will hurt himself. ("No, no! Don't climb on the chair. You may fall down." "Don't put the stick in your mouth. It's dirty and will make you sick.") Even a baby detects parental concern and adopts some of it himself. He's always thinking of his body or his safety instead of how to have fun with others.

Or his parents may boss him every minute. ("Mustn't touch." "Don't hold your spoon that way." "Hurry up and eat your meal." "Say *ta ta.* ")This bossing is apt to be a reflection of the fact that the parents themselves were prodded and corrected all through their own childhood. They developed a fundamental assumption that a child can be civilized only by constant nagging. This impairs his enjoyment of his parents and makes him somewhat antagonistic to them. As he grows a little older he develops the same bristly feelings toward others.

In another case the parents' pride in their firstborn, which is very natural, takes the form of showing him off constantly whenever there is any company around. ("Where is your nose?" "Tell Charlie your name." "Dance for Mr. Summers.") So the child comes to think of people not in terms of their being fun to do things *with* but as an applauding audience. When he becomes old enough to be with other children, he may not go forward to engage them in play but waits passively for their adulation. When it's not forthcoming his feelings are hurt.

Or the parents are so aware of their child and so delighted to pass the time of day with him that they always give the first greeting, always speak cordially no matter how grumpy he is, always make up new games to play with him. He's the prince; they are his servitors. He never has a chance to take the initiative or feels the need to be the charming person. There is nothing to stimulate and develop his outgoingness.

Of course, I'm not saying that parents shouldn't warn their small child of dangers that are really imminent or correct him when he's out of line or show him off occasionally. They'd be strange parents if they didn't do all these things sometimes. It's the constant fussing that I'm advising against.

And I'm certainly not suggesting that parents be cool or distant. The warmer, the better. I'm only suggesting that they go about their own business three quarters of the time and leave the initiative to the child. Of course, they occasionally should take the initiative.

From the time your child is an infant until he reaches school age, and especially when he first begins to walk, it's a good idea to take him, several times each week, to where other children play—to a playground or to a friend's backyard.

Don't interfere right away when he gets pushed or hit or temporarily robbed of a toy. Don't sympathize too easily with his hurt feelings, for this gives him the idea that he has been grievously injured or wronged. Let him find out that a little roughness is not fatal. Let him learn all by himself how to meet push with push or how to hang on to a toy when another child is trying to grab it. In other words, a child gets his basic feelings about the meaning of the aggressiveness of other children from his parents. If his parents consider it dangerous or cruel, he is frightened by it. If they take it casually, he learns to do the same.

Of course, you can't let your child be seriously injured or regularly intimidated by an unusually aggressive playmate. If the problem arises only occasionally, you can casually move in between bully and victim, which ordinarily will stop the attack. If it happens constantly, you'll have to take your child somewhere else to play, at least for a few months.

If your child is always the aggressor, you'll need some counseling from a family social agency or a child guidance clinic.

By the time a child is three years old, he should be able to profit from a good nursery school or day-care center. There he will learn to develop his bodily skills, his creativity, and his intellectual awareness as well as his sociability. The experience of school is particularly valuable for a first child, an only child, a child who lives far from other children, and a child whose parents find him frustrating to be with constantly. (In the last case the teachers should also be able to help the parents find a more comfortable relationship.)

If you have a backyard, you can install equipment in it—a swing, a seesaw, a sandbox—so that children will congregate there. If they need more luring, serve juice and crackers at mid-morning and mid-afternoon.

If your child is of school age and is still bashful or timid or unpopular, you can bribe other children to give him special consideration, to a degree, by inviting them, one at a time, to meals or to go on special excursions—on a picnic, to a zoo or museum, to visit a farm, a dairy, a factory. You can't make an obnoxious child popular with bribes. But you can ensure that your child's good qualities will be given fair consideration, rather than having him be thoughtlessly ignored just because he's a little bit different.

For a few parents the problem seems to be not how to attract other children to their child but how to break up a friendship that seems undesirable. There is, for instance, the friend who has offensive bad manners or who is always in trouble with the neighbors or who lies or steals or persistently seduces others into sex play despite firm requests to stop. If the problem is one of morals that seriously worry the parents, they will have to interfere. But if it's only a matter of the parents' tastes and preferences, I think they should be very hesitant about revealing their dislike.

If one child craves the company of another, this need has some real significance whether or not the parents can figure it out or approve. They should respect it for the time being and observe the effect of the relationship on each of the pair. If it seems to have no bad effect on their own child, they should be tolerant. Perhaps he will outgrow the friendship. (Some of the most intense relationships are short-lived.) If they believe their own child is being affected unfavorably, I'd suggest that they consult the school principal or teacher or a family social agency to get a more detached and professional opinion before interfering.

Friendship is not simply one of the pleasures of life, like ice cream or swimming. It's an absolutely indispensable ingredient of existence for ninety-nine out of a hundred people, whether they are skillful or clumsy in seeking it. Friendship is as important as food, health, shelter, sex. So it's sensible to cultivate the capacity in your child at the age when it is easily acquired.

▷ EXPRESSING ANGER

One of the healthiest trends in child rearing in recent decades has been the willingness of parents to discuss their children's resentful feelings toward them.

In the family in which I grew up, in the first quarter of the century, any such thing would have been intolerable, even unthinkable. By the time we became adolescents, my sisters and brother and I knew that we were often angry at our mother, who seemed to us unreasonably moralistic and arbitrary in her judgments and stern in her punishments. She never in her life, as far as we knew, admitted she was wrong or changed her mind.

We couldn't criticize her decisions or say we felt angry. We couldn't mutter under our breath or dart resentful glances or even argue persistently because she would interpret all these as signs of insubordination and would inflict rather severe penalties. (I can still remember being told at the age of seventeen, on the third day of Christmas vacation, that I couldn't go to any of the ten remaining parties because of minor disobedience. That seemed at the time the cruelest blow in my whole life.)

But in our early childhood years, though we must have felt extremely frustrated and oppressed at times, we also must have drastically suppressed our anger. This I realized only later in my professional training and experience, for a small child whose parents are severe does not dare show his resentment openly; furthermore, he does not dare allow himself even to feel it. He fears unconsciously that if he enrages his parents by defiance, they will either attack him or desert him, and he can't afford either.

(I should add quickly that our mother was also intensely devoted to her family, generous when in an approving mood, and one of the funniest mimics and storytellers I've heard, off or on the stage. She almost never used physical punishment—but, of course, she didn't need to. She herself had been reared with what we would call today a truly harsh discipline—though she and her sisters and brother also were well loved. My mother considered her treatment of us lenient by comparison.)

The intimidation my mother brought about in me in early childhood and the deeply ingrained habit of hiding my feelings from myself as well as from others has often interfered to a degree with my development of candid relationships with other people, even in adulthood. It also made me pass on a pattern of denial of feelings to my children.

When we habitually hide our feelings, we not only accumulate tensions and conflicts within ourselves; we make other people uneasy as well. They don't know what to make of us. They misinterpret our words and actions. Then their mistaken responses surprise and upset us. The further such misunderstandings go, the harder it is for those who hide their feelings to get back on the right track.

There are much better human relationships of all sorts—in business, in marriage, in friendship—when people can acknowledge their own feelings, recognize the feelings of others (these are two sides of the same coin), and allow these aspects of their relationships to come into the open, not just when misunderstandings threaten but all the time.

There is considerable variation in the amount of anger different children feel toward their parents, depending mainly on how tactful and sensible the parents have been in their general management. But there is no such thing as a child without some resentment at times. And there is no point at all in parents' trying to raise their children so sweetly and reasonably that no conflicts develop. The children will only test the limits until the parents can't help exploding.

Parents, to carry out their basic responsibilities, must keep their children from harming themselves and other people and things. They must teach consideration. They have to inculcate standards and aspirations. They must show their children that immediate gratification often has to be sacrificed for the sake of long-term goals.

The guidance in such matters doesn't have to be heavy-handed. Children—most of the time—try to be like the parents they love and admire, so they are willing and eager to do three quarters of the work of conforming. But as all parents know, young children are inexperienced, impatient, and impulsive. They have to be frequently told, "We must hold hands when we cross the street," and, "We hang up our coats when we take them off." "We put away our toys in the big box."

This kind of routine curbing and exhorting is bound to make a child slightly resentful. And when the parents on occasion become really angry and severe, the child's negative feelings will be correspondingly intense.

In addition to the open, conscious conflicts between parent and

child, there are the subtle ones way below the surface that Freud
discovered through psychoanalysis. They come particularly from
the rivalry that a son feels with his father and that a girl feels with
her mother. These feelings are so far from consciousness by the
time we reach adulthood that we never think of them; but psychoanalysts have always been impressed by the indirect evidence of
how bitter they are, even in children who on the surface are getting
along smoothly with their parents.

In previous centuries, when it was taken for granted that all
children were born savages and could be civilized only by relentless
parental vigilance and pressure, it was assumed that any disapproved behavior—whether it was hostility or sexual curiosity or
merely thumb sucking—must simply be squelched as vigorously as
necessary, by scolding or punishment.

Then Freud and other psychoanalysts and psychologists made
fundamental discoveries about hostile feelings. They are universal,
occurring even in the "nicest" people. It's not the curbing of a
child's aggressiveness that mainly civilizes him, but his love and
admiration for his parents. When parents are excessively strict and
disapproving, a small child may become anxious and also guilty
about his hostile thoughts. He fears not only that they may bring
harm to him but also that they may take some active form and
bring harm to his parents. (Magical thinking is common in childhood.)

Fear and guilt make such a child suppress his antagonistic feelings. He may end up a somewhat submissive person, or he may
develop neurotic symptoms such as compulsions or phobias that
can be disguised expressions of hostile feelings coated with guilt.

Child therapists have treated children for such symptoms by
getting involved in dramatic play with them. After the child has
developed trust in the therapist, he may show in his play how afraid
he is to admit any hostile feelings. These feelings—including antagonism toward the therapist—move closer to the surface.

As I have noted in the early days of child guidance, psychiatrists
allowed or even encouraged a child to actually take out his emerging feelings against the therapist by hitting him or abusing him
verbally or by damaging the office and its contents.

But experience showed that it is not advisable to allow a child to
carry his angry feelings into action. A child knows in his bones that
it is not right to abuse anyone. To do so gives him a *new* source of
guilt. And it frightens him to be in the care—at home, at school, or

in a clinic—of an adult who will allow him to go berserk. He may behave more and more provocatively to force the adult to get him back under control.

We all count on others, as well as on our own self-control, to keep us in line. And a child, because his self-control is less well established, senses that he has a greater need to be restrained by adults.

Further experience in child guidance clinics showed that excessive inhibition of feelings—especially hostile feelings—can be overcome successfully by just talking about them instead of carrying them into action. The therapist, seeing from the child's play or facial expression or grumpiness that he is angry, explains, in effect, "I think you are mad at me because I won't let you take the toy home (or go out in the hall or play with my pen). But you are afraid to say it because you think I might get angry with you and punish you or hurt you. I know that all children feel mad at grown-ups sometimes. I won't be angry if you do."

In talking this way—it's done in small installments—the therapist shows that he doesn't reject the child or consider him evil because of his angry feelings, that he considers talking about negative feelings quite proper and helpful.

Much the same approach may be used in a more casual and occasional way by all parents from their child's early years onward. When you have to interrupt the play of your three-year-old you can say quite sincerely, "I know it makes you mad at me when I do this." When your eight-year-old is furious because you insist he make his bed before running out to join his pal, you can say— sympathetically, not tauntingly—that you know how he feels.

When you are acknowledging a child's anger, don't in the same breath excuse yourself by explaining why you had to frustrate him. That turns the whole direction of the discussion away from a recognition of the legitimacy of *his* feelings, which should be your purpose, into a justification for *your* actions. This seems to him to be saying, "You don't have a right to be resentful because I have a higher right to control you."

The first step, to do any good, should simply give him a moment to feel your nonresentful recognition of his anger. Then if he wants to go on to ask reproachfully why you had to frustrate him in the first place, you will naturally discuss with him your legitimate reason. But this, if you can manage it, should not be given in an indignant or accusatory tone, for that tends to bring back his original anger. You should explain yourself as calmly as possible in order not to shatter your understanding attitude.

The helpful recognition of a child's emotions need not only apply to angry feelings. There are other emotions considered "negative," such as jealousy of a brother or sister: "I know how it burns you up when people pay so much attention to Linda."

There are other feelings not considered evil but that may cause shame or embarrassment in a child: "I think you are afraid of the dark, just as I used to be." Or sorrow: "You still miss your puppy." Or sexual desires: "I see you want to touch Mommy's breasts. All boys have feelings like that. But mothers don't let their boys do that because they want their breasts to be private," or however you want to explain your normal inhibitions.

By calling attention to children's feelings that a parent can acknowledge, I don't want to imply that a parent should watch a child all day and comment on every passing emotion. Parent and child would become unhealthily obsessed. These acknowledgments need to be communicated only occasionally, when it is evident that the child is in inner conflict.

It's also important for me to add that the parent needn't be and shouldn't be submissive and masochistic in attitude when calling attention to the child's anger, as if the parent were saying, "I know that I am an inadequate parent and that I deserve your resentment." It's not that the parent is a bad parent and deserves censure from the child. It's that good parents, in carrying out their responsibilities, have to impose restrictions and obligations. And normal "good" children are bound to be angry. But nobody is a bad person.

Inevitably a parent makes mistakes, as when, for example, he wrongly accuses a child or wrongly punishes him. Then there is good reason for the parent to admit his error and apologize. But even in this act the parent does not have to grovel. He is apologizing only because he was mistaken; he can still keep his self-respect.

I've added these cautions at the end to be sure that parents use these interpretations in order to increase mutual understanding and respect, not to establish an uneasy relationship in which the child is always the righteous accuser and the parent is always on the defensive as the wrongdoer.

▷ TEACHING CHILDREN THE IDEALISM OF SEX AND MARRIAGE

In the twentieth century there has been a tremendous shift in attitude regarding sexual matters, a shift away from shame and guilt. Psychologists, child psychiatrists, and educators have urged parents to overcome their uneasiness, to answer children's natural questions, and to get into discussions. These influences have made it considerably easier for the average parent to respond and converse. But it's foolish for professionals to give parents the idea that it's really easy to talk with children—particularly with adolescents —about these topics.

Most parents, even in these emancipated days, find themselves just a little bit surprised when the first question is popped, at two and a half or three, about physical differences between the sexes or the origin of babies. The question never comes in the expected form or place or time. And many adolescents (oftenest boys) are so self-conscious about their sexual changes and feelings that they further embarrass the parent, who is trying to explain, by claiming nervously that they know it all already. (That was what both my sons said.) However, if you are the exceptional parent and are not at all fussed by such a discussion, so much the better. On the average, mother-daughter discussions go easier.

Children between the ages of two and a half and six make the parents' educational job easy by their intense curiosity and their lack of self consciousness. They will sap up any information—or misinformation.

In this period—between two and a half and six years—there are several dramatic steps in the development of children's feelings and ideas about sexuality in the broadest sense. These are all interrelated. Together they make sexuality in the human being a *much* more complex and powerful and spiritual influence than it is in any other creature.

Most children discover the physical differences in the two-to-three year period if they have the opportunity. They are apt to worry because both girl and boy are likely to assume that a girl has somehow been denied or deprived of a penis and that the same fate might happen to the boy.

Between three and four, children want to know where babies come from and they want one to care for.

Boys, when they are told that only girls can grow babies in their abdomens, may insist that boys can do it too—they are unwilling to give up such an exciting privilege. Girls may show, in play or words, a wish for a penis.

But there are other emotional factors—pleasurable and worrisome—that complicate children's lives at three and four years. Most of them develop intensely adoring feelings toward the parent of the opposite sex. They "overestimate" the parent's qualities, as it's said. A boy will say matter-of-factly, "I'm going to marry Mommy when I grow up." A girl may say the same about her father. This adoration plays a large part in forming the romantic ideal that will guide the individual later in falling in love and in marrying.

Boys and girls want to play at being married, like their parents, and grow babies. They are apt to get involved in sex play, or doctor play, which expresses not only sexual feeling but also great curiosity about the genitals.

But gradually children come to realize, in the five-and-six-year-old stage that since the parents are already married, no additional marriages are possible. This leaves the boy and girl feeling left out, rivalrous, and resentful at times, at the unconscious level, as is revealed in the psychoanalysis of children and adults. At the conscious, everyday level, however, children go on being sensible, cooperative, affectionate people. Or they may become somewhat grumpy or uppity at times.

Psychoanalysis of children (and of adults) has also shown that when children feel angry and mean toward parents, they assume that the parents read their minds and feel equally mean toward them. So when a boy feels resentful toward his father for already possessing his mother, he assumes that his father is angry at him for wanting her for himself. In the same way a girl of five or six who feels rivalrous and resentful toward her mother assumes that her mother responds with rivalry toward her.

Despite the increasingly rivalrous feelings toward the parent of the same sex, boys admire and identify strongly with their fathers and girls with their mothers. This is how they set their ideals for what kind of people they want to be when they grow up.

Another factor that heightens the rivalry of a son with his father, which psychoanalysis of the unconscious has shown, is resentment that his father's penis is so much larger than his. (I saw this very clearly in one of my sons.) He feels, at times, like injuring it. He assumes that his father would like to retaliate by injuring *his* penis.

He gets the idea that this is a possibility from seeing girls without penises.

So this whole complex of interrelated ideas and feelings makes the boy increasingly anxious. In girls, the negative feeling is predominantly resentment over past deprivation more than fear of future injury. These concerns are one of the causes of bad dreams at six and seven years. And what children do when worried in such a way is to push the whole business out of their conscious awareness, into their unconscious minds, where it stews and sometimes causes neurotic symptoms such as phobias that don't make any logical sense.

Because of these anxieties in very young children, because their imaginations are frequently morbid, and because they hear bits and pieces of information and misinformation, their ideas about sexual matters become jumbled and contradictory even when the parents are excellent teachers. Long after they've heard the correct biological facts, they slip back into theories about storks and doctor's bags. So don't be surprised.

Incidentally you don't have to accept these findings derived from Freud if they strike you as preposterous. I include them because I was convinced during my own training and practice and because I think they help to explain children's behavior.

Between six and twelve years, because of the anxiety about rivalry with the parent of the same sex, children try to suppress much of the interest in sex, in marriage, and in having babies. They turn with relief to less personal, more abstract matters such as the three Rs, nature, and science. Now they find it more comfortable to seek and accept sex information in more scientific terms and are more comfortable hearing about sex in animals than in human beings.

But what happens, after the age of six, to the intense romantic attachments of son to mother and daughter to father, which I said were suppressed into the unconscious because of anxieties? What about the curiosity concerning the genital organs and the origin of babies? And what about the boy's admiration for his father and identification with him, which have been coexisting with his rivalry, and the girl's similar admiration for and identification with her mother?

All these emotions go through transformations in the six-to-seven-year-old period. The curiosity about sexual anatomy gets broadened into curiosity about many aspects of nature and science.

The admiration and identification with the parent of the same sex, which children now want to outgrow in order to become more independent, gets focused instead on their contemporaries; they want to dress like them, talk like them, have the same possessions. But some of the admiration is also deflected into the idealization of heroes of history, of sports, of invention, of exploration.

The romantic infatuation with the parent of the opposite sex stays mainly under repression until adolescence, when it re-emerges as crushes on teachers, movie actors, singers, who are seen in a highly idealized light. Then comes falling ecstatically in love with particular contemporaries who have some magical appeal of face, body, or personality. These early infatuations are often short-lived because adolescents imbue their beloveds with idealized qualities which they yearn to find but which are often there only in their own imaginations. But even when they become more realistic in their choices, some of their spiritual longings left over from their long-suppressed love of their parents of the opposite sex will reach out to music or poetry or literature or art, which they feel inspired to create or at least to appreciate. A classic example is that of Dante who was inspired to write some of the world's greatest poetry by Beatrice, a woman he never met, only glimpsed once in a crowd. I am one of those who believe, on the basis of psychoanalytic work with adults and children, that the deep love of the three- and four-year-old child for the parent of the opposite sex, which gets repressed (between six years and adolescence) is what gives power and mystery and spirituality to the phenomenon we call falling in love, and, to the human response to beauty in nature and all the arts.

So much for background theory and for the unconscious. How do you go about providing good sex education for your child? In order to answer children's questions about anatomical sex differences at about two and a half years, it's helpful if the parent realizes that girls and boys are both apt to assume that girls have somehow been deprived of the penises that boys have and that boys assume that the same injury could happen to them. So the parent can emphasize that no harm has been done, that boys and girls, men and women, are *meant* to be different. Children's first questions about the origin of babies are relatively easy to answer in terms of a seed growing in the mother's abdomen and the baby emerging from a special opening.

It may be a month or two years before it occurs to the child to ask about the father's part in creation. By this time (perhaps four to six years of age), I feel that it is important for the parent to refer not only to the father's penis in the mother's vagina but to emphasize their intense feelings of mutual love, their wish to please and serve each other, their desire for a baby to raise together.

I believe that human sexuality is as much spiritual as it is physical but that nowadays the spiritual aspect is too often left out. This, I think, is part of the reason why so many young teenagers have such a casual, experimental, exclusively physical attitude toward sex. They say, "Sex is a normal instinct meant to be enjoyed." It is that exactly in rabbits. But in humans who have been raised in loving, idealistic families it is much, much more.

I believe that parents should help their children to recognize and to respect the spiritual aspects of sex. When there is talk at the dinner table about the marriage of two high school students, they can point out that young people's marriages often break up because they are still changing so fast. When there is gossip about a divorce, they can explain, in a nonpreaching manner, how a good marriage doesn't just happen, it needs to be cultivated constantly, like a garden. They can set the example by showing their love and respect for each other and for the institution of marriage. No cheap jokes. When there is talk about a teenage pregnancy, they can point out that the young couple must not have realized their responsibility to avoid pregnancy and how seriously this will handicap their schooling, their lives. These comments need to be said not in a scolding tone but in the tone that adults use with each other when discussing problems. They can remember to talk with enthusiasm about good marriages, including their own.

Teenagers have many questions about life and love. They want to hear the opinions and experiences of others of their own age but also of teachers and their friends' parents, if these are friendly people. Underneath, they are curious about their parents' views, but they are reluctant to ask because they're afraid their parents will try to tell them what to do and what to believe. If you can bring up topics such as these for casual conversation, you make it easier for your teenage children to raise the questions that bother them, or you make it easier for all of you to start a more serious or thorough discussion.

Another way to get into talks about the facts of life with teenagers —or younger school-aged children—is through books. There are at least thirty such books in print for children of various ages, some of which you can find and look over in your public library or bookstore.

Books for children on sex can be valuable in several ways. They often contain diagrams and pictures that add a lot to a child's ability to understand the verbal explanation of even the most lucid parents and teachers. In the best of these books the wording has been carefully thought out to express the author's meaning. The shy kind of parent who would be embarrassed to answer questions—at least without help—can give the child a book to read or may read it aloud or give it to the child to read and follow up with discussion. At the very least, a book tells the child that his parents consider the subject suitable for thinking about, even if they are too shy to talk about it.

There are at least two reasons why conversations about sex between adolescents and parents are often difficult. When adolescents have become aware of the intense feelings involved, they are reluctant to reveal them to their parents, who have tended to be critical.

By the time they've played regularly with older children, young ones will have heard sadistic stories about birth—for example, that the doctor rips the mother open—so it is good when parent, teacher, author, or illustrator doesn't pass over the matter with the sentence, "Then the baby is born," but tells something about the naturalness of the process of labor, perhaps admitting, but not exaggerating, the pain.

Most modern parents find that discussion of sperm, egg, uteruses, and fetuses is not too difficult. What is hard is describing sexual intercourse and the intense feelings involved.

The parents can point out that even in this time of relaxed sexual standards there are still many young people who feel unready for intercourse despite the taunts of their bolder friends (who call them frigid or impotent) and who would like to postpone intimacy until marriage or until they are ready for marriage. To put it in other words, it is all right to say no. Parents can explain that many of the world's most creative people—composers, writers, artists, scientists —were shy about intimacy until they were well into their twenties.

▷ PETS

I can't discuss pets on the basis of my own childhood experience because I never was allowed to have any aside from the tadpoles I collected in egg form. Whenever I or my brother or any of my four sisters begged for a dog, our mother would say very firmly, "I've got six dogs already." This wasn't intended as an insult but as a reminder that she had enough to do taking care of us. And she never was known to change her mind. As we grew older we realized that she also objected vehemently to the fact that dogs have no sense of propriety: they take too much nosy interest in each other's anatomy (and even people's) and feel free to make love in public places in broad daylight. Cats at least have the delicacy to prefer the dark.

What I've learned about pets has come from those of my children, grandchildren, and patients.

Why, I've often wondered, are children so fascinated by animals —not just live animals, but also stuffed toy animals and animals in stories? I think that children of preschool age would rather hear a story about a rabbit than about a human being.

In Chapter Seven in the section "More on Comforters," I wrote about the soft toy animals, old crib blankets, and other cuddly objects that many children become deeply attached to. They stroke or feel them while thumb sucking during times of regression— when sleepy, anxious, or hurt.

I believe that these attachments begin gradually at about six months of age, when a baby starts to sense that he is a separate being from his mother; he now wants to do some things for himself and to assert his independence. The comforter reminds the child of the security his mother gives but is, in a way, a superior substitute because it cannot envelop or control him. With his comforter he can have his security *and* his tiny bit of independence.

Well, to get back to live animals, I suspect that one of their greatest charms to a child is that they offer companionship without bossiness. (It isn't just adults who boss small children; older children do it too.) The child becomes, in fact, the boss of the animal. You can see this in the amount of scolding he deals out. Along the same lines, the animal, which is usually small, allows the child to feel big. But even little children may boss large, live dogs this way, especially if the dogs are gentle-natured.

You can say also that the pet affords the child the opportunity to be a parent, a state all small children eagerly look forward to. Being a parent means not only being in control; it means providing love, tenderness, comforting, food. A child senses how much it has meant to him to receive these from his parents and he yearns to give them in turn to real or pretend children of his own or to other children and creatures.

What kinds of pets are most desired and which work out best? School-aged children dream of owning a pony. No wonder. A pony has the advantages of other pets and in addition the unique one of carrying his master wherever he wants to go, with the speed of the wind. I was never pediatrician to a child who owned a pony and I realize that this is an impractical kind of pet, at least for the city child—expensive to buy, house, and feed, requiring lots of care every day.

The dog is the great favorite because he is so obviously loving, loyal, enthusiastic, and playful. He gives a child the maximum of nonhuman companionship. And because he is affectionate to start with and responds so eagerly to the affection shown him, he will tend to foster a child's warmth and tenderness. (But I don't mean to suggest that all by himself he can cure a child of unfriendliness or meanness.)

The disadvantages of having a dog are that he must be patiently housebroken, trained not to jump on people in greeting, not to threaten strangers. He may alienate neighbors by digging up their gardens. His boisterousness may be too frightening for a timid child to get used to. And dogs (like cats) are often killed in traffic, which is hard on everyone in the family but may be particularly disturbing to a sensitive child.

A cat (and I hope I won't offend cat lovers by saying this) doesn't necessarily have the same insistent friendliness or exuberant playfulness as most dogs, so he may not appeal as much to the child who craves a constant, active companion. But a cat is affectionate in a subdued way and appreciates tenderness. He is easily trained, doesn't have to be taken for walks, is not aggressive in his friendliness or unfriendliness.

Among the animals that appeal to children's impulse to take care of a creature but that cannot demonstrate much visible love, companionship, or playfulness are rabbits, guinea pigs, hamsters, white mice, canaries, aquarium fish. The last four may be fairly acceptable compromises for the apartment-house child whose mother doesn't want a dog or cat.

Which child should have a pet? I don't think a pet is crucially important for any child in the sense that it can make the difference between happiness and unhappiness or the difference between a satisfactory and an unsatisfactory adjustment. But it can be more valuable to the only child, to the child isolated from companions, to the child who keeps begging for a pet whether or not his parents can figure out why he feels such a strong need. (If an isolated small child does have a pet, he should, if possible, be taken once or twice a week to where there are other children to play with. A pet is not a full substitute.)

Would owning a dog be helpful to a two-, three-, or four-year-old who has a phobia about dogs? Having a dog of his own may or may not make him feel more comfortable about strange dogs. A child usually acquires this kind of phobia not from having been attacked by a dog but because of an unconscious, guilty fear of a parent's anger, which finds expression in this disguised form. Getting used to a dog of his own does not change the child's underlying tension, though it may ease this particular symptom of the tension.

Meanness is not well curbed in many normal children before three years of age. Small children may bite each other when in the mood and they can be quite cruel to an animal. Therefore I would not ordinarily suggest giving a child a pet before the age of three. By this age his control over his aggressions, his appreciation of companionship, and his altruism usually will have become established. Of course some children show little or no meanness at two or even younger, and others always will be mean. At no age should a child be allowed to be cruel to an animal: it's not good for either of them.

The most constructive step is to try to train the child to submerge his hostile impulses in affectionate ones. Remind the child, repeatedly if necessary, with such words as, "It hurts the kitty when you hit him. Pet the kitty gently like this. You love the kitty and he loves you. He likes to have you stroke him and pat him gently."

Any child begging for a pet will swear by all that's holy that he will faithfully carry out the feeding, walking, cleaning, or any other care required. And experience through the centuries has shown that few children—especially young children—have enough sense of responsibility to deliver on such promises beyond a few days unless they have regular parental supervision.

But I think if a pet is bought for a child on the basis of such promises, it is preferable that he be held to them. In order to minimize nagging and recrimination, it's wise for parent and child to agree on a routine by which the child carries out the chores at the same time each day—right after breakfast or before supper, for instance, when the parent can easily see (and won't have to ask) whether they have been done. If necessary he can remind the child, "Time to feed Rover."

Or the parent can simply take over the care of the pet and not reproach the child. But it should be a consistent system, whichever method you choose. I'm arguing here against vacillation combined with chronic nagging: holding the child to the job one day, letting him slip out of it the next day without comment, letting him evade it the third day but scolding him later. Parental inconsistency actually encourages a child to dodge his obligations.

If a pet dies or has to be sent away, it is normal and proper that the child feel upset and depressed—for days and even weeks. Parents with the best of intentions may try to minimize this mourning by cheerfully offering a new pet at once. But this is a mistake.

The right way to recover from the loss of any creature or person, psychiatric experience has shown, is to feel it, to talk about it, not to repress it. And if a child sees his parents apparently untouched by a death that is tragic for him, he may assume that his parents' love for him is equally shallow and transitory. Let the child come to his own desire for a substitute pet.

Death should not be thought of as an entirely negative matter for a child to face. It is an aspect of life with which each of us must come to terms, first as a theoretical threat, then in the loss of pets, friends, and relatives, finally in our own dying.

At each of these stages death teaches us to be humble and to get on with our living. It asks of us courage and dignity. In these matters the parents should set the example for the child—in words, in manner, and in attitude. The death of a pet is not usually as devastating as the death of a close relative. So it provides parents and child with a more readily comprehended lesson.

Young children have a natural inclination to solemnize the death of a pet with a ceremony, if only the placing of the body in a cotton-lined box and burying it with dignity. Parents should enter into these ceremonies in the same reverent mood as the child does.

Child psychiatrists have learned that a young child—especially one under the age of six—may be seriously upset if a pet has to be put to death because of illness, injury, or extremely unsuitable behavior such as viciously attacking people. The child concludes

that the same fate or punishment may be dealt out to him. Better
to explain that the doctor says the pet must live in the country, or
somewhere else, for the rest of his life and that the doctor (or the
parents) will find a new home for him.

If the parents decide for some reason or combination of reasons
that they are opposed to getting the pet their child is begging for—
or any pet, for that matter—it is important to announce their decision quite definitely. Nowadays many conscientious parents are
uncertain whether they have the right to deny their child something
that is within their means, no matter how much the granting of it
would go against their desires or convenience. They may finally
decide in their own favor. But then their feeling of guilt may be
very obvious. If it is, it will spur the child on to endless pleading,
whining, and reproaching.

I believe firmly that parents have the full right to make all the
final decisions about their child—after considering the child's
wishes, the customs of the community, and their own desires. If
they can make their decisions without feeling guilt (by thinking
them through together) and announce them without guilt, the child
will be much more likely to accept them cheerfully.

▷ GOD AND RELIGION IN THE AGNOSTIC FAMILY

Talking with children about religion has been made more difficult in the past hundred years by the changing religious attitudes
and weakening beliefs of many people. But the concept of the universe as a purely physical system and of the human being as merely
a contraption made up of cells and chemicals, developed through
the process of evolution, leaves many of us who are agnostics or
are only vaguely religious feeling unsatisfied. We crave more meaning for our existence. We strongly sense a spiritual force within us
and in those around us. We want to give that force a name and
identity and to define our personal relationship with it.

This section is not primarily for the firm believers. They have the
least trouble explaining religion to their children. Nor is it for those
atheists who assume they should pass on their disbelief. It is mainly
for those who stand in between: the vague believers who are inclined to think there is a God but are at a loss as to how to charac-
terize God to their young children; the agnostics who are uncertain
about how to explain their doubts; and what I'll call the democratic

atheists, who want to let their children come around to their own decisions about religion.

Many such parents ask questions like the following: What can we teach children about religion and spiritual values? Should we confess all our doubts if and when the children ask? Should we pretend to be firmer believers than we are to give our children something definite to lean on, at least for the time being? Or should we pass on all the responsibility to the children, telling them they must decide for themselves sooner or later? Of what importance is the advice that children from Christian and Jewish backgrounds should know at least something about the Bible, as part of their cultural education? What about Sunday school? What about the psychological effects on children of the deep guilt that is implanted by some churches and of the threat of hell and damnation?

To understand the significance of some of these issues for children, I think it's helpful to consider what a religion like Christianity or Judaism means to children at different stages of their emotional development and how their feelings at these stages contribute to their eventual religious attitudes in adulthood.

At three, four, and five years of age children admire and adore their parents. They are emotionally very dependent on them for their sense of security. They believe their parents are the wisest, richest, most powerful, and most attractive people on earth. They are eager to imitate their parents' behavior and attitudes. If the parents are reverent believers, these very young children will adopt their own version of the same attitude; they will accept God on the parents' say-so. There will be no arguments, though there may be questions.

Since parents are the most important people in the world by far, young children will usually picture God as something like their father—or grandfather—in appearance and attitude. (This is an aspect of the sexism in our society, for there is no reason why God shouldn't be a woman, as in some other societies.)

The association between God and parents works out in another way too. If the parents are gentle, loving people, they will tend to present God as kindly and approving. If the parents are stern, they probably will accentuate the judgmental aspects of God. So it is particularly in the age period from three to six that the child's readiness to love and depend on God or to fear God develops. Those individuals who were unloved in early childhood usually do not come to religion later.

In the six-to-twelve-year-old period, children are trying to overcome some of their dependence on their parents and to begin their adaptation to the outside world. Even if their parents are nonbelievers, these children will be picking up references to religion and asking their parents questions. When my older son was seven and we were spending a weekend with some friends, he first heard about hell and damnation for disbelievers from the cook. Since we didn't attend church, he wanted to know whether we thought there was any danger to us of hellfire. It was also evident that he wanted to know how our family lined up with other families in regard to religious beliefs. Did we belong to some regular, recognized category, even if it was a category of disbelievers? He was ready to accept our explanations and our reassurances about hellfire.

So it can be seen that the desire at this age to be more independent has to do with superficial matters about which children characteristically rebel against parents: they have an urge to resist family regulations by being messy, dirty, noisy, bad-mannered, rough-talking. They do not rebel against their parents' more serious beliefs about morals and religion.

Most children between six and twelve have little inclination to mull the meaning of religion or to yearn for a personal relationship with God. It is a relatively impersonal age in which deeper feelings tend to be covered up. But questions of authority do concern children now when they are attempting to outgrow their previous total, voluntary subordination to parents and feel the need to substitute some other authority to respect. They may ask their father and mother whether they, the parents, have to obey the mayor, whether the mayor has to obey the governor, and whether the governor has to obey the president. It rather appeals to them to find that their parents must bow to higher-ups and, if they are being raised in a religious family, that everyone acknowledges God's supremacy, including fathers and presidents.

Consciences are stern and arbitrary at this time. Right is right and wrong is wrong. There is no gray zone, no tolerance for human weakness.

The strengthening of conscience and the sense of guilt, plus the readiness to acknowledge a higher moral authority, make up, you might say, the second stage in the readiness for our Christian and Judaic religions.

In adolescence religion is apt to become a different thing altogether. Feelings of all kinds have come surging to the surface—

feelings of physical attraction and adoration, of idealistic dedication to causes, sensitivity to beauty in all its forms, and responsiveness to the spiritual side of human affairs. Adolescents yearn to form intense and meaningful relationships. This includes a personal relationship with God, if they have been brought up religiously or have been converted to religion.

Adolescents also are confused and frightened by their new bodies and new emotions. They've lost their old, familiar identities as children, and it will take them years to find their full identities as adults. So they reach out to a trusted teacher, a member of the extended family, an older brother or sister, a tried-and-true friend for confidences, advice, and security. (They often don't turn to parents because there is an increased rivalry now between the generations and because parents are too apt to scold.) Some turn to God directly, or indirectly through a clergyman. They may do this individually or they may join a church youth group.

On the other hand, the rivalry with parents causes some youths to reject the parents' religion, or all religions, at least for a while.

Throughout the rest of life the elements that work for a continuing tie to God and church are the same human needs that have been developing during successive stages of childhood. There is the desire to have someone to depend on for understanding and love under all circumstances, to have a moral code for guidance, and to have the promise of relief from guilt if one will renounce what parents, society, or God considers wrong.

In trying to understand complex matters, children are likely to want to take one small step at a time. If and when their curiosity reaches out further, in a minute or a month, they will ask more questions. So it is well to answer only the question the child has asked, not to volunteer more.

Preschool children ask thousands of questions about the things they see and have heard of and especially about things that might worry them: "What happened to that man's leg? Why is grass green? Is a cat a boy or a girl? Why did the bug die? Well, do I have to die?" But their curiosity usually doesn't reach out into matters that have never been brought to their attention; that comes later.

In a churchgoing household where God is often spoken of, small children are apt to ask such down-to-earth questions as: "Where does God live? Can I see God? Does God like me?" Meaning, is God disapproving, as my parents at times are? "Does God have a mommy?" By this they are asking who takes care of God, such as a mother or wife. (They don't distinguish too sharply between mother and wife when thinking about adults. Occasionally I was asked by young, affectionate patients whether I had a mommy, even after I was white-haired.)

A highly conscientious, honest parent may be troubled when answering questions such as where God lives, because even the Bible is vague about the location of heaven; yet children want a definite answer. But this isn't as much a problem as it seems to parents, who are always anticipating the next question and the next. It may satisfy a small child to answer, "In a place called heaven." He is no more apt to want to know its geographical location than he wants to know just where St. Louis is.

I think that questions such as, "Can I see God?" or, "Why can't I see God?" from a child of three, four, or five are hard to answer, even for churchgoing parents, because a spirit is intangible. They can help the child to see that it's not just his problem by saying, "Nobody can see God." Then parents can try to define a spirit by giving an example. "God is a spirit. That means God doesn't have a body like you or me. We believe God is everywhere, watching over us, listening to our prayers, loving us. You can't see the wind, can you? But you can feel it and you know it is there."

Nonbelieving parents can give the same kind of explanation, but instead of making it their own explanation, they can preface it by saying, "People who believe in God believe that God doesn't have a body like you or me. God is a spirit. That means God is everywhere," and so forth.

And if a child asks, "Do *you* believe in God?" I think that parents can say, "We do, but we don't know just what God is like." Or, "We don't, but we have a lot of friends who do. We believe in some of the things that Jesus taught." Or, "We don't. But when you are older, you may decide to believe in God."

Whether or not the family is religious, children from six to ten years of age will pick up remarks of friends, parents, and others and ask penetrating questions, if the parents have encouraged questions in general. I think it is often easier for parents who are unsure of themselves as interpreters of religion to refer to the Bible or to the clergyman as the authority rather than to try to be the experts themselves. Then they can hide behind the Bible when they feel stumped. Believing parents can refer to the Bible in a manner that indicates they believe it totally or with reservations. Nonbelieving parents can show that they consider the Bible to be a book of history written in ancient times by many people, without necessarily intruding their own belief or disbelief—at least until they are asked.

Vague believers and nonchurchgoing parents may answer questions about God and the Bible and heaven along the following lines: "The Bible is a book that was written thousands of years ago. It tells how a person named God made the whole world in the beginning. It says he made the sun and the moon and the stars, and the mountains and the oceans. It says he made all the animals and birds and fishes, and finally he made people. Lots of people go to church on Sundays to sing songs to God and to thank him for all the good things they have, like delicious food and a nice house and warm clothes. These people also go to church to ask God to help them be good. The Bible says God lives in heaven, but we don't know where that is. Some say it is in the sky. People who go to church can't really see God there. But they feel he is there just the same, not as a body, but as a spirit."

What can religious parents do to foster religion in their young children, aside from answering questions? It's simple, I think. They can love their children (while asking for respect from them) and set an example of what they consider to be good Christian or Jewish living. The children will do most of the rest by imitation and identification. They will remain in their parents' religion at least into the rebellious period of youth. If they then reject it, they may later return to it, or to another religion, when they have achieved adulthood and independent identity. Even if they don't go back to a formal religion, they may very well remain ethical, idealistic people because of the spirit of their upbringing. Of course, parents who have not been religious but hold seriously to a system of values and share them with their children can also expect their children to end up with strong values, though not necessarily identical ones.

I think it's wise for religious parents to discuss their own principles and their church's principles with their children when issues of behavior or belief come up in regard to the family or the outside world. In other words, religion is not just for Sundays. But it is more effective to do this in a positive, cheerful manner than in a scolding one. And it's not necessary to preach a lot. The aim is to clarify the meaning of the principles rather than to hammer them home.

I believe too that religious and ethical ideals should be balanced by discussion of how natural it is for human beings to be greedy, selfish, procrastinating, lazy, irritable, angry, jealous, and impelled by sex, so that individual children won't get the idea that only they are naughty.

Yet I feel that children shouldn't be taught, either, that human beings are predominantly bad and that only God is good. For the positive drives in people—love, generosity, cooperation, loyalty, and the drive to nurture—are stronger than the negative drives, provided that individuals have had the benefit of growing up in a loving family.

I believe strongly that children, especially small children, should be spared any talk about hellfire or God's wrath. The picture conjured up in a young child's imagination is much more terrifying and threatening than in an older child's or adult's.

I'm also against inculcating heavy guilt. I was brought up with an excessive amount of guilt, though it was not tied directly to God, and I see how it made me afraid of everyone when I was a child and interfered with my effectiveness later. (As a student about to take an examination, I felt so guilty about any part of a subject in which I was not completely prepared that I would manage to drag that part into my answer and thus reveal my ignorance, even though that subject had not been a part of the question at all. And I still have unpleasant dreams about going into examinations totally unprepared.) So I learned that *excessive* guilt can be destructive without having any compensating moral advantage. I italicize *excessive* because all good citizens, in childhood and adulthood, need a conscience to keep them reasonably in line and a moderate sense of guilt to prod them when they are straying.

I feel that Sunday schools—as long as the teachers have a positive attitude—have much to offer, even in the case of the children of agnostics and atheists. Judaism and Christianity are integral parts of the history and culture and attitudes of most of the people in the United States, even of those who have rejected these religions; it's an important aspect of education to understand our pasts. It's also valuable for all people to be familiar with the biblical stories that their fellow citizens often refer to and to be familiar with the hymns that are often sung outside churches as well as in them. These are part of our shared cultural experience.

Parents who never go to church can't, in all fairness, insist that their children attend Sunday school, but they can recommend it.

Of course there are parents who are emphatic disbelievers and who think it would be dishonest and misleading to talk to their children as if they thought there was a possibility that God existed, or as if they themselves would be content if their children eventually became believers. My own recommendation would be that, in addition to setting their children a good example of their ethical standards, they occasionally discuss their own spiritual beliefs with them—not suddenly, out of the blue, but when conversation is brought near such topics by world or neighborhood or family events.

The reason I mention this is that often the reaction of agnostics and atheists against established religion makes them shy away from even referring to any spiritual beliefs. Even the word *spiritual* may make them a bit suspicious, as if it might be a disguise for religion. But spiritual only means feelings (of a positive kind) as opposed to material things—feelings such as love for others, dedication to one's family and community, courage, the response to music and scenery. All but the most materialistic among us hold to strong spiritual values and beliefs, even if we never speak of them, and our children absorb them gradually and silently by living with us. But to hear them spoken of and to discuss them with us helps children to clarify spiritual beliefs and values, to select those aspects that have the most meaning and to adopt them as their own.

More specifically, in relation to the topic of this section, the discussion of spiritual values with parents (and teachers) will enable children—particularly in that age period from six to twelve, when they want to be moral and want to belong in a category—to see that though their family may not go to church, they are not entirely different from religious families and are not adrift without a definite system of beliefs. Furthermore, such discussion will help them to understand that their family does not stand alone—that there are other families that do not attend church either, but nevertheless also live by a system of values and morals.

Those who believe firmly in an established religion tell us that religion is what is lacking in so many peoples' lives, and some maintain that we all need to be born again. Certainly religion has given direction and inspiration to peoples' lives in most societies. But if, in some individuals' minds science has undermined the credibility, the authority, and the mysticism of religion, there is no way that it can be reinstated by a command, someone else's or one's own. (This can happen on a deathbed, but that's different.)

I have hopes that enough people will come to recognize the social ills and tragedies stemming from our spiritual poverty, or be shocked by some economic or environmental disaster, or be inspired by a spiritual leader, so that they will dedicate themselves to the ideal of service to their fellow humans, whatever their gainful occupations, and inspire in their children a similar ideal. I literally believe that without such a conversion, our singleminded dedication to materialism will do us in. I'm not basing this on religious or moral grounds but simply on the evidence that our society is disintegrating.

▷ FAIRY TALES AND OTHER STORIES FOR CHILDREN

Ever since I finished my training in pediatrics and psychiatry, in the early 1930s, and began pediatric practice, I've been aware of the endless controversy over whether cruel fairy stories are good or bad for small children. "Psychologist declares fairy stories are a wholesome outlet for children's hostile feelings," says one news report. The next week a child psychiatrist is quoted as saying, "Grimm's fairy tales cause nightmares and phobias."

Certainly it's true that most children generate their own hostile feelings and mean fantasies in the early years, as a result of having to be frustrated by their parents and because of rivalry with their brothers and sisters. They have a natural inclination to deny and suppress this hostility because, to the degree that their parents show disapproval of hostility, they feel guilty.

Because of this almost universal sense of guilt about hostility, it is comforting to children to hear that other people get angry too, that anger and cruel thoughts can be talked about, that thinking angry thoughts doesn't kill people or even injure them. (In the same way, it relieves the guilt of conscientious parents to find out that other parents get furious with their children at times and feel like strangling them.) It is on this account that some psychiatrists and psychologists have looked favorably on the reading of cruel fairy stories to small children.

On the other hand we all have known young children who have become upset, have had trouble going to sleep, and have had nightmares after they heard scary stories or watched violent television programs. The owner of a large movie theater told me years ago that after *Snow White and the Seven Dwarfs* had played for several weeks he had to redo all the seat upholstery because it had become saturated with the urine of small, frightened children. Such symptoms prove that children are experiencing more anxiety than they can comfortably cope with.

My impression is that the most harmful kind of frightening experience is seeing live actors on film apparently being battered, cut, or shot by other actors, being hurled off buildings and cliffs, being chased by thugs or wild animals—because these scenes look so real. Small children can't easily distinguish between make-believe and actuality. A little less harmful, because they are less realistic, but still harmful, are animated cartoons and pictures in storybooks.

When children are listening to fairy stories and trying to form a mental image from the words being read to them, they are limited by their own experience and vocabulary, so they may not get the full impact of the story's cruelty. On the other hand, they may misunderstand the words and draw a worse conclusion than was intended by the author.

There certainly are great differences among children, even children of the same age, in their response to frightening dramas and stories. Active, outgoing children seem on the average not to get such a strong impact from troubling experiences. And they further protect themselves by what's sometimes called turning passive into active: they quickly shift from feeling like the victim to becoming the aggressor. For example, if they have received an injection from a doctor, they may promptly pretend to give a shot to their doll and thus get rid of a lot of the anxiety.

At the other end of the scale are the children who have always tended to be quiet, intently observant, and easily upset. They are acutely sensitive to anything the least bit frightening. And once something has frightened them, they remember it for a long time.

Age is another factor in how much children are worried by stories and dramas. The younger they are—down to the age of two or three—the greater the likelihood of their being upset. As they mature they can distinguish better and better between what is real and what isn't. They don't all make equal progress, though, I've known teenagers and adults who've become seriously upset on seeing a movie that hit them in a sensitive or neurotic spot.

I myself would not read even mildly cruel stories to children or let them see even slightly disturbing programs on television. This is not just to keep them from being frightened but also to keep them from becoming tolerant of violence. There are plenty of life experiences that inevitably disturb children (and adults too) without our creating them unnecessarily.

I want to emphasize that you have to be on guard against television programs and movies—especially cartoons—that are presumably intended for children. Fully three quarters of them go in for sadistic incidents, one episode piled on top of another. The rabbit falls off a cliff, gets his hair all burned off in an explosion, is smashed into a flat pancake by a train, is sliced in two by a buzz saw. The adults in the audience laugh but the small children cringe.

I would firmly and consistently see to it that my young children did not have a chance to view frightening or violent television programs, no matter how much they begged or complained. (I wouldn't let older children watch violence either.)

I wouldn't read any story to a young child that I hadn't glanced through first. There are hundreds of harmless stories that young children find fascinating and that can be bought or borrowed from the library. I discovered as a parent that there were some stories I enjoyed reading aloud and others that irritated me. Since children want their books read to them again and again and again, it's wise for easily irritated parents to choose books to buy that are pleasant reading for themselves.

CHAPTER ELEVEN

Health and Nutrition

▷ TEACHING HEALTH ATTITUDES

▷ TEACHING GOOD EATING HABITS

▷ INFANT DIET

▷ AVOIDING FEEDING PROBLEMS

▷ SERIOUS ILLNESS

▷ HOW TO TALK TO CHILDREN
ABOUT SEXUALITY AND LOVE,
IN GENERAL

▷ TEACHING HEALTH ATTITUDES

The aim in building sound attitudes about health is to educate people away from ignorance and neglect but at the same time try to avoid turning them into worriers, hypochondriacs, and other types of neurotics. This is not always easy.

Most health attitudes and habits date from early childhood. But that doesn't mean you can teach your child good habits exactly as you'd like them to be learned, the way you teach the multiplication tables. For some attitudes spring from very early experiences that the parent did not plan in any way.

An adult phobia about cancer, for instance, is apt to have its roots in unusually strong guilt feelings buried deep in the unconscious in childhood and may have little to do with any specific health teaching by the parent. A hypochondriacal tendency is often partly based on a self-centeredness and insecurity that developed way back in the first two years of life.

Deliberate neglect or abuse of health may be quite contrary to what the parents have preached; it can be an expression of pretended courage and manliness (like whistling in the dark) or of masochistic self-punishment.

So the most basic preparation for good health attitudes is to bring up children to be generally comfortable with themselves and with others, which is a prescription too vague to be of much assistance. A baby or a young child is helped to be outgoing by not being excessively fussed over, bossed, or warned (as first babies are sometimes treated by uneasy parents); rather, a child can learn to be outgoing if he is allowed to develop his own pursuits, to make contact with his parents when *he* feels sociable, to have opportunities to learn give-and-take with other children from the beginning.

Deep feelings of guilt and self-punitiveness can be avoided when parents take most of the responsibility for keeping young children from doing the wrong things—by eliminating some of the temptations in the one-to-two-year-old period and by stopping misbehavior promptly, casually, and consistently, rather than by stern moral disapproval before or after the act. A parent can be affectionate, cheerful, and companionable most of the time without encouraging the child to get out of hand. In other words, parental leadership does not need to be grim in order to be effective.

A suggestion that I want to make in the beginning is for parents to steer between overemphasizing injuries and illnesses and denying them. If a parent acts as if each little symptom or hurt is potentially dangerous, it can certainly make a child a lifelong worrier. And if a parent is generally critical or standoffish with a child and becomes attentive only when he is sick, then the child learns automatically to exaggerate every complaint he will ever have to try to draw people closer and more sympathetically to him.

On the other hand, if a parent has a great fear of giving in to illness (as I was taught to have in my childhood), he will have the impulse to teach the same thing to his child: "Don't fuss, you'll feel better soon." "That doesn't hurt. Stop crying." "Don't be a baby, be brave." This may not seem a bad thing to teach. It would counteract any tendency to hypochondriasis or exaggeration of aches and pains; it should inculcate bravery and stoicism—virtues that have been prized since the days of ancient Sparta and are still admired greatly in some families.

But one trouble with an attitude of denial of illness and pain is that an individual may learn to ignore the symptoms of disease in himself until he is in very serious condition. Doctors frequently encounter patients—even patients who are physicians and should know better—who have had clear-cut symptoms of a disease such as cancer for many months and who not only did not mention them to anyone but also managed to persuade themselves that the symptoms were of no importance at all.

A more troublesome consequence of excessive stoicism about pain and discomfort in some individuals is that they eventually may come to suppress feelings of other kinds too—anxiety, sorrow, anger, or even joy. Worse still, they also may tune out the emotions of other people. They won't recognize unhappiness or worries or resentment in their spouses, children, friends, and fellow workers. They become difficult, uncomfortable people to live with.

For the only satisfactory way in which human beings can get along with one another is by communicating their feelings along with their thoughts. We all watch constantly the face, especially the eyes, of the person we are talking with, to be sure that he understands and sympathizes with what we are telling him about ourselves, or to see whether the proposal we are making pleases or irritates him. If he is the kind who conceals his feelings, we are uneasy. Or we assume that his feelings are unfriendly and then we turn unfriendly ourselves.

So the sensible balance to aim for in raising a child is to allow him to show the pain or other discomfort that seems realistic for the injury or illness he is suffering, but by reassurance or firm reminder to counteract any strong tendency he may have to exaggerate his misery.

Of course, this is a rather theoretical piece of advice because parents already have built-in attitudes that are difficult to hide. A mother who is frightened by the sight of blood, no matter how insignificant the wound, or a father who harbors a sense of shame about showing any fear is naturally going to have difficulty striking the best balance with the child. We all deviate from the average in some such respect.

Psychoanalysts believe that many worries about bodily inadequacy start from unnecessarily stern warnings about masturbation. Around one year of age, when a child is identifying all parts of his (or her) body, he explores his genitals too. It's good to realize that this is only one aspect of his curiosity and his growing sense of self and is normal. You don't need to do anything, if that suits you, or you can smile and say, "That's your penis" (or "your vulva"), or whatever you want to call it—an entirely acceptable part of one's body. Or if his handling of his genitals bothers you (as it does some parents), you can easily distract him at this age by offering a plaything or just chatting about something that interests him. The main thing is to avoid giving him the idea that a part of his body is evil or that he might injure himself by touching it.

The same consideration applies to the three-to-six-year-old period, when occasional experimentation with the genitals and sex play with other children is very common. Depending on your own feelings, you can casually ignore these signs of normal sexual development. Often just the presence of the parent is enough to interrupt the play. Or you can divert the children by suggesting another activity. Or you can tell them matter-of-factly that it's not polite to do that when there are other people around, or simply that you don't want them to do that. But it is better not to imply to your child that sex play is harmful to physical or mental health (it isn't) or that it will turn you against him.

The most efficient time to encourage toilet training is around two to two and a half years of age. There is a natural readiness then in a majority of children. Dr. T. Berry Brazelton, as a result of observing fifteen hundred consecutive children in his practice, came to several conclusions about training. It's wise to avoid any pressure or persuasion. Present the child with the kind of seat that fits over a potty on the floor and tell him that this is his very own seat. Don't mention its other purpose at this time. Leave the lid on, let him sit on it as often or as little as he wishes. After several weeks during which he has gotten used to it and developed friendly possessive feelings toward it, put a potty under it, raise the lid, and tell him that he can use his seat to go poo-poo (or make a BM, or whatever term you use), just the way Mommy and Daddy use the big toilet. Leave off his diaper at the time he usually performs. Let him try this as little or as much as he wishes. If he sits briefly and then gets up, don't try to detain him. The idea is to let him feel not that you are trying to get his movement away from him and into the potty, which arouses possessive and balky feelings in many young children, but that using the toilet is a grown-up skill that he may want to learn *by himself*.

Dr. Brazelton found that children not only do learn toileting by themselves but that they learn urine and bowel control at about the same time. The most convincing result of letting the child learn by himself was an extremely small number of cases of persistent bed-wetting. This suggests that persistent bed-wetting (past three or four years) is a protest—at the unconscious level of the mind—against too much toilet-training pressure from the parents.

It's also important that children not be taught, by the parents' words or facial expressions, that the bowel movement is not only disgusting but also dangerous to touch, as if it were poisonous. Many individuals have received such impressions in early childhood, impressions that then persisted into adulthood and caused chronic worries about such matters as irregularity in the timing or amount or consistency of the bowel movements. These worries sometimes lead to frequent use of cathartics, enemas, and high colonic irrigations.

Actually there is nothing unhealthy about irregularity in movements, the amount passed is not important, and the only harm in hard movements is the discomfort. When an individual has been led to believe that the bowel movement is inherently poisonous, he is easily convinced that headaches, sallowness of the skin, bad breath, and fatigue are caused by constipation.

He may then begin to feel debilitated or ill when the timing of the passage of the movement or the amount of movement seems less than ideal. But bowel movements are not poisonous inside or outside the body. And even the disgust at their smell is something that is taught.

The common denominator in these various suggestions is that to bring up our children to have healthy attitudes toward health, we should focus our concern not on the injuries and diseases that threaten them, but on preserving their good feelings toward their bodies, toward themselves as people, and toward us as parents.

▷ TEACHING GOOD EATING HABITS

We Americans have the world's highest standard of living. We consume the lion's share of the world's protein. (The grain that's fed to cattle to make our beef would go a long way toward relieving the world's hunger.) We have such an abundance and variety of fruits and vegetables that the inhabitants of even the other industrialized countries envy us.

Yet a majority of our own people—adults and children—are eating a poor diet. Despite increasing prosperity, it has been getting steadily worse since World War II, according to nutritional scientists.

The poor diet is due partly to maldistribution of income. Government figures show that increasing numbers of Americans are living below the poverty level. And a few years ago a congressional committee found that hundred of thousands of people—adults and children—are slowly starving. They don't lie down in the streets and fields and die relatively quickly, as in some famine-stricken lands; the adults here are partially incapacitated by deficiency diseases and die prematurely of other diseases, such as pneumonia, to which they have a lowered resistance. The children become stunted —bodily and mentally.

But the malnutrition I want to focus on occurs just as commonly in middle- and upper-income families that can afford a good diet. And it more often manifests itself as obesity than emaciation. I'm thinking of the excessive consumption of sweets, refined starches, and animal fats. Together they favor obesity; the tragic result is fat people who are laughed at all their lives and who have difficulty believing in themselves. Excesses of sugars and starches also contribute to decay of the teeth and sometimes to diabetes.

The harm from eating large amounts of sweets and refined starches is double, since not only are these foods deficient in themselves, but by satisfying appetite they keep people from eating enough of the other, more valuable foods.

A new accusation comes from the surgeons dealing with cancer of the large intestine. They now see evidence that this killer is caused mainly by our high consumption of refined foods, which cause the passage of food from mouth to rectum to take several times longer than in those parts of the world where people eat chiefly fruits, vegetables, and whole grains, with all their roughage.

Then there are the increasing numbers of people who get arterio-sclerosis and die of coronary heart attacks or of strokes at younger and younger ages. In part this is believed to be caused by an excessive consumption of animal fats (including excessive amounts of milk, cream, butter, and cheese) and of cholesterol, especially from too many eggs.

The link between animal fats, cholesterol, and arteriosclerosis has not been finally proved yet, but it is accepted by most scientists in the field. It was first suspected from the death statistics for coronary heart disease in Denmark during World War II. When the occupying Germans appropriated most of the butter, cream, cheese, and choice meats, the death rate of Danes from coronary attacks fell dramatically, only to rise again to the previous high rate after the German defeat.

We don't know today what other diseases will be discovered, years hence, to be caused by other deficiencies, overrefinements, and additives in our unnatural diet.

Dietary habits get set in childhood and tend to persist through the rest of life. We are allowing a majority of our children to form atrocious dietary habits. They eat corn cereals that, to start with, contain less-valuable protein than wheat and oats. Then many of the cereals, in being refined, have lost most of their germ, protein, roughage, and vitamins. Some have been made even less desirable by being sugarcoated or mixed with marshmallows or other candies.

The cooked starches that children eat for dinner are often spaghetti, noodles, or white rice, which are relatively deprived foods. Bread that children prefer is most commonly white bread or white buns. The white flour is "enriched," which sounds good and is better than nothing. But that term means only that after the roughage and wheat germ and most of the vitamins are removed, a part of the vitamins are replaced.

Eating a little refined starch at times won't hurt anybody, of course. But what I'm concerned about is that millions of children are eating refined, deprived starches every day in quantities far out of balance with nutritional requirements. To keep their families from slipping into these patterns, parents ought to make hard-and-fast rules and think of them every time they enter a market or plan meals.

It's a good idea not to serve puddings composed of refined starch and sugar. Ice cream, cakes, and pastries should be reserved for very special occasions.

Between-meal snacking as commonly practiced by school-aged children is a crime against good nutrition: candy bars and sticks of gum feed the germs that make the cavities in the teeth. The sugar in carbonated drinks similarly produces cavities, and the acid dissolves away the enamel directly. Rich snacks reduce the appetite for healthier foods at mealtime.

Sugary foods as snacks are doubly harmful because it's the number of hours during which the mouth is syrupy that determines the amount of tooth decay. Sugar at meals and between meals keeps children's teeth in a pool of syrup from breakfast time well into the evening.

Schools (even medical schools!), which should know better, sometimes have vending machines that offer candies and carbonated drinks.

I've condemned so many foods that by now you may have an uneasy impression that all foods are unhealthy. But our markets bulge with valuable foods as well as deprived ones:

Fruits—fresh, frozen, or canned (pour off the syrup)—should be the dessert every day after lunch and after supper and also should be used as snacks if snacks are needed. (It's better to train children by school age to omit snacks.)

A green or yellow vegetable should be eaten daily.

Cereals and breads should be made of whole wheat, oats, or rye. Read the labels carefully.

Nutrition authorities are not ready to recommend that all children hold the animal fats they eat—including milk, cream, butter, cheese—to a limited total. But they do recommend, in families in which there have been early deaths from coronary attacks, that children receive blood tests early to see whether they have an unusual susceptibility to arteriosclerosis. If they do, they should be on strict diets for life.

I myself think it is sensible to hold all adolescents and youths (as well as adults) to sensible, moderate limits of animal fats and cholesterol-rich foods. So meats should be lean. Since prime and choice meats are "marbled" with fat throughout the red portions anyway, make it a family habit to cut off the visible fat from the edges of steaks, chops, roast beef, lamb, and ham.

Adolescents and adults, I think, should drink skim milk. It is wise for them not to eat more than one egg a week.

Chicken or fish should be substituted for red meat at least twice a week, because it's believed these foods don't foster arteriosclerosis and fish oils may in fact aid in lowering body cholesterol.

A variety of beans and grains will supplement the protein in meat without encouraging arteriosclerosis.

In *Baby and Child Care,* from the very first edition through later editions, I've stressed the superiority of whole wheat and oats and advised against sugary foods and drinks. But I left a lot of leeway and allowed for exceptions. Now I feel I should be more emphatic and more arbitrary. Don't offer the "undesirable" and the "less-desirable" foods at all.

I'm changing my tune because so many children's diets are poor and getting worse. This means that many, many parents don't take good diet seriously. Or if they agree that diet is important in the long run, perhaps they feel that there is plenty of time to get around to improving it later. Or at least they believe that exceptions should be made, and then they let the exceptions become the rule.

Parents of babies and young children have the opportunity to get their children off on the right foot from the start—to make the diet so good and the rules so definite that their children accept them as a matter of course.

Children plead and argue—about food or anything else—only when they sense that their parents lack conviction or that their parents feel guilty about denying their children the delights other children are enjoying. So my job is to support parents in their intention to be firm.

▷ INFANT DIET

There are a number of factors that play a part in obesity, including national diet, family habit, heredity, individual bodily configuration, and emotional states such as unhappiness or anxiety. Tangled in with these factors is that mysterious matter of appetite, which may be easily satisfied in one person, never satisfied in another, and in the same individual may vary inexplicably from day to day.

The easiest and quickest way to produce fatness in infancy is through a lot of sugar in the diet. Starches and fats play a part too.

In earlier times some babies who were on formulas made with highly sweetened condensed milk puffed up like balloons. (Let me say quickly that this doesn't mean that young babies shouldn't have a moderate amount of sugar in their diets. Human milk is twice as sweet as cow's milk. Infants in the early months don't have the digestive juices to get nourishment from starches and they can't handle too much fat or protein, so they have to count on a moderate amount of sugar.)

In our part of the world most parents have always taken great pride in plumpness in their babies and have been a bit ashamed of skinny ones. (When my wife was a baby, her father wouldn't allow visitors to see any part of her but her face because she was so thin.) Perhaps plumpness seems a proof to parents that all systems are go, as they say in the space program. Perhaps it also is assumed to mean that the parents are doing a superior job.

When obesity persists into later childhood and adulthood it predisposes to arteriosclerosis and diabetes. It brings ridicule and self-consciousness. It interferes with many activities.

Bottle-fed babies have a greater chance of becoming plump than breast-fed babies—another advantage of breast feeding—perhaps because bottle-feeding parents are quite often tempted to urge just a bit more formula, which is visible in the bottle and which most babies are willing to accept. Nursing mothers, on the other hand, are inclined to take their baby's word for it when the baby stops suckling.

One of the means that can be taken to restrict the caloric intake of an infant who has reached the age of five or six months, who is eating solids, and who therefore no longer needs a sweet formula is to remove the additional sugar from it. This is easy to do when the formula is made from a combination of evaporated milk, water, and syrup. Simply omit the syrup by gradual steps, ¼ tablespoon each day, so that the difference will not be too noticeable. Babies who are on commercially prepared formulas, which include added sugar, can be shifted to whole milk or evaporated milk, and water without added sugar.

How about solid foods for babies? The way to prevent obesity and—just as important—to ensure a well-balanced diet, is to feed the baby generous amounts of fruits, vegetables, and meats, adding eggs after nine months, and to limit to moderate amounts the starches and sugars.

It is important in the long run that the starches consist mainly of whole-grain cereals—though the tradition still persists of giving babies refined white cereals for the first few months. It also is important to concentrate on wheat and oat cereals, which have better-quality protein than corn. (The protein in rice is better in *quality* than the protein in corn, but the *quantity* may be less.)

Up through the 1930s parents prepared their own baby foods. Beef was seared and then scraped vigorously to get the shreds of red meat out of the white connective tissue. Fruits (fresh and dried) and vegetables were cooked and then mashed through a fine sieve. (There were no blenders.) Cereals were cooked in double boilers for two hours, because at that time there were no precooked cereals.

Since then baby foods in jars and precooked cereals for babies have taken over because their great convenience has far outweighed their expense, in the judgment of parents.

When baby foods were first introduced, each jar contained one vegetable or one fruit or one meat or one pudding. As the years have passed, more and more of the jars have contained mixtures—mixtures of fruits with starches, mixtures of vegetables with starches, "dinners" containing meat, vegetable, and starch.

The large print on the label may not reveal that the jar contains a mixture. "Creamed beans," for example, may really mean beans and cornstarch. So wise parents will make it their business to read the small print on the label, which lists every ingredient, beginning with the one in largest amount, as the law requires.

Though babies do need a moderate amount of starch, I feel it's a mistake to give them more than a moderate amount of even the best starches (oats, whole wheat, and rye). And it's a further mistake I feel to feed the less valuable starches (corn and rice) combined in jars with a baby's other foods (meats, fruits, and vegetables), since the baby probably is also taking cereal separately a couple of times a day.

Therefore, in buying baby foods in jars, I would not buy mixtures but straight fruit, straight vegetables, and straight meat.

Give your baby fresh or frozen vegetables and fruits when the family eats them. In the first year when you cook these for the whole family you may then puree some for the baby in a blender or hand grinder. When the family eats canned vegetables and fruits, serve them to the baby too. Buy fruits packed in fruit juice or pour off the syrup in which many canned fruits swim. This will remove some of the excess sugar, but most of it will, of course, stay in the fruits, which already have absorbed it.

Fruits—fresh, frozen, or canned—make better desserts than

puddings, especially cornstarch puddings and gelatin desserts. Of course rennet desserts and rice puddings made mostly with milk have their uses, particularly for children who drink little milk. But fruits make the ideal dessert.

Don't begin cookies and cakes and candies—even though your baby will love them and will look cute gobbling them and smearing them all over her face.

Give the baby the meats and fish the rest of the family is eating, minced fine.

Up until recent years doctors strongly urged egg or egg yolk by a half year because of the risk of anemia and because egg yolk has more iron than any other food. But recently it was discovered that the iron in egg yolk is not absorbed. So there is no longer any point in hurrying egg since it is one of the foods most likely to cause an allergy if given young. Egg is still a source of good protein, especially in the absence of meat and fish in vegetarian families. Nowadays the usual recommendation is three or four eggs a week beginning between nine and twelve months.

Dietary habits are formed early in life and then tend to persist. You can easily get your baby on the right track if you pay attention to a few simple rules rather than to your own human impulse to indulge your baby.

▷ AVOIDING FEEDING PROBLEMS

I often see parents gently urging their babies to eat just a little more solid food or to drink just a bit more formula or milk. The baby turns away. She doesn't really want any more. She bangs on the tray of the high chair or squishes a lump of food that has landed there. The mother or father tries to charm her, to make her forget her refusal by turning the next spoonful into a pretend plane that swoops in circles, to the accompaniment of engine noises, as it approaches her mouth. When the baby smiles the parent quickly pops the spoon into her mouth, before she quite realizes what is happening and has time to balk. Or the parent distracts her completely from the thought of food by making faces or singing comic songs and then slips the food in when the baby laughs.

I remember a mother who did this kind of distracting and urging for five years. In the beginning she needed to distract her son only at the end of meals when his appetite was satisfied. But over the intervening months and years the mother's bribing and pushing progressively eroded all positive feelings the child had about food. Finally, he was disinterested even at the start of meals. By the time I first saw him, when he was five years old, his mother, who was an ingenious storyteller, was reciting a long tale about some imaginary animal before each mouthful. "Now, this story is going to be about Ellie the Elephant," she would say, or "about the duck that hated water." It was a painful bargain on both sides. As if taking nasty medicine, the child obviously was close to nausea as he swallowed each spoonful, but he loved the stories. And the process was painfully boring to the mother because each small meal took one and a half hours. Only her anxiety that her child would actually starve to death kept her going. The child's appearance made this fear seem not too farfetched, for by the time he was five years old, he was spectacularly thin.

One way you can be sure that some mysterious disease is not malnourishing such a child is that the revulsion appears greatest against foods the parents consider vital foods such as milk and vegetables. The child's appetite remains better for items the parents consider unimportant or even unsuitable. Several children I've known whose appetites were killed by parental urging eventually wanted only olives or pickles or frankfurters. They came from families in which these foods were considered harmful to children. And the boy who was told all the animal stories used to beg for the dregs of his parents' martinis and for the anchovy canapés they often ate with their drinks.

Another characteristic of children with food aversions is that many of those who want almost nothing at meals—in fact, will gag if urged too hard—begin hunting for snacks as soon as a meal is safely over. It is parental pressure at meals that has suppressed the child's appetite; when the pressure is off, the appetite begins to return—at least to a small degree.

Aversion to foods that are pressed on a child often seems to start at certain points in the child's development.

A baby getting her first teaspoon of solid food is a comical sight. She looks bewildered and slightly disgusted as she wrinkles up her nose, opens and closes her mouth with a clucking noise, and oozes most of the food down her chin.

It's natural for babies who have been accustomed only to sucking milk from breast or bottle for five or six months to be puzzled by their first taste of solid food. The consistency is strange. The hard spoon is strange. And the act of swallowing is quite different from the act of sucking; it requires a new set of techniques.

Be patient at the beginning. If a parent tries to get too much into the baby at first, the child may resist. Instead of becoming more expert and pleased, she may grow more obstinate. The right method is to proceed in a gentle, friendly spirit, starting with just a taste of solid food and increasing the amount only as the baby develops skill and, more important, enthusiasm. My own preference has been to start babies not with cereal but with cooked fruit or mashed, raw, ripe banana, avocado, or papaya, which many of them find more appealing.

A time at which a problem may begin is when the ravenous appetite of early infancy eases off, at about four, five, or six months of age, when the rate of weight gain normally decreases and the variety of solid foods increases. Another such point is when the child is teething, a process that definitely suppresses appetite in some babies. A feeding problem can begin when a baby or a child has had an infection that has killed her appetite temporarily and her worried parents start pushing foods before her normal appetite has returned; it is very easy to turn a temporary aversion into a permanent one at such times.

The commonest time of all for eating problems is when the child is about a year of age, when variations in appetite are frequent. This is when a majority of children develop temporary aversions to foods they took well enough before, especialy vegetables, cereals, and milk. Why babies turn against foods that they liked before is one of those mysteries that I cannot completely explain. It's partly because weight gain decreases at this time and so appetite drops. Also, between the ages of one and two most babies are able to feel and express their likes and dislikes much more definitely than before. They may already have been bored with vegetables, cereals, and milk but were too ferociously hungry to turn them down. Now they refuse to eat what doesn't please them.

It's worth remembering that small children like crisp food and soupy foods but they tend to dislike sticky, in-between consistencies such as stiff mashed potatoes or firm-cooked cereals.

Why are parents, especially new parents, so easily seduced into pushing and urging food? It may be partly instinctive. But surely the anxiety about eating enough was injected into most of us during our own childhood, and we carry it over to our children. There are ethnic groups in various parts of the world that believe children will starve if not stuffed and who prize obesity. Such anxiety is totally mistaken. Human babies, like the young of other species, have wonderful appetites unless they are sick or unless they've become disgusted by too much urging or forcing. (When the urging in infancy is gentle and is not repeated too long, the baby's natural appetite usually is strong enough to survive in spite of her overanxious parents.)

In actuality, there is never a need to urge food on a child; it always defeats the purpose in the end. A mother may say, "But I can always get a few more spoonfuls of food [or swallows of milk] if I'm patient." That is true at the moment, but if you get more into the child than her growth pattern calls for, her appetite will be that much less at her next meal. And if you persist, even gently, you gradually will reduce the child's desire for food to below normal. So you're not really gaining anything; you're actually losing.

It's easy to state the rule: always let a baby or a child stop eating just as soon as indifference appears. That's the way to preserve the child's God-given appetite at its very best. That's also the way to keep the child ideally nourished. However, I know well, from dealing with hundreds of conscientious, intelligent parents, that this advice is hard to follow, especially after a baby or a child has already developed a pattern of balking.

You don't have to worry about a one-year-old baby who has turned against most vegetables. Certainly you should stop serving the vegetables to which she has developed an aversion. To keep offering them will only make her more obstinate and suspicious and will increase the list of foods she won't touch. But keep serving the few vegetables she does like. You can offer raw vegetables such as carrot sticks, green beans, avocados, tomatoes. Some of these can be held in the baby's hand, which encourages her to learn to feed herself. You can also try some of the less commonly used, less commonly liked, strong-tasting vegetables, such as boiled onions, cauliflower, cabbage, broccoli, and turnips, but they are not likely to be accepted. Do not serve raw peas or cooked corn; they may cause choking.

When dealing with a balking one-year-old, it's most important to realize that fruits—stewed or raw—contain the same minerals and roughage and some of the same vitamins as vegetables. (Their carbohydrate is sugar instead of starch.) So fruits, along with vitamin A in drops, will replace the vegetables that have been temporarily rejected. Most fruits remain popular during that difficult second year too, so don't worry if your small child takes no vegetables for months or even a year or so.

Cooked cereals often are spurned during the second year—and sometimes for life. But there are lots of substitutes: dry cereals, breads, crackers, potatoes white and sweet. Cereals, bread, and crackers should be made of oats, rye, and whole wheat. Quite a few children give up all starches for a year or two but they usually eat enough other foods so that their nutrition doesn't suffer.

Why is it that most children (and probably a majority of adults too) love the sweetened foods that undermine nutrition and cause cavities in the teeth? Dr. Clara Davis, in experiments done many years ago, worked with babies between nine and twelve months of age who up until then had been fed nothing but formula. She offered them a wide variety of natural foods and discovered that they tended to pick what any nutritionist would consider a well-balanced diet. They didn't overdo the fruits, which were the only sweet foods served to them.

Then how do children's appetites become corrupted? I believe that parents are often the culprits, though they don't mean to be. They serve their children plain food and then offer sweetened desserts and candy as a reward for eating the wholesome food or for behaving well at the dentist's or doctor's office. Many parents were rewarded with sweets themselves when they were children, and it's natural to carry on the same tradition. The result is that love equals sweets, generation after generation. It would be better if parents said, "You can't eat your spinach until you've finished your dessert."

Many children cut down on milk intake during infancy and early childhood, often to well below a quart a day, but most continue to average a pint or more, and that usually is enough. In any event, parents should keep in mind that milk is just as valuable—particularly for its calcium and protein—when cooked into cereals, soups, and junket. Many babies like cheese, and an ounce of firm cheese contains as much calcium as eight ounces of milk. (Cottage and cream cheeses are not nearly as rich in calcium as firm cheeses.) If a child is taking meat and poultry and eggs (meat and poultry remain popular), these will make up for some of the protein missed if her milk intake has fallen below a pint.

But even if the child's diet is not ideal, what are you going to do about it? You can't force a child to eat, and urging only increases the aversion to food. So you have to put all your hopes into reviving the child's appetite *by serving only the wholesome things that she still likes,* no matter how lacking or bizarre the resulting diet. Your hope is that by offering only the foods that the child likes and doing this for months, you will be able gradually to train yourself out of urging and the child's natural, positive feelings about eating will slowly return. But this takes enormous self-control and patience on the part of the parents.

▷ SERIOUS ILLNESS

I received a letter from a mother who had learned, seven months before, that her four-year-old daughter had diabetes. She described vividly the emotional stages she herself went through—suspecting, denying and acknowledging the diagnosis, and then turning bitter and guilty. Eventually, because of her honesty and her sound personality, she worked through the turmoil of her feelings and came to a healthy acceptance of the situation.

The insights offered by this mother's letter should be valuable to parents contending with problems other than diabetes—and not just serious problems either, though it's easier to see what's happening when they are dramatic.

Parents are made at least slightly guilty by a wide variety of situations—for example, ordinary childhood accidents, the homeliness or awkwardness or relative unhappiness of a child, or the fact that the parents feel less enthusiasm and warmth for one child than for another. Guilt—whether justified or not—will get in the way of the parents' management of the child until they can understand it and be freed from it.

Here is Mrs. T.'s letter:

"Last March we were told that our four-year-old, Linda, had diabetes. I had been worried about her since the previous autumn because she was sometimes drinking excessive amounts of water and getting up two or three times a night to urinate. I had heard that these were symptoms of diabetes, but I found excuses to put off going to the doctor. The symptoms would come and go and I didn't want him to think I was neurotic or overanxious.

"When the diagnosis was definite I felt that I had accepted it, but my husband, George, became very upset and refused to believe it for several days. Then he accepted it but I turned bitter and also very guilty. I kept thinking, why didn't I take her to the doctor sooner? He would have caught it earlier and then she wouldn't need insulin. No matter how much my pediatrician stressed that this wasn't true, I didn't believe him—at least, not for several months.

"The doctor hospitalized Linda for a few days. Although we tried to prepare her for this, she couldn't seem to understand, because she didn't feel sick. The reason she was going to the hospital, we said, was that she drank too much water and went to the bathroom too often and we wanted to know why.

"In the hospital she was given a blood test, and I was told later that she screamed, 'Please, *no*, Doctor! I won't drink any more water —I promise!' That broke my heart, and I realized I had to stress to her that she drank the water only *because* she had a problem, not that her drinking it was *causing* the problem.

"Another thing that upset me terribly was seeing other parents at the hospital going through so much. One six-year-old had cancer of the lung, a two-year-old had cystic fibrosis, and there was another two-year-old who needed a pacemaker. Linda was actually the best off, but that didn't make me feel any better. I just kept asking myself why any of us had to suffer while others in the world went on worrying about making more money and buying fancier houses.

"I soon found I didn't want to talk on the phone to any of my friends and relatives. There was nothing helpful they could say, and I didn't want to hear their advice or 'how sorry' they were. Their remarks only made me angry, so I decided I'd rather not even get into a conversation.

"After about three or four days in the hospital, Linda cried and said, 'I know I'm never going home.' 'You are—soon,' I promised. But she kept crying. Two or three days later, on her way home, she was very quiet. She didn't seem at all happy. Then we found out why.

"While my father was taking her for a walk, she ran into her best friends, two little boys her age. 'Bad news, you guys,' she said. 'I can't play anymore.' No wonder she wasn't happy! We all assured her that her life would be just the same, with only a few exceptions, but she didn't really believe us at first. We sent her back to nursery school the second day home and I had kids over every afternoon, and after a while Linda began to act like her old self again.

"My own bitterness finally began to go away as I realized that the problems of living with a diabetic child aren't so great. What bothers me most is our strict mealtime schedule: we must eat every meal at the same time each day. Also I'm sure that if Linda were more pleasant about her insulin injections, it would help me.

"This has been one of my biggest problems. In the beginning she'd shout at me, 'Big deal! So I drank water and went to the bathroom in the night! Big deal! Who cares!' And for months, when I gave her the insulin shot she would scream, 'Pig yoke!'—an expression she made up. It was probably the worst thing she could say without coming right out and calling me a pig.

"She also kept asking, 'Why are you doing this to me?' And I would repeat like a broken record, 'I'm doing it because I love you and I want you to stay healthy.'

"Although George knows how to give the insulin injections, he has done it only twice. Linda wants me to give them to her, and George prefers this too, although he won't admit it. I sometimes resent this.

"Linda's illness was the first real trouble in my life. I was an only child with loving parents and I had a wonderful childhood. I married a fine man who is a great husband and father. When I wanted a baby I got pregnant. When I worked I had a wonderful job as secretary for a child-development study. So I had no preparation at all for this devastating experience. There were two things that helped me to cope.

"One happened after a staff meeting of the child-study group. Dr. Lowell, one of the doctors I work for, asked me if I had any suggestions as to how he, as a pediatrician, could help parents in a situation like mine. Then he said something that stunned me. 'Does any part of the parents' upset,' he asked, 'have to do with the fact that their child is no longer perfect? That they now have an imperfect child?' I looked at him and nodded. I was choked up because I realized it was true.

"All along, my friends have envied me for my parents, my husband, my children, and my job. And I guess I counted on that. Now I was human, with troubles like everyone else, no longer to be envied. That was not easy for me to admit! But once I dealt with this in my own mind, I improved a lot.

"The other thing happened when my cousin came over to tell me she had heard about Linda. I spent one hour telling her about my problems. As she left I apologized for spending all the time on my own troubles. She said that one day she would tell me about hers. After prodding her, I finally learned that her husband had cancer of the lung. (He recently died.) I was so ashamed! That's when I decided that everyone had problems and that I couldn't burden anyone else with ours again.

"When Linda first came home from the hospital, I used to sit and watch her from the window, tears running down my face, torn between my fear of letting her out of my sight and my knowledge that I had to raise her to be a normal human being.

"I didn't realize how much I'd changed in half a year until something happened this autumn. When Linda started kindergarten the school nurse called to ask about her condition. I explained that the diabetes was well under control.

" 'You know,' she said, 'when you have a sick child you must stay at home while she's in school and always be near the phone.' If I had heard this in March, I think it would have been the last straw. But by September I was a hundred times better.

" 'With a great deal of professional help,' I told her, 'my husband, my daughter, and I have come to accept this. We're not going to make a big deal out of it. I'm a person with things to do and places to go. It's ridiculous to expect me to be home every minute of the day. I assume if anything happens, you will take her to the hospital.'

" 'Yes, of course,' she said.

" 'And you wouldn't just sit there and watch her die,' I added.

" 'Of course not.'

"So I told her, 'Well, that's what I would do too. And if you can't reach me, just go ahead as if she were your own child.'

"When I told George the story, I said I knew I had finally accepted Linda's disease and I was not going to be scared by it anymore. He couldn't believe I had talked to the nurse like that but he was glad I had."

The letter that follows was written some years later, by Linda at the age of fifteen. We include it here just as she wrote it.

D.B.S.

"It doesn't matter how many times I'm reminded that God isn't responsible for my diabetes—I still have to wonder. It doesn't matter how hard I try to keep myself in good control, there's still a-lot of times I'm out of control, otherwise being known as having high blood sugar. A-lot of things make me so scared that I can't help myself from crying. No-one but a diabetic understands what it feels like to hear about other diabetics dying, or getting complications & going blind, or ending up on a dialysis machine. Don't people (doctors, parents, etx.) understand how many times a-day were reminded of what will happen if we don't stay in good control?! It's weird too, how cold some people can be to us too. Could you imagine what it feels like being only 8 years old and developing diabetes and coming back to school knowing that you physically have had a change internally, but expecting everyone else to treat you the same—only to come back to school and having your class-mates actually bring bottles to school labeled "cootie spray," to keep you away? It hurts. I also remember once in sixth grade a classmate told me that I "deserved" diabetes. You try not to think of yourself as being different, but when people who *were* just like you, keep coming arund telling you "you are different," you eventually believe it yourself. Up to this day, I will not tell anyone I have diabetes due to what I experienced years ago. I think for this reason, with every-one trying to make you feel and believe you're different, that is why I sometimes eat foods I *know* I shouldn't eat. I guess I try to "brain-wash" myself and eat the same foods "normal" peole eat to make myself fit in somewhere/somehow with them. I also hate it when my parents acuse me of eating just because I'm in the kitchen. As long as I have diabetes, I'm going to try to keep making myself believe that I'm just like everyone else, but how can I when I can't eat when and what like everybody else. In the mornings, as I'm filling my syringe, a lot of feelings go through my mind. Sometimes I can't help but hate God for "chosing" me—what did I ever do?! I also hate my parents after all if I were never conceived I wouldn't have to go through the pain, physically and mentally of this disease. I also get to the point where I feel like *really* committing suicide, when I see how much easier financially and emotionally better my parents would be off without me. I feel like I've let them down. All you hear about is how parents feel about how *very* important it is to have a healthy baby. I remember how I used to thank God that I was four years old and too old to be killed for not being "perfect." Sometimes I wonder if my mom would have wished for an abortion if she would have known her "baby" would soon end up not being "perfect," and she would have to worry about me to the point that she cries. But I have to admit, the only one person in my whole life who's *always* been there for me, from the first hospital visit to the good check-ups from the eye doctor, is my mom. Without her help and support—I don't know where I'd be now. But all I have to say now is diabetes won't be the cause of my death. I just hope I'll be the one to kill it."

On the day Mrs. T. wrote her letter to me—a month after she

talked back to the school nurse, seven months after the diagnosis was made—she added a postscript: "Today I walked into the room to give Linda her insulin and she was standing there with her pants pulled down, ready for the injection—and *smiling*. My God! Does that mean she has finally accepted the insulin shots?"

I'm grateful to have a letter like this to form the core of a discussion. There aren't many people in a society such as ours—which generally urges us to keep smiling, to keep a stiff upper lip, to keep our feelings hidden from others and even from ourselves—who can recognize the nature of their emotions and express them as honestly as Mrs. T. does. I believe that her words will get through to other parents and help them more than the generalizations of a professional person. I'll just add my comments on some of the matters Mrs. T. has made so real.

Mrs. T.'s bitterness is common. "Why does God (or fate) pick on me? I don't deserve this!" That is a healthy way to ward off a too-painful sorrow and guilt for a while. In the long run bitterness is not a constructive reaction, because it doesn't lead to any solution. It's an angry form of self-pity. But it allowed Mrs. T. to lash out—in her imagination—at the well-meaning friends who tried to "console" her with irritating remarks. It was good for her to be able to turn on somebody else.

Mrs. T. was surprisingly honest in being able to acknowledge early, with the assistance of Dr. Lowell, that Linda's "imperfection" was a blow to her own pride and ego. This admission of an attitude she felt as unworthy (though it is really natural and inevitable) hastened her recovery.

I imagine she is right in assuming that having had no very painful previous experiences in life, she was caught off guard. But her happy lifelong adjustment was not basically a disadvantage. It was surely the major factor in enabling her to make a very mature readjustment to the situation in the end, without long delay.

Guilt, to some degree or other, is inescapable. We are taught from early childhood that we are responsible for our failures and sins, whether we are brought up to be religious or not, and the forming and care of our children is one of our major obligations. If this were not true, we would be dangerously irresponsible parents. When our child falls seriously ill or has an accident, a wave of guilt sweeps over us. Usually this is eased, step by step, by the realization that we aren't really so bad—or at least that we are no worse than the average. The doctor's reassurances eventually get through to us.

But if the disease is a serious one and if the guilt goes on not only for months but for years, then the individual needs psychiatric help to trace and uproot the hidden causes of the exaggerated guilt.

Guilt about not having faced the symptoms earlier tortured Mrs. T., made her watch Linda constantly at first, and caused her difficulty in explaining the disease and the injections. I imagine that it was a guilty, slightly cringing attitude in Mrs. T., when she kept explaining that the shots were well-intentioned, that encouraged Linda to take out her own tensions by stalling on the shots, reproaching her mother, and calling her bad names.

To me the most revealing part of Mrs. T.'s testimony is that having worked through her guilt at last, she was able to speak to the school nurse and set her straight in no uncertain terms about the fact that she was not going to sit anxiously at home, waiting for an emergency call from school, but expected the nurse to be able to act sensibly if the child should need emergency care.

Dramatic evidence that Mrs. T.'s guilt was what had stimulated Linda to torture her mother—and herself—was that when Mrs. T. had finally outgrown her guilt (I imagine that writing the letter helped her gain a sense of perspective), she found Linda with pants down, smiling, ready to take her medicine.

I agree that it would be much better if fathers shared fully in the care of a sick child—especially in treatments that are unpleasant and cause resentment, such as the administering of bad-tasting medicines to young children. It eases the mother's tensions somewhat to be relieved of half the responsibility. More important, the mother doesn't have to be the only "mean" parent. The father shouldn't be excused just because the child asks the mother to do the job.

Perhaps the most valuable thing that all parents, including those whose children have no serious disease, can learn from this story is how children can misinterpret and draw excessively morbid and guilty conclusions about a situation they don't understand. Linda had concluded that she had caused her disease by drinking too much water and that she'd never be able to go home again. When she got home she assumed that she couldn't ever play again. It reminds me of a study of children's views of why they were in the hospital to have their tonsils removed. For example, they thought, guiltily, that their tonsils were enlarged because they had not worn their coats or rubbers when it was stormy. A girl believed that the surgeon would slit her throat from ear to ear, tip her head back, and reach into her throat to do the cutting. A boy who'd been moved from one hospital room to another assumed that his parents would never be able to find him to take him home. (Similarly, when parents divorce, most children believe that it was their bad behavior that somehow broke up the marriage, perhaps because they've heard their parents arguing angrily about them.)

The answer, for parents, is to keep their ears open for cues and hints of what their child may be worrying about during an illness or any other family crisis. Ask sympathetic questions to clarify the child's anxiety. Don't laugh, in an effort to be reassuring; children are sensitive about being ridiculed. Be sure you understand the child's concern before you try to reassure, for reassurance that misses the mark is only frustrating. A general suggestion in these situations is to listen as much as you talk.

It was healthy, in one sense, that Linda could be so open in her reproaches and could even shout, "Pig yoke." This is better for the child than bottling up all her anxieties and resentments. But when I say this I don't mean that parents should regularly invite or permit direct rudeness, for parents only do that, in general, when they have a guilty or submissive attitude (it can come from other sources besides a child's serious illness): and such a parental attitude usually makes life more difficult for the child.

But since Mrs. T. *had* to feel guilty for a number of months, it was good that Linda had such a forthright character—and such a trust in her mother's love and understanding—that she could express her reproaches openly.

Linda will do well in life, despite her handicap.

▷ HOW TO TALK TO CHILDREN ABOUT SEXUALITY AND LOVE, IN GENERAL

We tend in this "scientific" age to explain human sexuality only in terms of anatomy and physiology (how the body works). That might cover the matter well enough for rabbits, but human beings are vastly different. For example, they compose music, they paint pictures, they write poetry, they build beautiful buildings, they worship God, they deck themselves in clothes and ornaments.

And sexual love, in humans, is very much more complex than in other creatures—more powerful and more spiritual. It is intimately interwoven with other emotions and other relationships, like the threads in a tapestry. This comes about during the stages of emotional development in childhood as has been discovered in the psychoanalysis of the unconscious levels of the mind.

The early adoration of the parent of the opposite sex which I have discussed in Chapter Ten, explains in part why an individual later "falls madly in love" with one sort of person, and not at all with another whom others might consider equally attractive.

By the age of five or six children realize that their parents belong to each other sexually and romantically. This arouses feelings of jealousy and resentment. They assume at this age that their parents of the same sex have the same jealousy toward them. This very uneven rivalry scares them underneath. So at six, seven, eight, and nine years they suppress many of their intense positive feelings for their parents and their own excitement about being married and having babies. Instead they shift their admiration to the heroes and heroines, real and fictional, whom they read about in books and comics and see on film: the scientists, the explorers, the inventors, the military and civic leaders, great women like Florence Nightingale and Marie Curie. They dream of being heroes themselves.

In the preteen (ten to twelve) and teen years (thirteen to nineteen), when children's glands demand that they turn their thoughts and feelings back to love and sex again, these feelings are still imbued with some of the intense idealism and spirituality that were in them when the children were three and four and five. Now they may idealize and love, in their imaginations, popular musicians, singers, actors, writers, artists; they feel inspired to be like them. They may develop crushes on teachers. And when they fall in love with people their own age, they dream of performing heroic deeds for them, of dedicating their lives to them.

In adulthood the spiritual aspect of sexual love is part of the inspiration of painters, sculptors, novelists, poets, dramatists, songwriters. And it is part of ordinary people's pleasure in viewing pictures, reading books, and hearing music. Most important of all, the spiritual aspect of sexual love is part of what inspires good wives and husbands to have high aspirations for their marriage, and to think the best of each other—which brings out the best. The spiritual feelings toward the loved one—whether in marriage at twenty-four or sixty-four years, or in playing house at four, or in day dreaming at fourteen—include such emotions as faithfulness, respect, tenderness, helpfulness, wanting to please, and eventually, in most cases, a desire to create children and cherish them.

Sex education really begins back at two and a half years, when boys and girls themselves are likely to raise slightly anxious questions about why a girl doesn't have a penis like a boy. ("Nothing bad has happened to it, a girl is meant to be different, like mommies are different from daddies.") Boys want to grow babies inside themselves. By three or three and a half, children usually ask where babies come from. ("They grow from a tiny egg in the mother's uterus.")

By four, five, or six years children are likely to ask, What does the father do? The parent can explain that when a husband and wife are feeling very loving toward each other and are lying in bed the man puts his penis in the woman's vagina and his seed, called a sperm, comes out of the penis and gets into her egg and makes it start to grow into a baby. The emphasis is on the mutual loving feeling.

By answering questions, the parents not only satisfy legitimate curiosity but show that it is all right to ask about sex.

Teachers and parents can keep the subject open when the child reaches five or six years by keeping pets that have intercourse and give birth. Thus children are encouraged to continue to question. But parents can emphasize the difference: rabbits mate with any other rabbits, and they take care of their babies for just a few weeks. Human beings fall in love only when they love each other very specially. They get married because they want to live together, take care of each other, help each other, please each other, have children to care for until they are grown up, and to love as long as they live. If parents are religious, they want God to bless their marriage.

Before children reach the age of nine it is wise and helpful for parents to talk about the puberty growth spurt and how its time table varies in different individuals—lacking such reassurance, this variation may worry early developers and late developers. The average girl begins to shoot up in height at ten; her breasts begin to develop and pubic hair appears. Her first period is apt to occur at twelve. But plenty of girls start developing as early as nine or as late as eleven, a few at eight or twelve. Boys on the average start their growth spurt at twelve, two years after girls; many start at eleven, a few at ten or fourteen. The rapid growth in height and weight lasts for two years. Then it slows down progressively for two more years and stops. These differences are not abnormalities—they are normal variations, which tend to run in families.

It is wise for parents to get into teen-level discussions about sex, love, and ideals when their children are still in the preteen (ten to twelve years) stage because teenagers, through their instinct to gain independence, are apt to become increasingly impatient with their parents' ideas, and to take the opinions of their peers as the only truth.

By the time children are ten, eleven, and twelve (preteens), when their feelings are becoming more romantic and sexual, some of them become shyer about asking questions. But they do make comments about friends' infatuations. Parents can be on the lookout for chances to add their own comments and open conversations especially about the spiritual aspects of love: how natural it is to fall quickly in love now, but also to fall out quickly, too, since young people are changing in all ways, including their taste in boyfriends and girlfriends. Parents can point out that young people naturally want to be popular, but many of those who are popular at ten or twelve because they are easy talkers, jokers, kidders, and easily get involved in petting have lost their special appeal a few years later; and those who are shy at first may later be appreciated for their good qualities. Parents can explain in a sympathetic way that the physical attraction of sex may be particularly exciting in the preteen and teen years because it is so new, but in the long run what makes for lasting love and marriage is spiritual qualities added to the physical attraction.

When there is family gossip about a schoolmate's pregnancy, parents can point out that sexual freedom calls for responsibility; that the couple must not have been thinking of each other's future since it is so hard to go back to school afterward and since the baby may be unhappily deprived of the security of a stable family; that pregnancy will surely follow regular intercourse, sooner or later, unless there is careful contraception. When there is a neighborhood divorce, parents can wonder out loud whether the couple did not get to know each other well enough before marrying or did not try hard enough to help and please each other afterward.

It is good for preteens and teens to hear that the statistics show, even in these days of sexual freedom, that many young people feel that they want to postpone sexual intimacy until marriage or at least until they feel very sure of their compatibility and of the depth of their love; this usually takes many, many months, since both partners are still growing and changing.

It's good for teenagers to know that feelings of unreadiness for sexual experiences of various degrees are not a sign of abnormality, as some of their tougher, taunting peers will try to persuade them. This shyness has been a common pattern of belief and behavior throughout the centuries, particularly among young people brought up with high ideals. Some of the world's greatest writers, artists, and scientists have been too shy to date in adolescence, though they were inspired by longings for idealized lovers. These shy young people can become great lovers when they feel ready.

It will help teenagers to hear from parents and teachers that it is all right to say no. This won't give them a bad reputation or make them unpopular—except with those who want to exploit them sexually. In fact, it will make them more appealing in the eyes of those young people who have similar ideals and who will be searching for others who have them, too.

Parents can point out how much education and hard work go into making a living for a family, and how much planning and going without are necessary to stick within a budget; therefore the spirit of cooperation and thoughtfulness is crucial in a marriage.

These points are made by parents to overcome the preteens' and teenagers' inclination to think that infatuation is the same as a tried-and-true love, that pregnancy only happens to others, that having a baby to love and be loved by, without marriage, will solve the search for happiness.

Such comments shouldn't be made grimly or sourly, but in the spirit of affectionate concern. Parents should offer them as their own beliefs, not as if they are the absolute truth just because the parents are older. Most important is that the parents keep asking for their children's views and listen respectfully to what they say. That doesn't mean that the parents have to accept their children's opinions. They can pay attention to them and then explain further their own beliefs, being still careful not to give the impression that they think they have a monopoly on wisdom. In the end the child may not act convinced and the parent may wisely decide not to argue. Yet the child may be much more impressed than she or he admits. To put it another way, the parent may persuade better by showing respect than by arguing.

I feel that it is important for parents to discuss these various aspects of sex and love, and to have found a comfortable way of talking with their children before they go into the subject of venereal disease. Otherwise the whole subject is upside down and children get the impression that their parents are saying that sex is mainly disease and evil.

I'd start by explaining to preteens (age ten to twelve) that different infectious diseases are spread in different ways: measles, for instance, by fine spray coughed out by measles patients; impetigo, a skin infection, by touch; and venereal disease by contact of the genitals.

Gonorrhea is an infection of the surface of the urinary tract in males and of the vagina (and fallopian tubes) in females, with a thick, creamy, irritating discharge.

Syphilis is quite different: It starts with a sore on the penis or in the vagina. The germs quickly get into the blood stream and soon cause a mild skin rash all over the body. The last stage, which takes years to develop, consists of inflammation of the lining of the heart and arteries, or of the brain.

AIDS is quite different still. It is caused by a virus (a germ too small to be seen through an ordinary microscope). It can spread from the genitals into the blood, and manages to destroy the body's ability to develop immunity to other, ordinary infections. So, a person with AIDS can die of a commonplace infection which, in a normal person, would soon be cured by a quickly developing immunity. AIDS is most commonly transmitted from semen to blood in intercourse, and also from blood to blood in drug abusers who share needles without sterilizing them. It can also be transmitted from a woman to a man by intercourse, by a blood transfusion and from infected mothers to their unborn babies. So AIDS is transmitted only from semen to blood or blood to blood. It is not a highly contagious disease but is highly lethal. And it is spreading throughout the world.

The frequency of AIDS is high in homosexual men who practice anal intercourse because the lining of the rectum is more easily injured than the lining of the vagina.

AIDS is *not* spread by hand or body touch, or by kissing or by living in the same family or by sitting in the same classroom, or by swimming in the same pool with an AIDS victim, or by eating or drinking from the same utensils or by sitting on the same toilet.

So much for the facts. Now, how to talk to preteens and teens about AIDS? I've explained why I believe that the positive aspects of sex and love, including the spiritual side, should come first, over a considerable period of time. The main reason for getting well started in the preteen years is that children before age thirteen or fourteen are much more willing to listen to their parents. If preteens or teens have become anxious about AIDS, they need to know all the ways in which the disease is *not* transmitted.

About how to avoid AIDS in future years—children should know that the surest way, of course, is for both partners to avoid intercourse until marriage or until they have felt a deep attachment to one another for at least one year, preferably several years, and know who else that person has had intercourse with in the past. And about the present health of past lovers.

The greatest risk of AIDS, they should know, comes from promiscuousness, from having intercourse with a number of people who are also likely to have had intercourse with many others. For, the greater the number of sexual partners, the greater the chance that one of them has AIDS or is carrying the virus without having developed the symptoms.

Teenagers should also know the risks drug addicts take when sharing unsterilized drug equipment with other addicts.

They should know that condoms (long, thin rubber caps worn over the penis during intercourse) will offer much, though not total, protection if they are having intercourse.

How much to tell a preteen or teenager about the homosexual aspects of AIDS should depend, I feel, on the age, the personality, and the sophistication of the individual child. I myself wouldn't tell an innocent-seeming child about anal intercourse until the age of fourteen or fifteen unless the child asked earlier. I think it might shock the child unnecessarily. On the other hand, I'd casually tell a ten- or eleven-year-old boy that some men don't feel like making love to women but want to make love to men and boys instead. Children of both sexes should be told not to accept invitations to visit homes or hotels of grownups, whether known to them or not, without permission of their parents. It is surprising how much some kids know these days, as a result of videos, movies, literature, and gossip, though such information may be confused and inaccurate.

The two greatest protections against AIDS, I feel, are education and a belief that the spiritual aspects of sexual love are as important and as worthy of respect as the purely physical.

Index

About the Author

Benjamin Spock, M.D., is a contributing editor at *Redbook* and has been writing a regular column for the magazine since 1963. His first book, *Baby and Child Care,* has comforted mothers in 26 languages since 1945. He is also the author of *The Problems of Parents, Dr. Spock Talks with Mothers,* and *Raising Children in a Difficult Time.* He and his wife Mary Morgan now make their home in the Virgin Islands.